IMAGES
of America

MAINE STATE PRISON
1824–2002

On the cover: After 178 years of operation, the Maine State Prison closed its doors and moved to a state-of-the-art facility. This 1800s photograph shows the interior of an inmate housing block. (Courtesy of Maine State Prison Archives.)

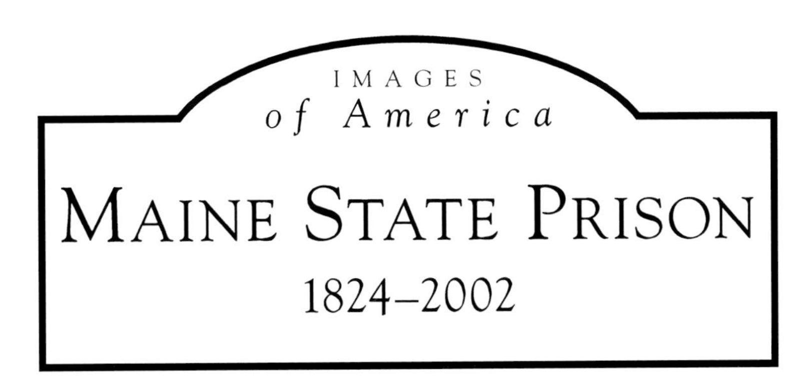

Warden Jeffrey D. Merrill Sr.

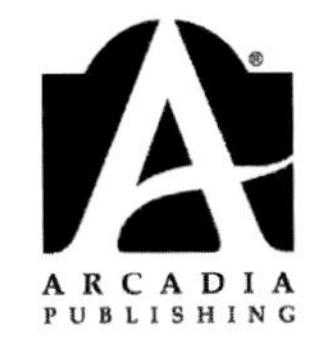

ISBN 978-0-7385-6244-5

Published by Arcadia Publishing
Charleston, South Carolina

Printed in the United States of America

Library of Congress Control Number: 2008934410

For all general information contact Arcadia Publishing at:
Telephone 843-853-2070
Fax 843-853-0044
E-mail sales@arcadiapublishing.com
For customer service and orders:
Toll-Free 1-888-313-2665

Visit us on the Internet at www.arcadiapublishing.com

I dedicate this book to the citizens of the state of Maine and to former and present staff of the Maine State Prison.

Contents

ACKNOWLEDGMENTS

Our history book offers a look into a world that most people do not have the opportunity to experience. One hundred and eighty-five years ago, staff at the Maine State Prison was entrusted with the responsibility of carrying out the law of Maine citizens. Former and present employees have accepted this responsibility with honor, courage, and commitment. With this book, we recognize that the almost 200 years of service by Maine citizens for Maine citizens did not come without a price.

After the demolition of the Maine State Prison–Thomaston in 2002, the only vestiges of its 178-year existence are a few artifacts, pictures, and countless memories. Over the years, many people have come in contact with the Maine State Prison, or Thomaston, as it became known. For some Thomaston residents, the prison was part of their community and neighborhood and represented a vigilant friend. This publication is not only our way to remember the Maine State Prison's rich and sometimes turbulent history, but also a way to allow a look inside for those who are curious and wonder, "What was it like in there?" The creation of this book is also our way of memorializing staff that sacrificed so much to keep the citizens of Maine safe.

As the last warden of Thomaston and the first of the Maine State Prison in Warren, I wanted to take this opportunity to thank those individuals from both the public and private sectors who have given their expertise, photographs, and time to make this journey back though history a reality.

I especially want to thank the following individuals without whom this project would not have been possible: Leida Dardis, deputy warden of programs, and book editor; Nelson Riley, deputy warden of operations; James O'Farrell, deputy warden of security; Karen Carroll, deputy warden of support services; Dwight Fowles, acting deputy warden of operations; Robert Costigan, prison administrative coordinator; Robert Walden, industries supervisor; David George, captain; Bonnie Johnson, training officer and book planning layout coordinator; Louann Thompson, secretary and digital media; Martha Hodgdon, administration office associate and book liaison coordinator; Valmore Blastow, Thomaston town manager; Margaret McCrea, Thomaston Historical Society; Walter Breen, retired assistant training officer; Ed Barrett retired officer; officer Dale Tobey; and officer Freemont Anderson.

Unless otherwise noted, all images appear courtesy of the Maine State Prison archives.

Introduction

Maine is known for its abundant natural resources, its beautiful scenery, and its miles of pristine coastline, lakes, and rivers. Imagine what it must have been like in 1824, riding in a handmade wooden boat up the St. George River past rolling farmland and coastal estuaries, docking in the port of Thomaston with its stately Federal-style captains' houses. You are met by uniformed men waiting to take you to your journey's end. Manacled in leg and wrist chains, you are marched up a hill to the foreboding monolith known as the Maine State Prison and imprisoned in an underground cell. You have just come "up the river," a colloquial expression meaning you are sent to prison.

As detailed in a report dated November 30, 1882, by Joseph Porter, chairman of the Board of Inspectors of Prisons and Jails, the Maine State Prison was erected in Thomaston in early 1823 under the supervision of Dr. Daniel Rose, a medical doctor who practiced in Boothbay Harbor and Wiscasset. Having been elected to the Maine Senate in 1820, Dr. Rose was politically well connected and held strong views about criminal reformation. In a report to the state legislature on January 23, 1823, Dr. Rose and the Honorable Benjamin Greene submitted their proposal for the construction and administration of the Maine State Prison: "that State Prisons should be so constructed that even their aspect might be terrific, and appear like what in fact they should be, dark and comfortless abodes of guilt and wretchedness."

Before Maine achieved its statehood in 1820, convicts were shipped to Boston to serve their sentences at Castle Island (later known as Charlestown Penitentiary). As a new state, with its own government and judiciary, Maine required a correctional facility of its own.

The coastal town of Thomaston, located on the St. George River, was a prosperous port and shipbuilding center in the early 1800s. Its centralized location in the state, its accessibility by boat to transport convicts, and its natural resources made it an ideal place for the new prison.

The 10-acre prison site was purchased from ex-governor William King for the sum of $3,000. The site, known as Limestone Hill, contained abundant limestone deposits from the precambrian age that would be mined with convict labor at a profit earmarked for the state. For many years, Revolutionary War hero Gen. Henry Knox used this land to work the limestone quarry. The prison quarry became a place for convicts to perform hard labor as penitence.

Pursuant to the legislative mandate to build the prison, Dr. Rose was appointed warden, and he supervised the construction of the prison in 1823. The initial construction consisted of a wooden cell house that sheltered 56 underground cells. Underground cells were a unique feature of the prison and reflected Dr. Rose's theories of punishment and reformation. Stark living quarters were the cornerstone of Dr. Rose's theory of convict rehabilitation.

Dr. Rose's correctional philosophy was documented in the January 23, 1823, legislative report:

> The convict shall be furnished with a hammock in which he may sleep, a block on which he may sit, with such coarse though wholesome food as may be best suited to a person in a situation designed for grief and penitence, and shall be favored with so much light from the firmament as may enable him to read the New Testament, which shall be given him as his sole companion and guide to a better life.

On July 3, 1824, the first 20 convicts arrived at the Maine State Prison, followed by 14 more on July 14, and 10 additional on July 25. Convict number 1 was Richard Pelham, convict number 23 was sentenced to two months for the crime of blasphemy, and convict number 58 was a boy 13 years of age sentenced to one month.

Prison industries have always been a fundamental mainstay of the prison from its inception to today. The early convicts not only worked in the limestone quarry as stone cutters but also in the blacksmith shop that was added in 1824, as cooks, tailors, and shoemakers. Some had to cut and split firewood, and the invalid picked oakum. In 1824, the operating cost of the prison amounted to $5,000. By 1828, cabinetmaking and chair making, painting, and joinering were added industries. The per annum cost per convict was under $40. By the early 1900s, prisoners were making carriages, sleighs, harnesses, and brooms for sale, and some of these turned a profit.

Although an 1836 commission recommended that a new prison be constructed on the Auburn plan, no action was taken until Warden Benjamin Carr and prison inspectors decried the dungeonlike underground cells and called for reform.

On December 22, 1851, a fire that originated in the guardroom destroyed the convicts' housing area and the warden's residence. These were reconstructed during a prison expansion that was completed in 1854. This was just one of many fires that plagued the prison during a 100-year period from 1824 to 1923. Many of them were suspicious in origin, although no convicts escaped during these incidents. Until 1855, the prison was surrounded by a wooden barrier, which was replaced by a stone wall that took years to complete.

Convicts worked at cutting slabs of granite and limestone in the quarry, chair making, blacksmithing, tailoring, painting, and cabinetmaking. The 1864 warden's report showed the prison made a profit of nearly $2,000 from its industries work. In that same year, the prison held its first execution. Although the death penalty was "on the books," it had never been carried out until the Maine State Prison's warden was murdered.

In 1861, Richard Tinker of Ellsworth was appointed warden and became the first prison staff person murdered by a convict. On May 14, 1863, Warden Tinker was killed when convict Francis Spencer stabbed him in the neck. The convict, who was serving a five-year sentence for assault, approached Warden Tinker from behind and without any known cause, stabbed him, severing the carotid artery. Warden Tinker died on the spot. Spencer was indicted for murder, pled guilty, and was sentenced to death. He was executed by hanging on June 24, 1864, in the same place where he murdered Tinker.

Three more executions took place before the death penalty was repealed by the legislature in 1876. In 1883, the death penalty was reinstated, and three convicts were executed in the next four years. It was abolished again in 1887. Maine is noted as the only state to have abolished the death penalty twice. The last execution was a double hanging on June 25, 1875, and created controversy and outrage that led to the abolishment of capital punishment.

In the prison's early years, programs for the convicts were limited to religious services provided by community chaplains who would conduct a service on the sabbath and take other "opportunities to convey religious instruction and advice" as noted in an 1836 annual report. Bibles were routinely dispensed to convicts. In many of the prison's early annual reports, the chaplains wrote about their successes in teaching prisoners to read and write. An 1870 annual report recommended the hiring of a full-time chaplain "to devote his time and ability wholly to the improvement and reformation of the convicts."

In the 1930s, the prison farm was constructed two miles from Thomaston as a farm barracks for the Maine State Prison. It became one of the largest dairy and beef farms in the state. In his historical review of the prison, Warden Allan L. Robbins wrote, "The Prison Farm represents one of the more advanced stages of penological development in the Maine prison system."

A destructive fire, coupled with a changing work world, resulted in the farm redesigning its purpose and function to provide vocational training opportunities for prisoners to learn a marketable job skill. The farm was later named the Bolduc Correctional Facility after Ronald Bolduc and remains a key place for prisoners to learn new skills.

In 1951, Allan L. Robbins was appointed warden, first serving 2 years as deputy warden followed by 20 years as warden. His length of service is the longest, and his progressive ideas marked a new chapter in the prison's history. Not only did he spearhead reform inside the prison by promoting programs and activities, he also connected the prison with the community in unique and creative ways.

The Maine State Prison or Thomaston, as it became known in later years, has had its share of controversy and bad times. Like most prisons, Thomaston has had escapes, riots, lockdowns, and even murder. Despite the dismal brick and mortar, concrete walls, and mystery, the Maine State Prison stood as a living testimonial to the development of progressive penology. Originally designed "for the purpose of having each convict confined in a separate cell, and entirely secluded from all intercourse with any mortal" as written in the January 23, 1823, legislative report, the prison found itself in the reform movement of the 1960s and 1970s. Prisoner sweatshops and hard labor were replaced with vocational classes that afforded prisoners the opportunity to learn a viable skill or trade. Prisoners received medical care that rivaled that available to free citizens. The philosophy of the prison changed from a punitive to a corrective rehabilitation model. This change allowed for a more effective means of holding the prisoner accountable for his actions.

Public sentiment toward crime and punishment changed yet again, as reflected in the abolishment of parole and calls for "truth-in-sentencing," meaning a prisoner sentenced to life remained incarcerated for his natural life. In 1994, the Maine legislature reduced 15 days a month good time credit for time served down to 5 days as part of the truth-in-sentencing initiative. These actions created a significant increase in the prison population. To alleviate overcrowding, some cells were turned into double occupancy, a dangerous practice given that many prisoners had violent histories.

Although the prison underwent physical plant upgrades over the years, its antiquated structure remained. Walking into the haze and din of the east wing cellblock was like walking into a James Cagney movie. Opening the heavy steel door, one was met with the monolithic site of rows upon rows of iron bars and concrete four tiers high. At one point, the east wing alone housed almost 230 prisoners amid the pungent odors of 178 years of cigarette smoke and perspiration that permeated every crevice.

On February 11, 2002, Maine State Prison staff transferred its 400 prisoners from "Box A" to a state-of-the-art facility in Warren, built for $76 million. After 178 years in operation, the Maine State Prison–Thomaston closed, and the Maine State Prison–Warren opened. The long-standing connection between the town of Thomaston and the prison was broken.

On March 21, 2002, demolition of the once mysterious, awe-inspiring fortress began. Gone were not only the inhabitants of the imposing structure in an otherwise quintessential New England neighborhood but also Thomaston's largest and most watchful neighbor.

One

Going to Thomaston

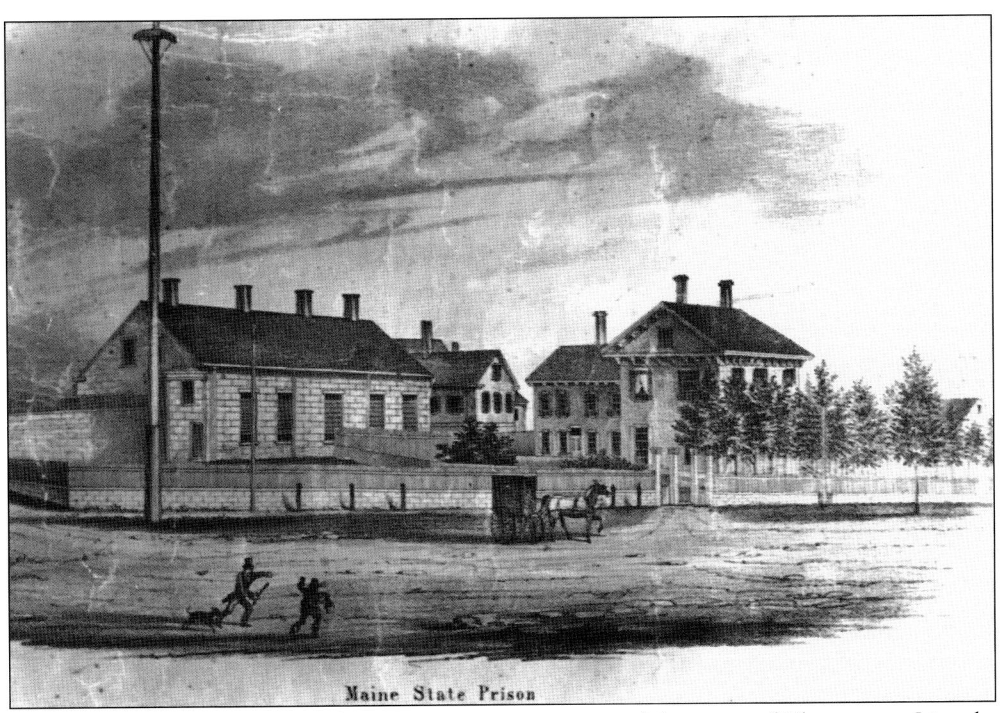

This engraved image of the early prison appears on a map of the town of Thomaston, Lincoln County, by D. S. Osbourne and published by E. M. Woodford in 1855. Thomaston was part of Lincoln County before Knox County was established in 1860 from parts of Waldo and Lincoln Counties. The east wing appears on the left and the warden's residence on the right. (Courtesy of the Thomaston Historical Society.)

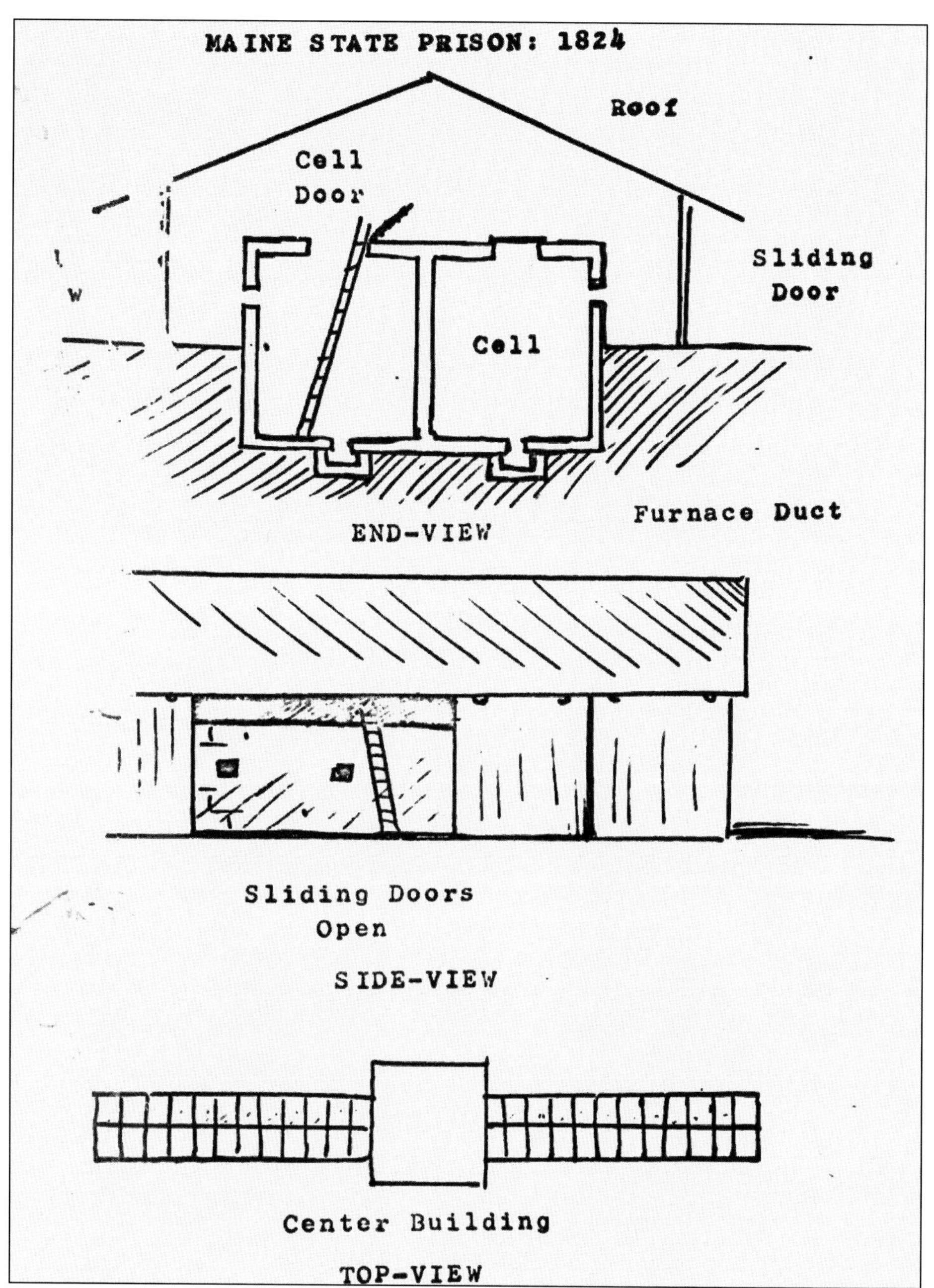

The new prison consisted of two wings adjoining each end of the prison hospital. The underground cell walls were constructed of thick stone slabs and were 9 feet in length and 10 feet deep. Openings on the top of the cells allowed natural daylight and air to filter in. After working in the quarry all day mining limestone, the convicts would be lowered down into their cells, known as "stone jugs," with a ladder through a two-foot hatch and left in isolation for the night to reflect upon their transgressions against society. Rainwater and snow fell into these underground cells, making existence a struggle, and convict deaths from exposure and respiratory ailments were not uncommon. Joseph Porter in his November 1882 *Report on the State Prison* noted that the initial cost of the prison was $25,000.

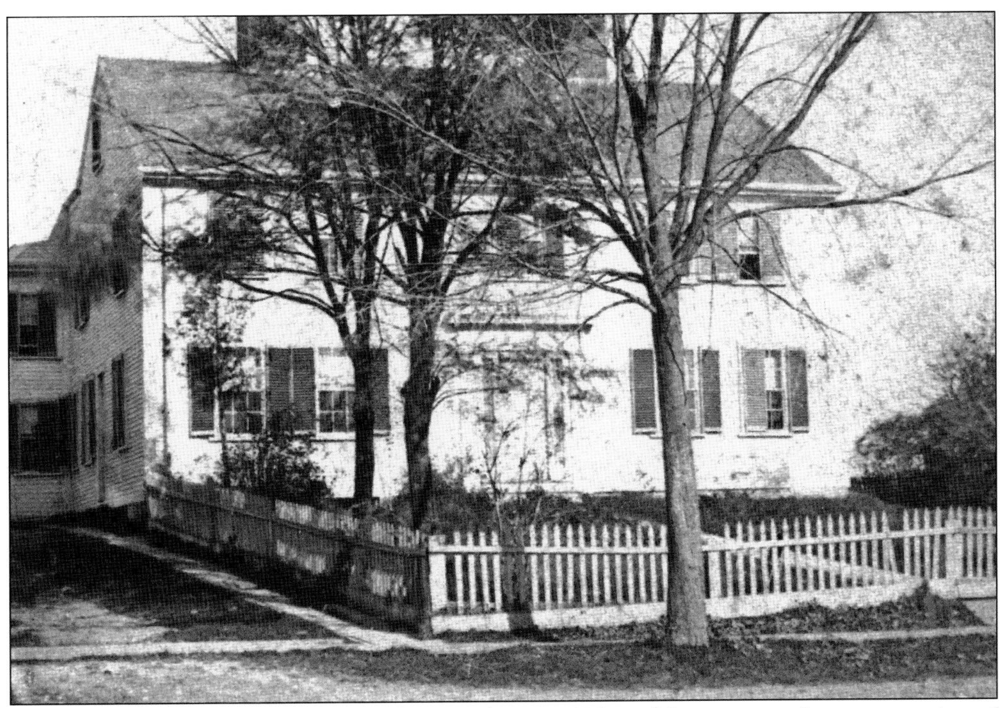

Dr. Daniel Rose was appointed the first warden in 1823, and he oversaw the construction of the new prison. He developed the unusual concept of the underground cells that reflected his theories of punishment and reformation. In his report to the legislature on January 23, 1823, he wrote, "State Prisons should be so constructed that even their aspect might be terrific and appear like what in fact they should be, dark and comfortless abodes of guilt and wretchedness." The photograph above shows his home on Main Street in Thomaston that he shared with his wife and seven children. The photograph below shows Dr. Rose's trunk, which is on display at the Thomaston Historical Society. Following the closure of the prison in 2002, prison artifacts and memorabilia were placed on loan to the historical society. (Courtesy of the Thomaston Historical Society.)

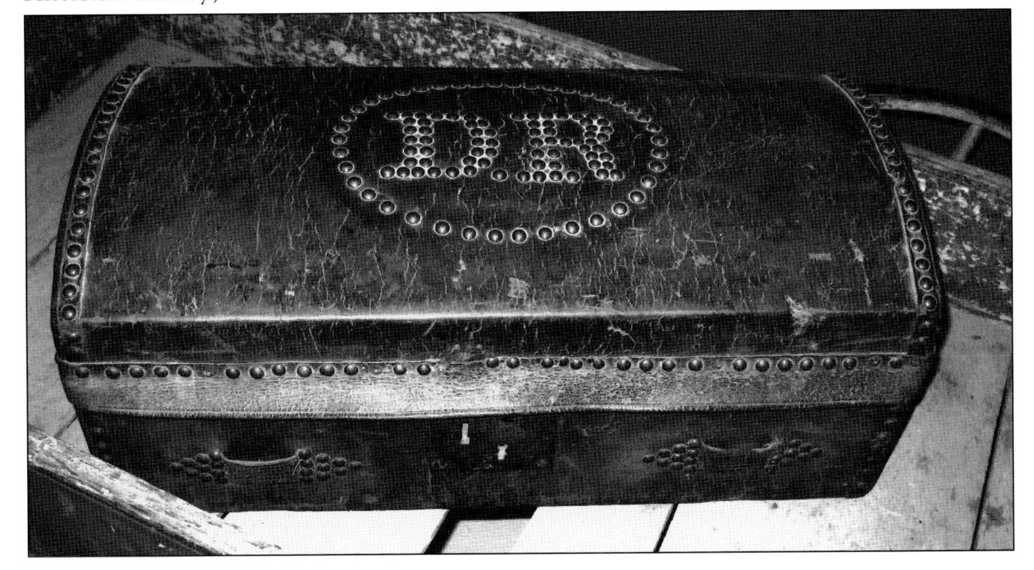

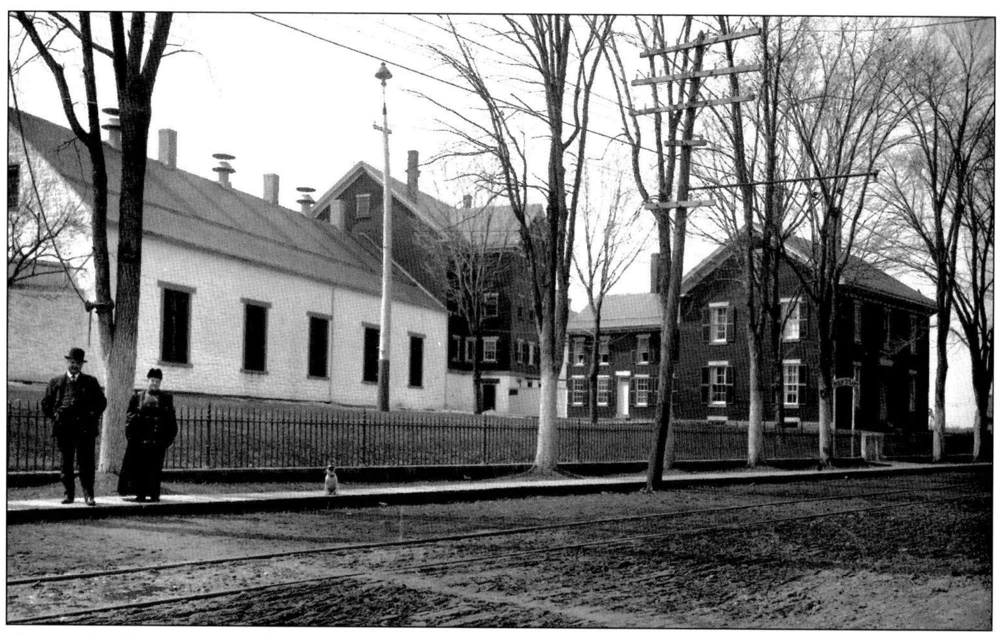

This early-1900s picture shows the east wing housing entrance and the warden's residence. The devastating 1923 fire destroyed nearly all of the prison buildings including the warden's residence. In 1936, the state purchased from Edward K. Leighton one of the lovely captains' houses across the street from the prison for $4,500 for wardens and their families to reside in.

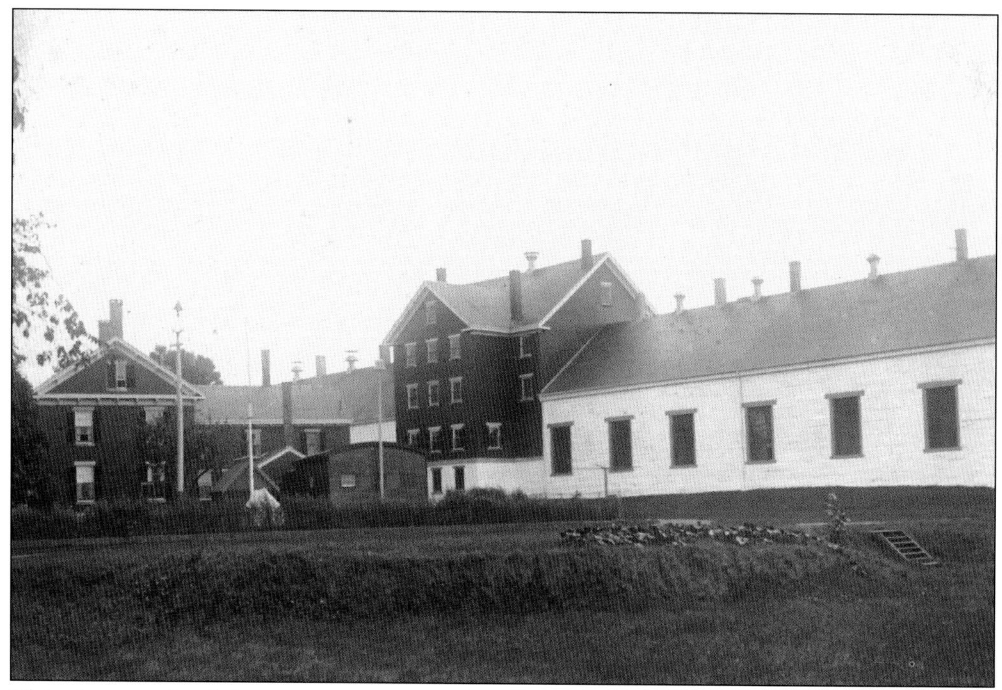

This photograph of the west wing convict housing was taken in the mid-1800s. (Courtesy of Paula Hopkins Dayboch.)

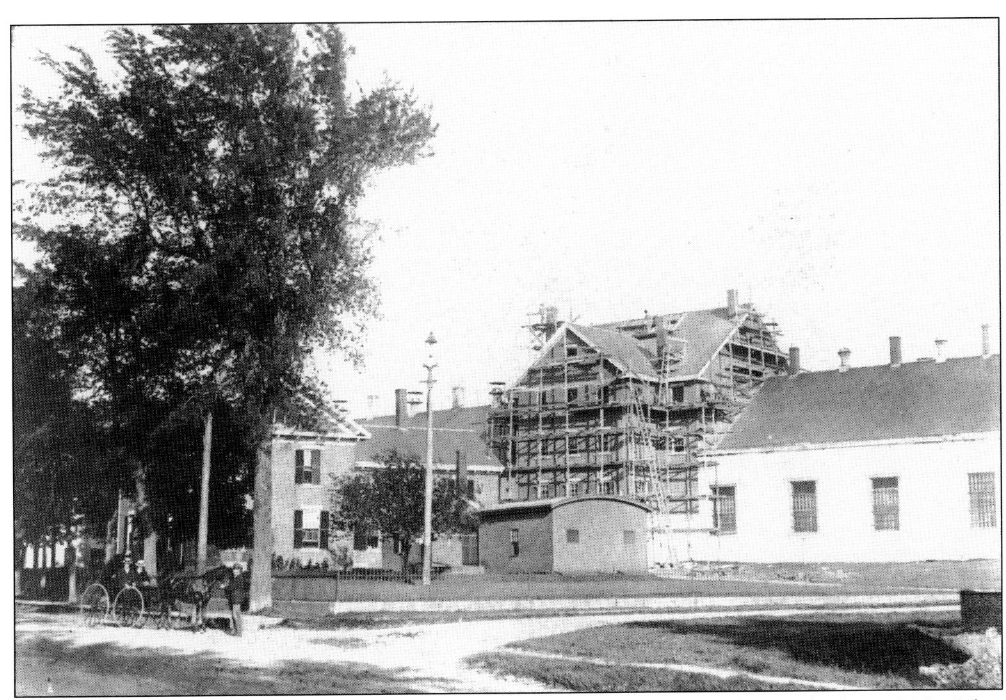

Above, the prison is shown undergoing one of many structural upgrades in the late 1800s. This view is from U.S. Route 1, or Main Street. Below is the addition of the cupola. (Courtesy of the Thomaston Historical Society.)

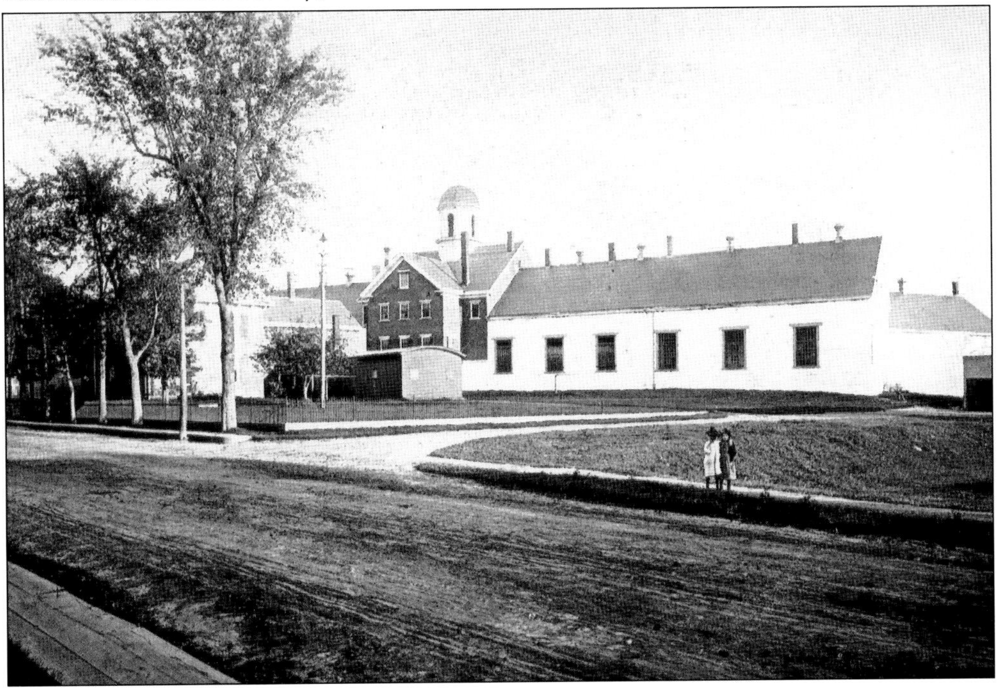

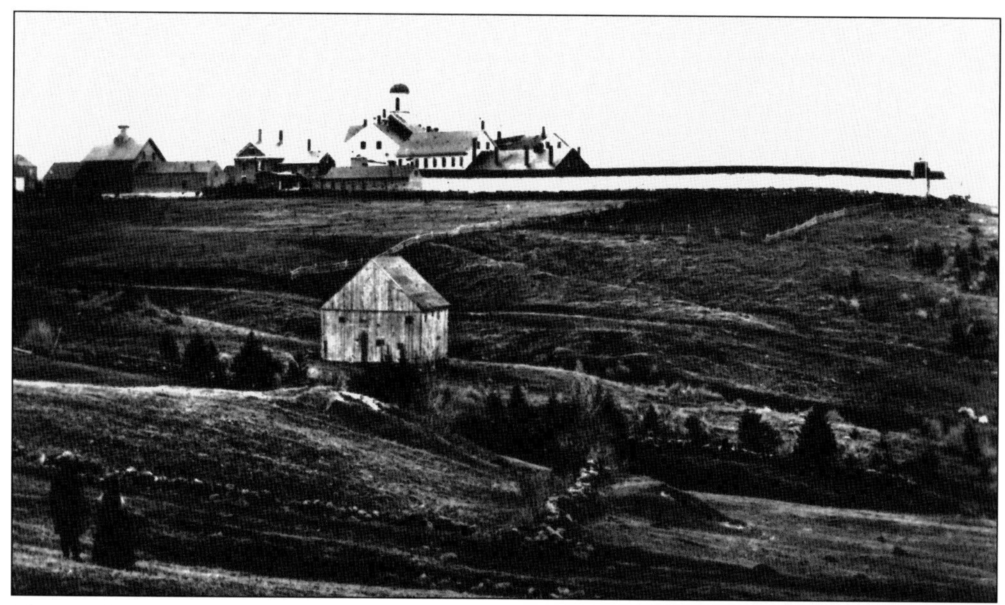

This 1870s view is of the prison as seen from the hill to the west near the former site of the Chapman and Flint shipyard on the St. George River. The shipyard relocated to Bath when the Knox and Lincoln Rail Road divided the property from its river access. Gardens were planted in the fields below the prison, in which convicts grew produce for the prison. (Courtesy of the Thomaston Historical Society.)

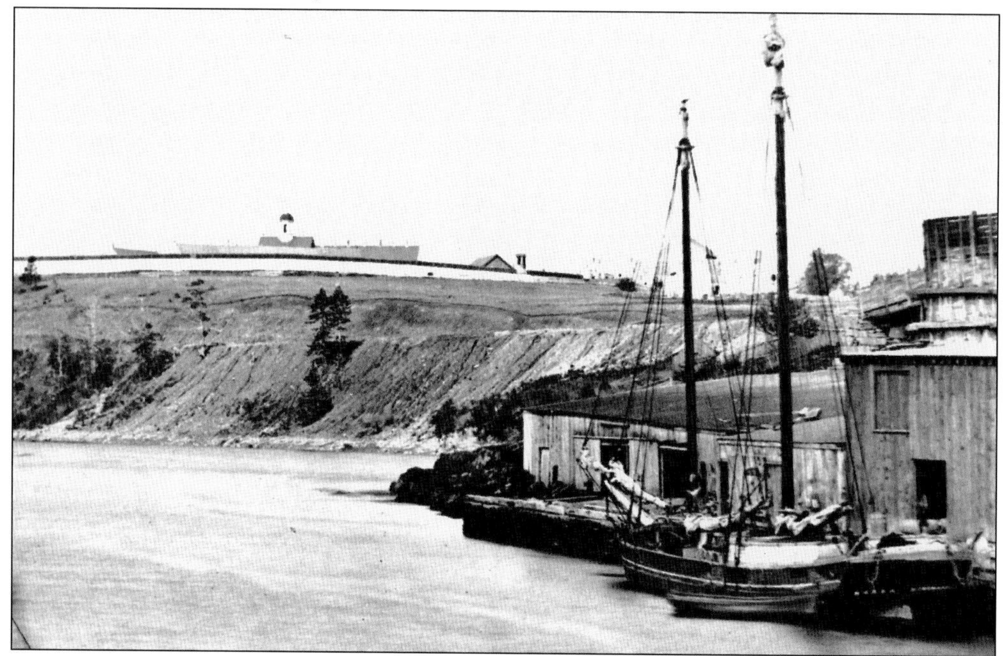

The schooner *Morea* lays dockside at an early Thomaston limestone kiln below the prison on the St. George River. The prison had a wharf above this area from which lime-carrying vessels would load quarried rock destined for faraway ports. The demands for limestone and granite created a need for vessels to transport the products, thus creating a major shipbuilding industry along Thomaston's waterfront. (Courtesy of the Thomaston Historical Society.)

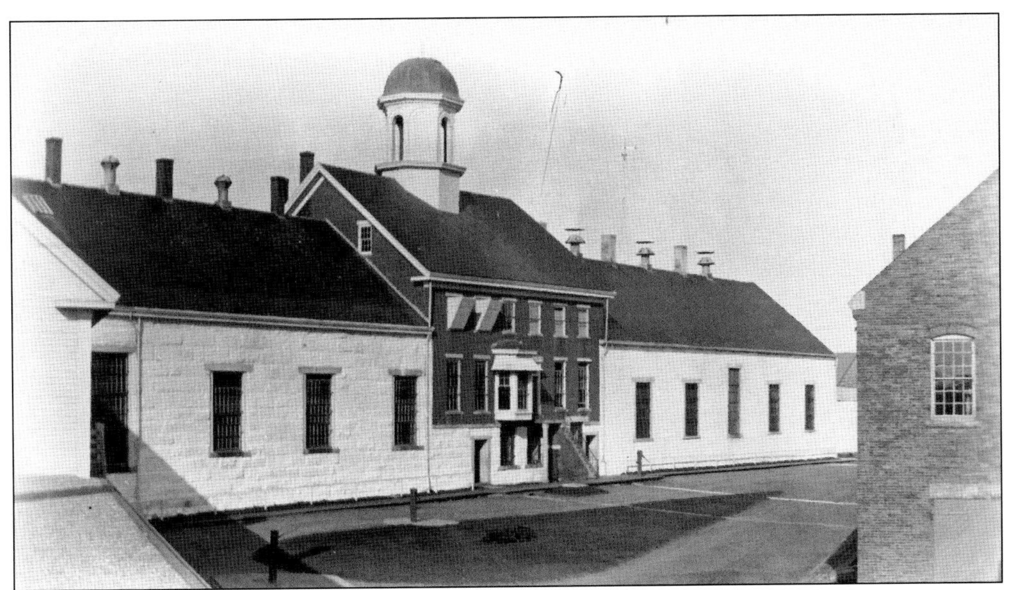

The first female convict was housed at the prison in 1839, and a separate living area had to be modified for her confinement. Reverse awnings were installed over women's windows to prevent them from seeing men, but still allowing natural light in. In 1935, the females were moved to the Women's Correctional Center in Skowhegan. The photograph below is an early 1900s view of the stairway entrance on the right leading to the guardroom below the women's living quarters.

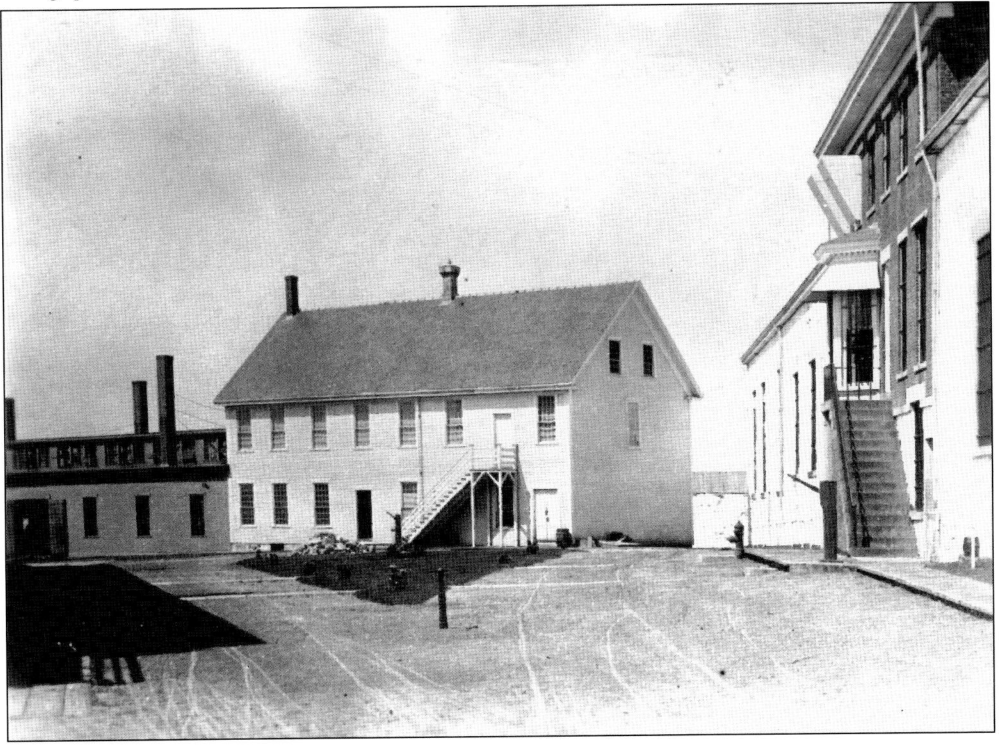

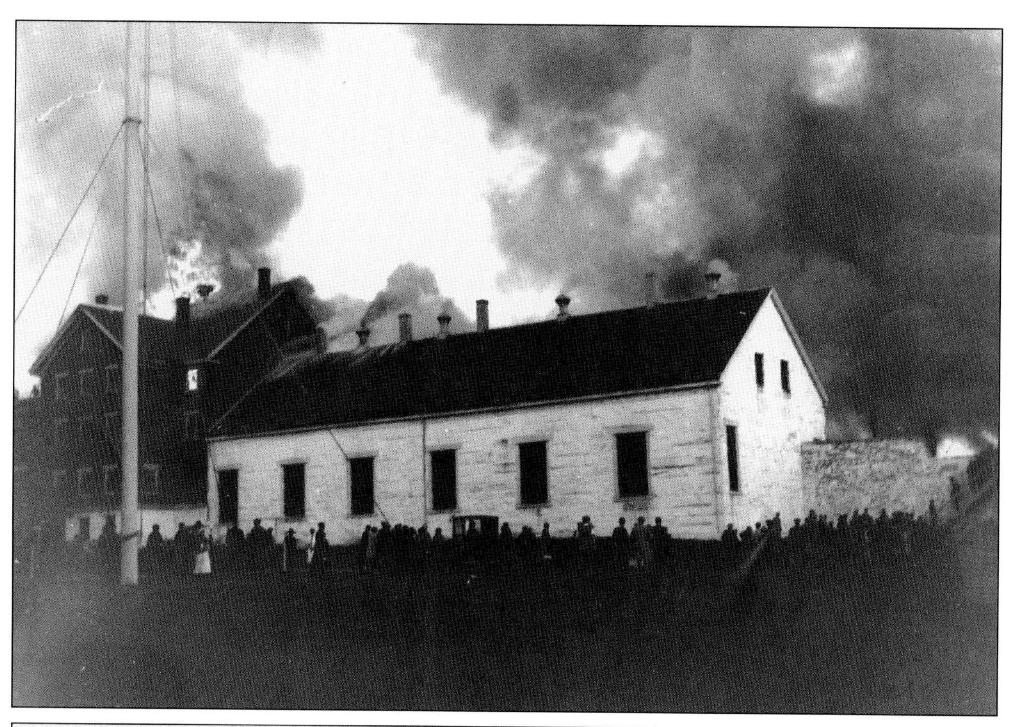

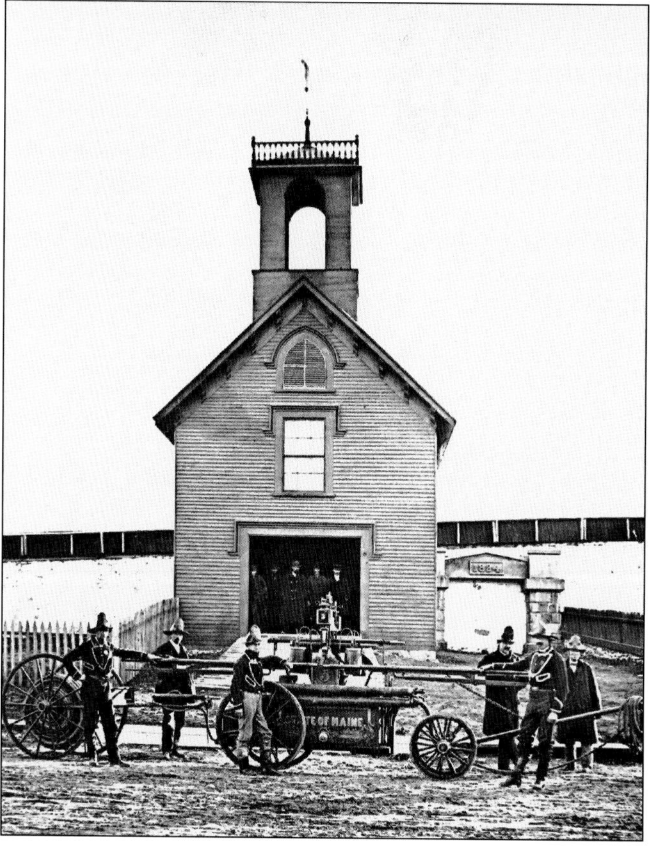

On December 22, 1851, fire broke out inside the prison. It originated from a stovepipe in the guardroom and spread rapidly, destroying the entire center and west wings of the prison, including offices and the warden's dwelling. Not one convict was lost. The prison was rebuilt and expanded in 1854, and a fire engine was purchased by the state. A group of citizens composed the State of Maine No. 3 Fire Department. This was later named the W. W. Rice for a prison administrator who had served as foreman. (Courtesy of the Thomaston Historical Society.)

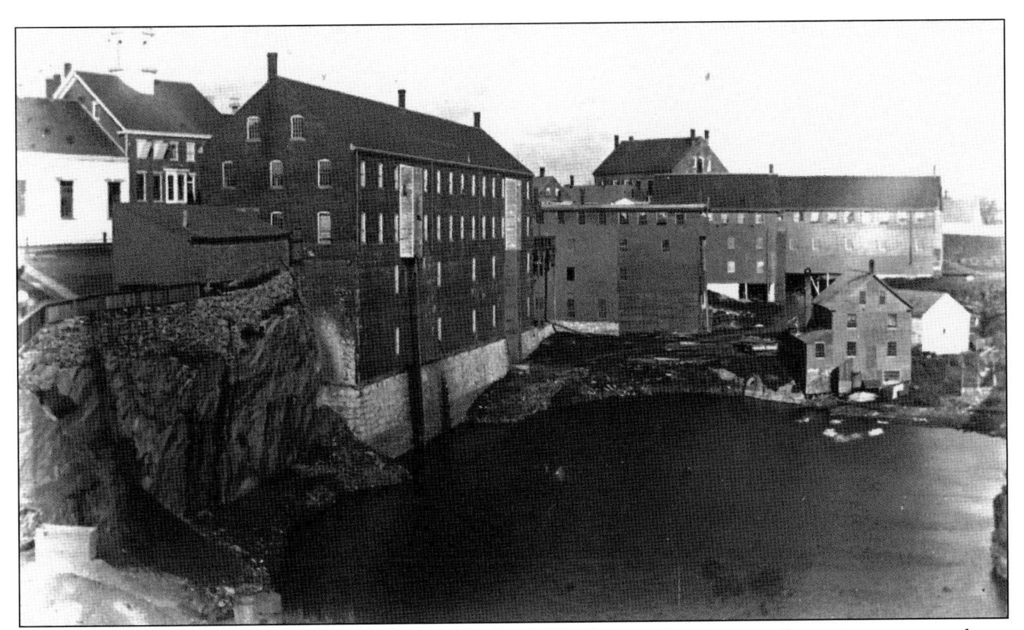

This 1885 photograph shows the quarry that had filled in with water and seeping sewage from the prison. As early as 1886, the prison physician, H. C. Levensaler, M. D., recommended the drainage of the cesspool for health reasons. By 1903, drainage was completed with the installation of hundreds of feet of pipe laid down to the St. George River.

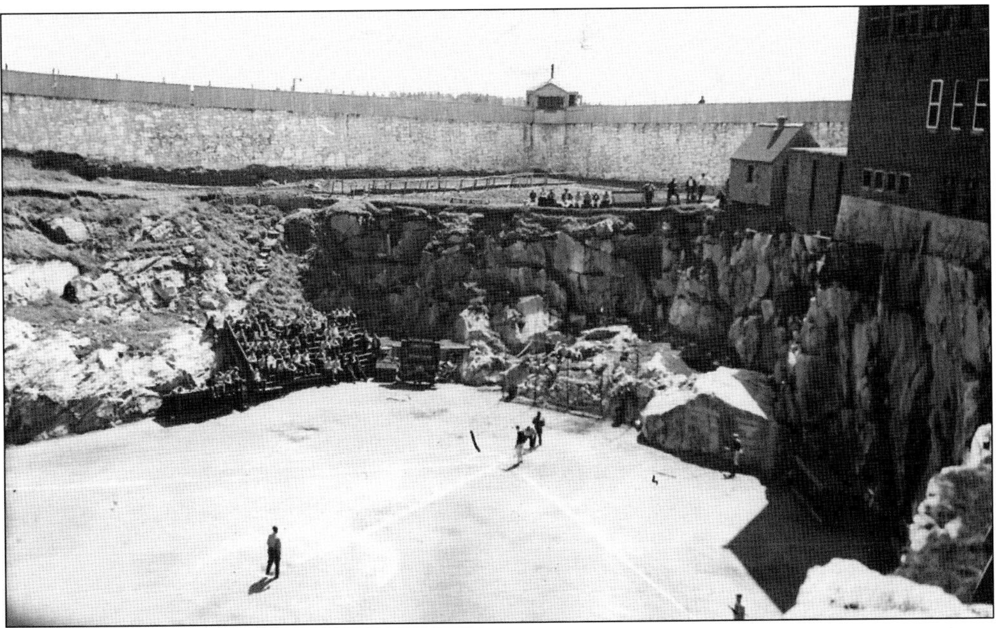

Warden Hillman Smith wrote in his 1903 *Maine State Prison Report*, "the old quarry with its filthy cesspool, an unsightly nuisance for so many years, is today a clean, attractive lawn." The cleaned-up quarry became the background for many recreational activities such as baseball. (Courtesy of Sue Dow Thurston, Rebecca Dow Burnham, and Nan Dow Mulford.)

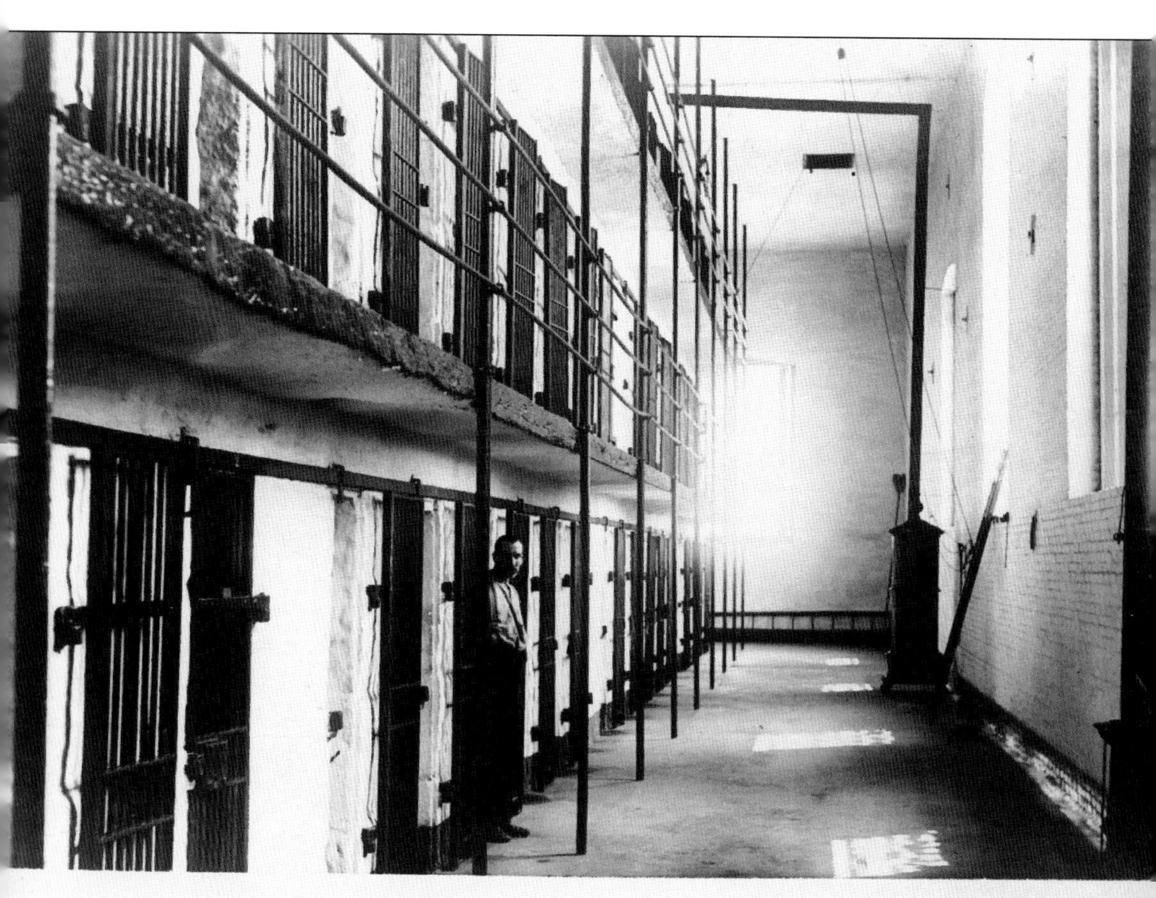

This late-1800s or early-1900s photograph is of the interior of a housing wing prior to the 1923 fire. After the fire, the wing was rebuilt much the same except for the addition of a stairway and second-level security post at the far end to improve observation. The catwalks were closed in to prevent anyone from "accidentally" falling off.

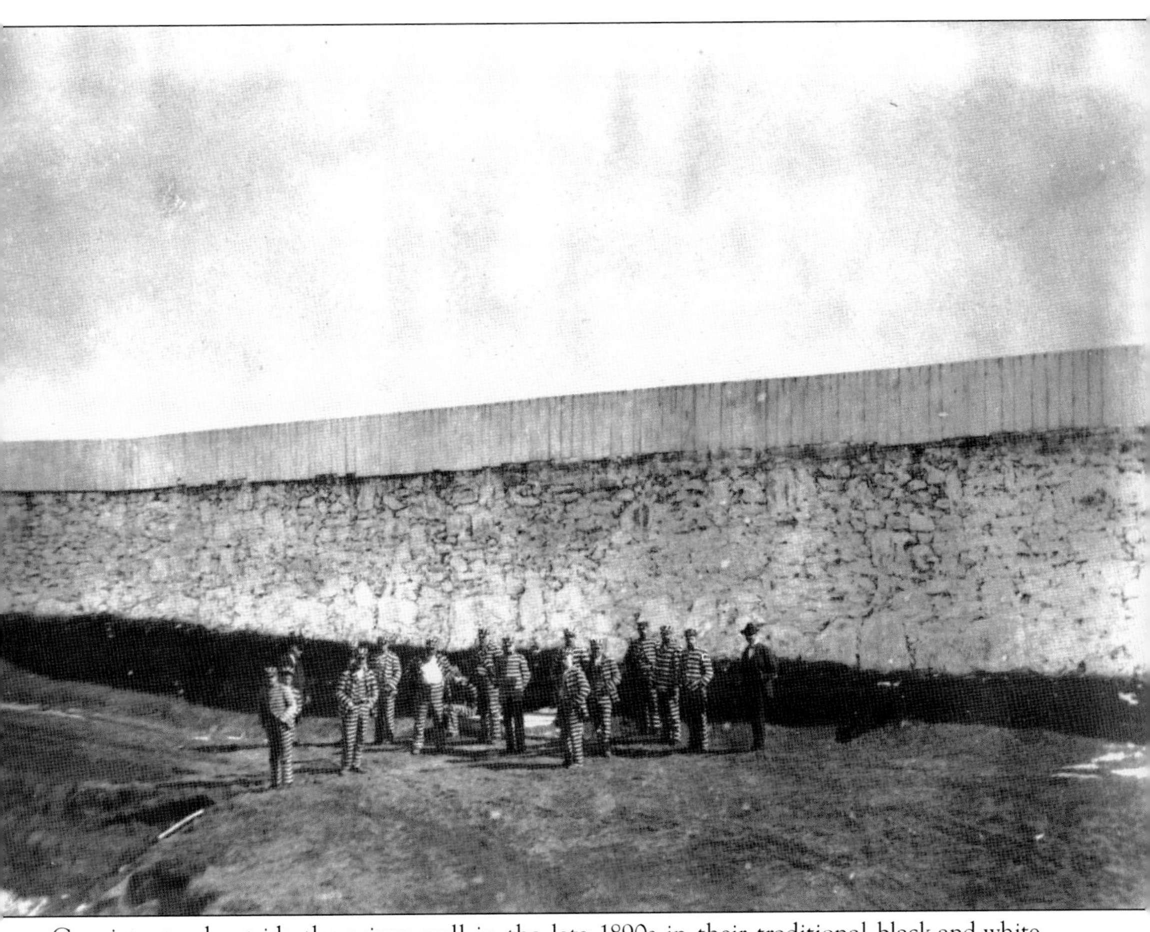

Convicts stand outside the prison wall in the late 1890s in their traditional black-and-white striped uniforms, conspicuous and often thought of as "cruel garb," as shown in the above picture. Earlier uniforms consisted of shirts with one red sleeve and the other black. Their trousers were similar in appearance.

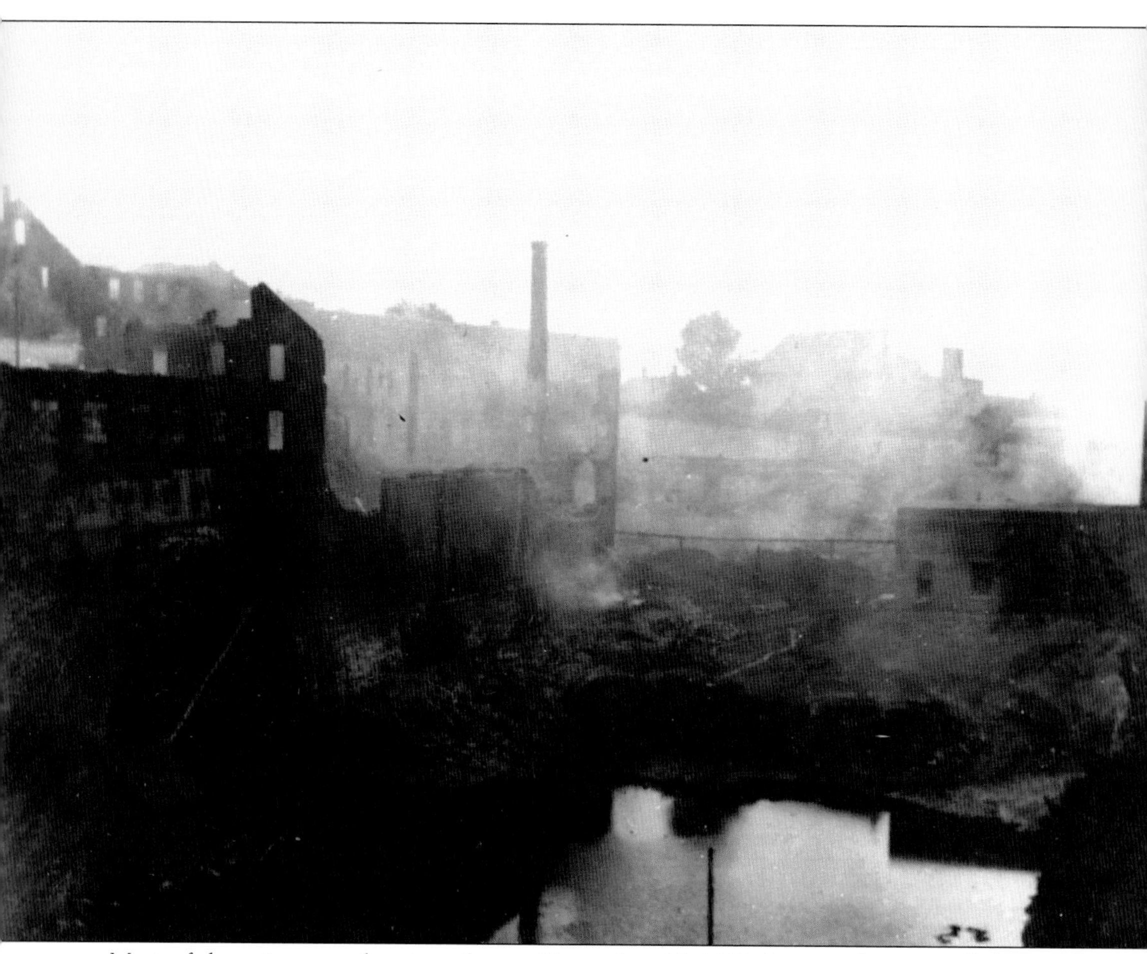

Most of the prison was lost in a fire on September 15, 1923. It started as a small fire in the broom shop and spread rapidly to other shops, including the woodshop that contained 75 cords of wood. Convict living areas were also destroyed, but with no loss of life, and the convicts remained orderly. The estimated loss was $500,000. In 1924, the rebuilt prison was dedicated by Gov. Percival P. Baxter.

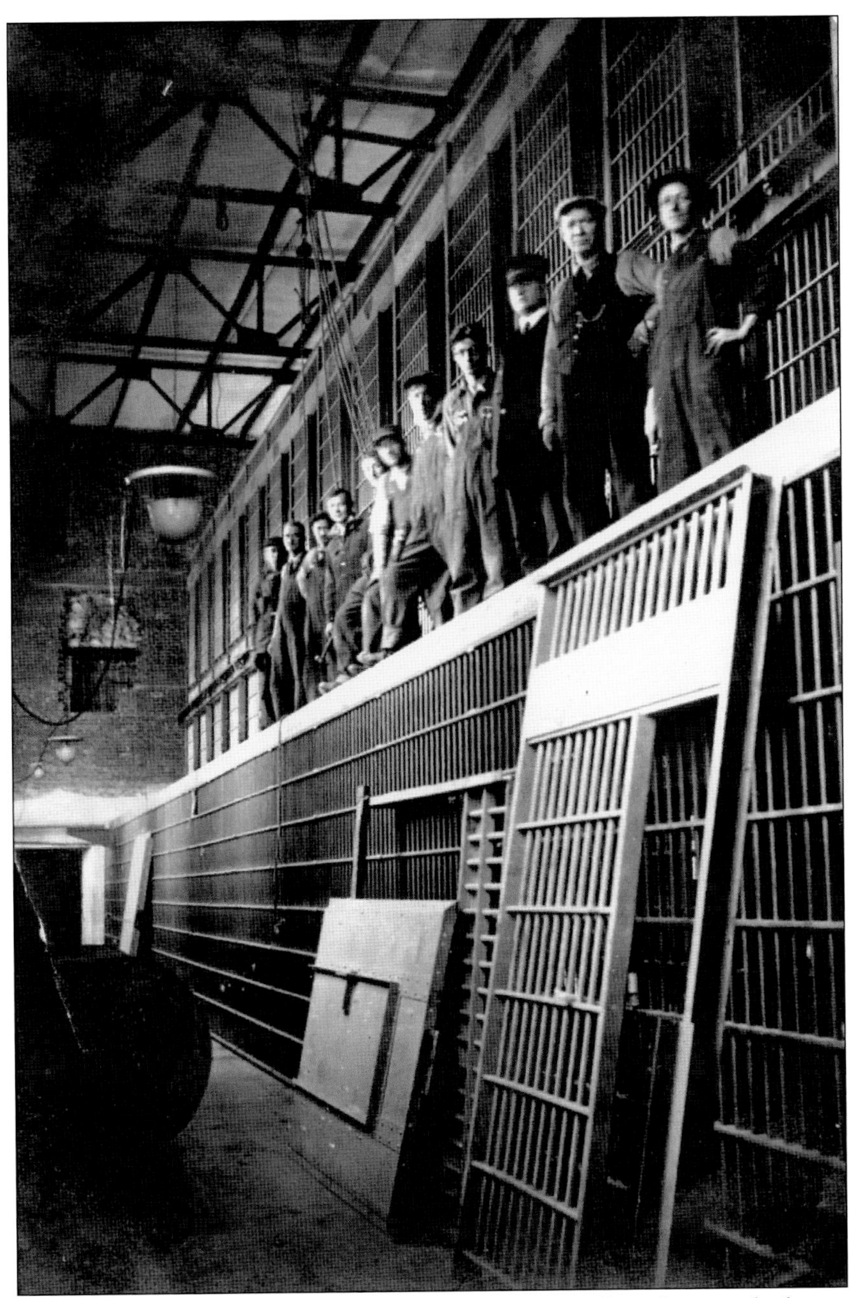

After the fire, convict labor was used to rebuild the prison. This photograph shows a group of convicts installing cell doors in one of the housing wings. The rebuilt prison was on the same footprint as the former one. Coincidentally, the dedication of the new prison took place 100 years after the dedication of the original prison. The 1924 prison marked a new era in penology. Convicts were permitted to converse with one another under limited conditions, and they would receive pay for their labor, ranging from 30¢ to 50¢ a day. Some of their earnings were sent to their families, and some were set aside for their release. A unique Welfare and Honor League was established whereby convicts would govern themselves through a board of five elected "governors." (Courtesy of John Struk.)

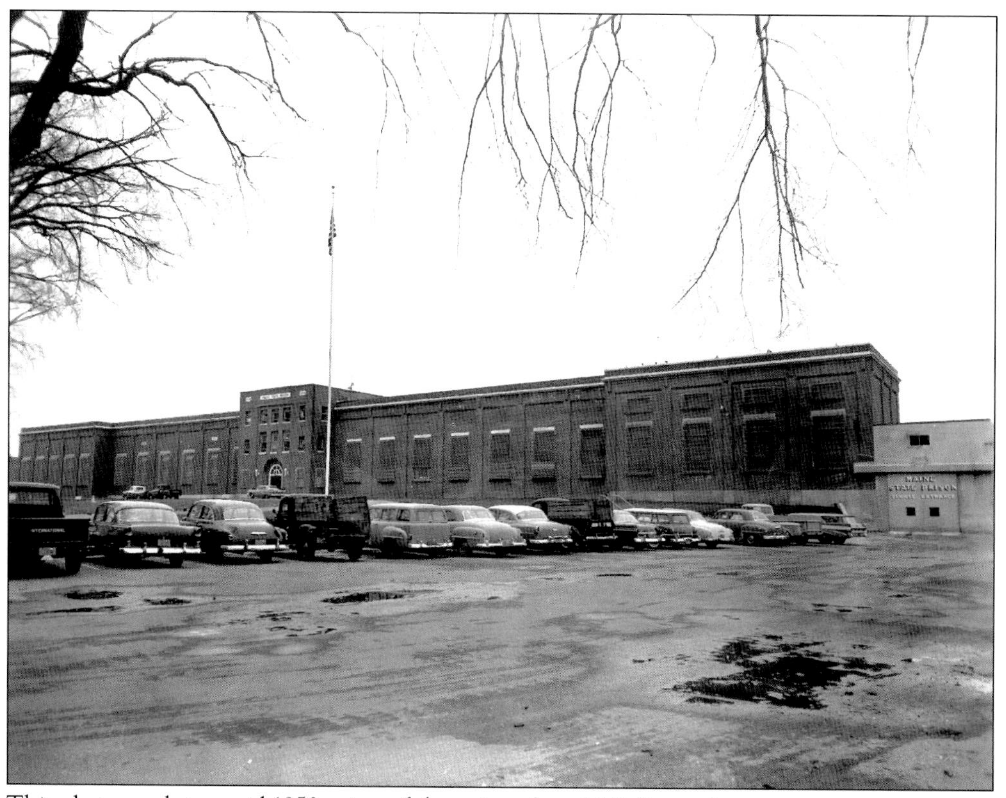

This photograph is a mid-1950s view of the prison from U.S. Route 1.

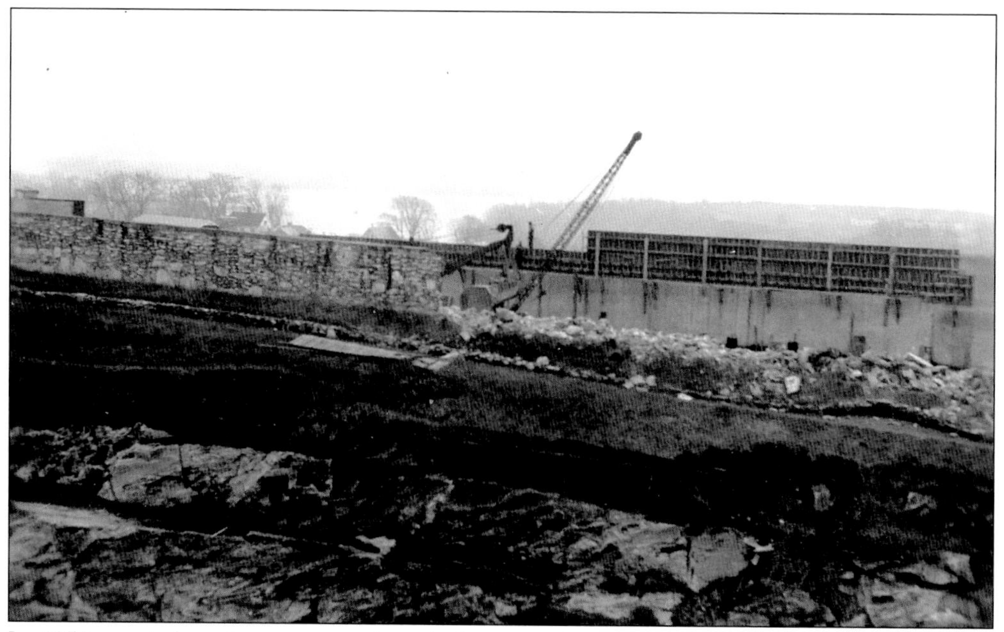

In 1958, a reinforced concrete wall with five guard towers was completed. Each tower was equipped with shatterproof glass, electric heat, and communication capability with the deputy warren's office. An armed officer was on duty at each tower.

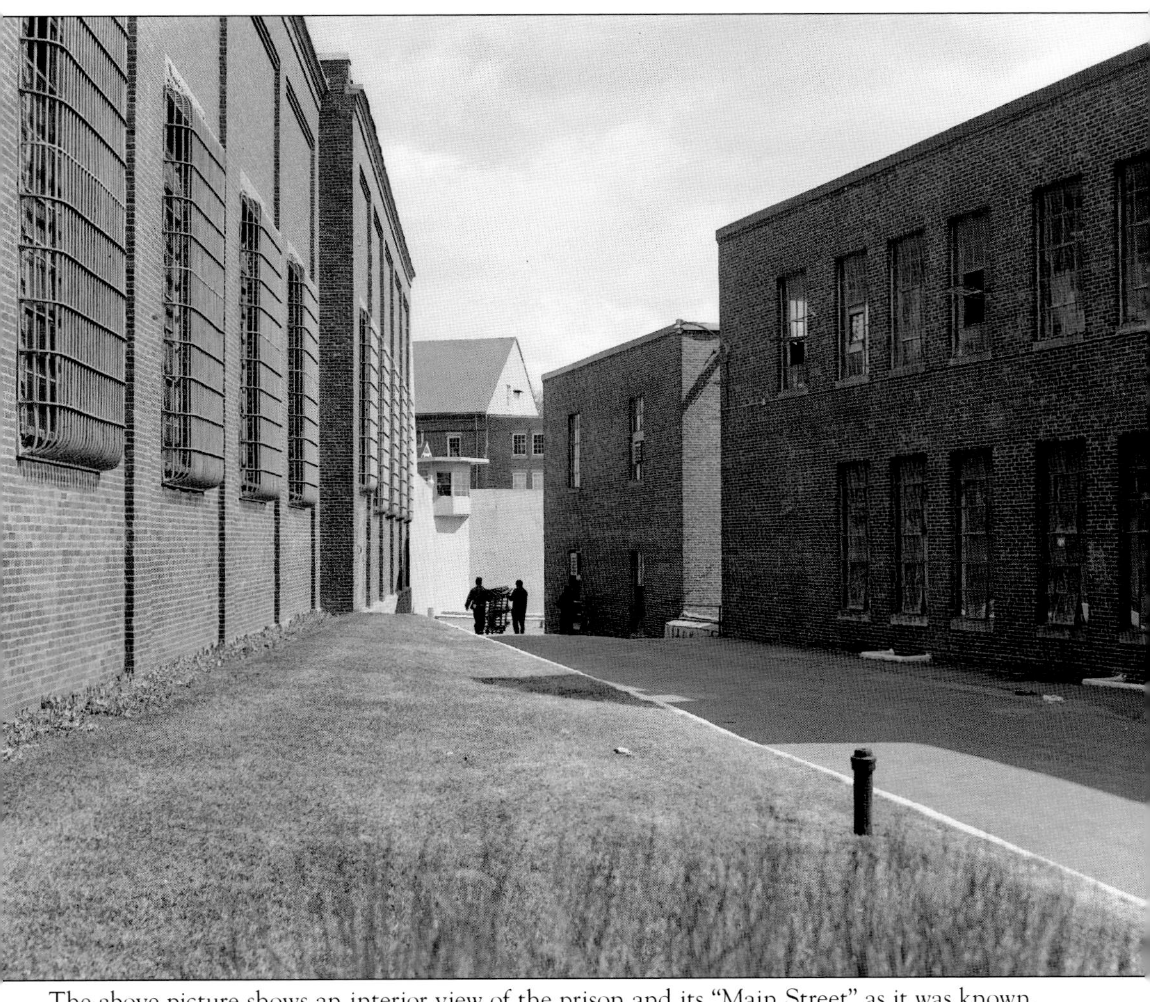

The above picture shows an interior view of the prison and its "Main Street" as it was known. Main Street continues on past the craft room on the right and the east wing on the left. In the far background beyond the wall post is the prison showroom building.

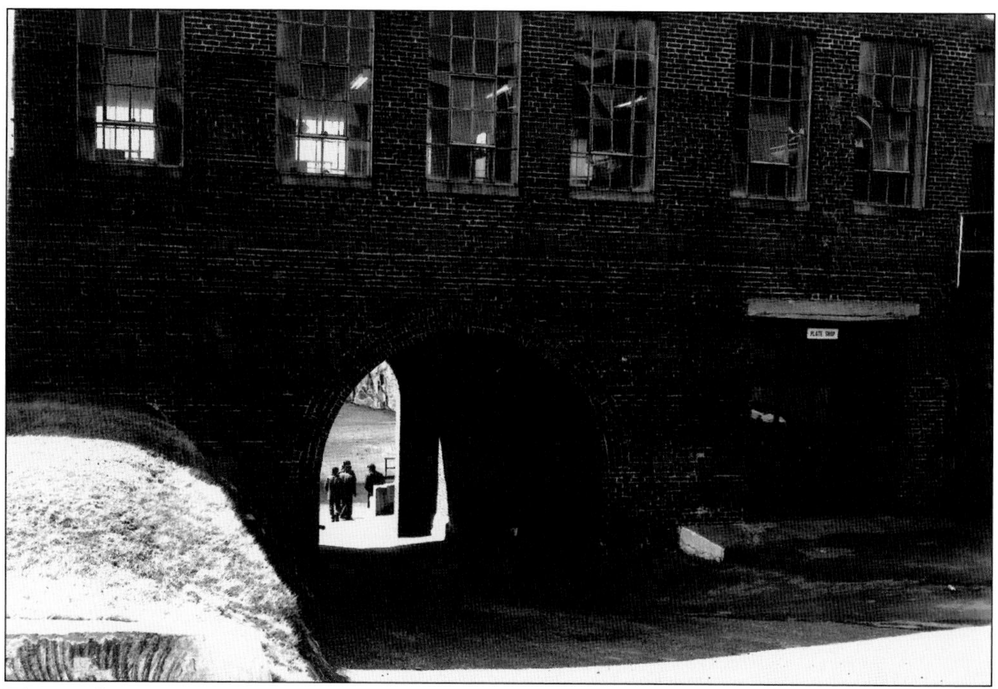

The "archway" was the only egress to the lower yard where recreation and the canteen were located. Its enclosed angle made visibility difficult, and inmates took advantage of this to transfer contraband or to assault other inmates and staff. In the winter months, the 30-degree pitch became icy and dangerous for foot and vehicle traffic.

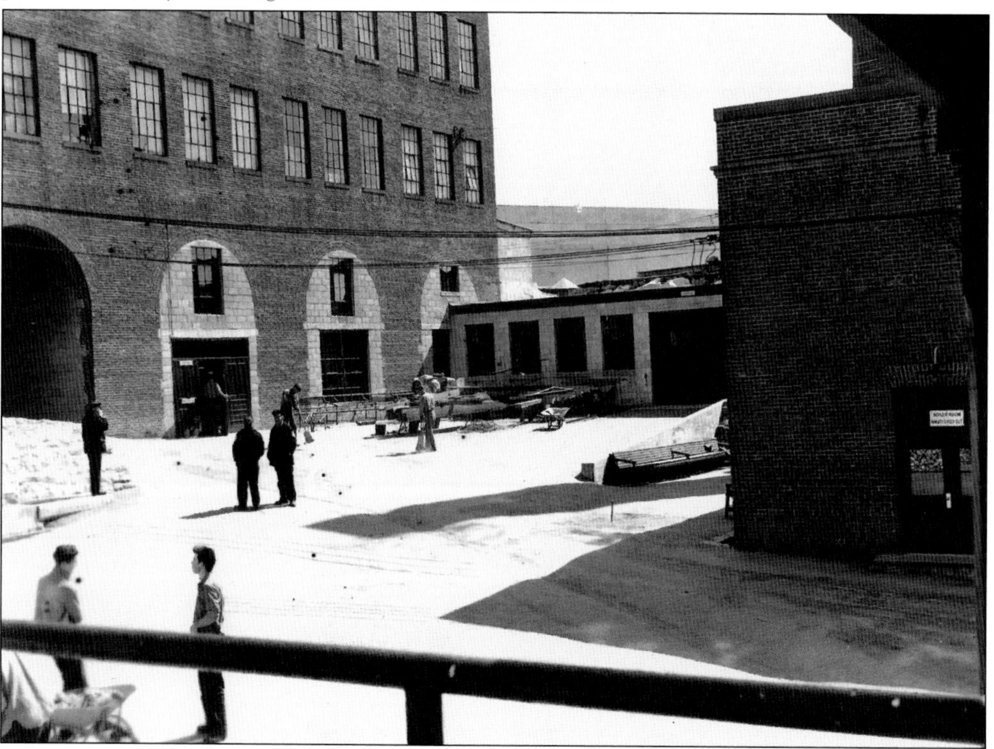

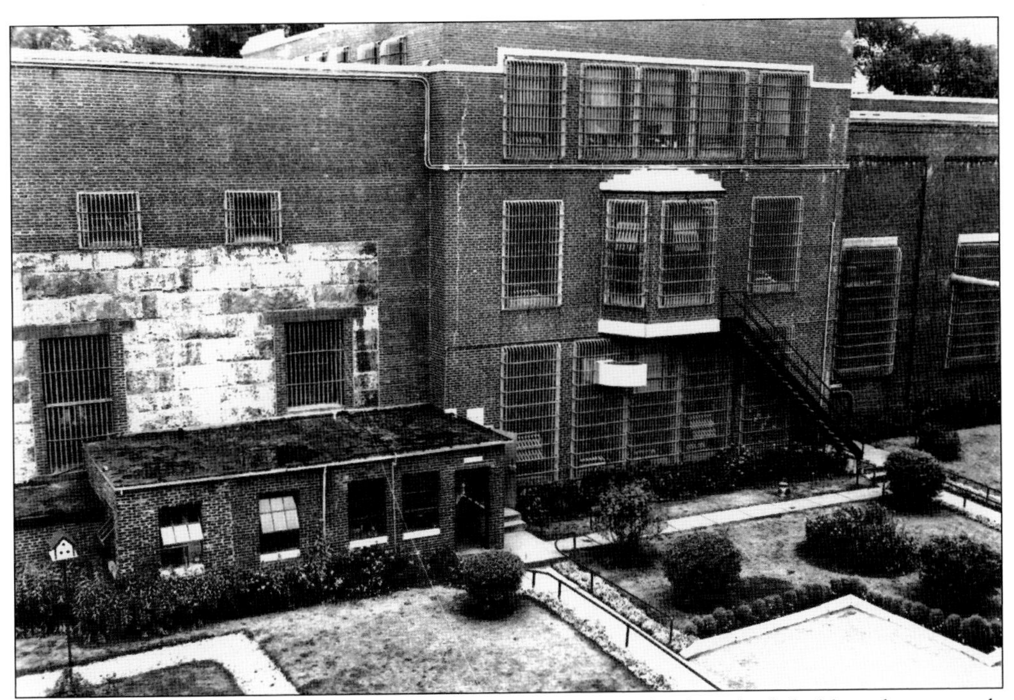

This 1960s picture of the interior prison shows the "garden shack," which held gardening tools for inmates to maintain the gardens and lawns inside the prison.

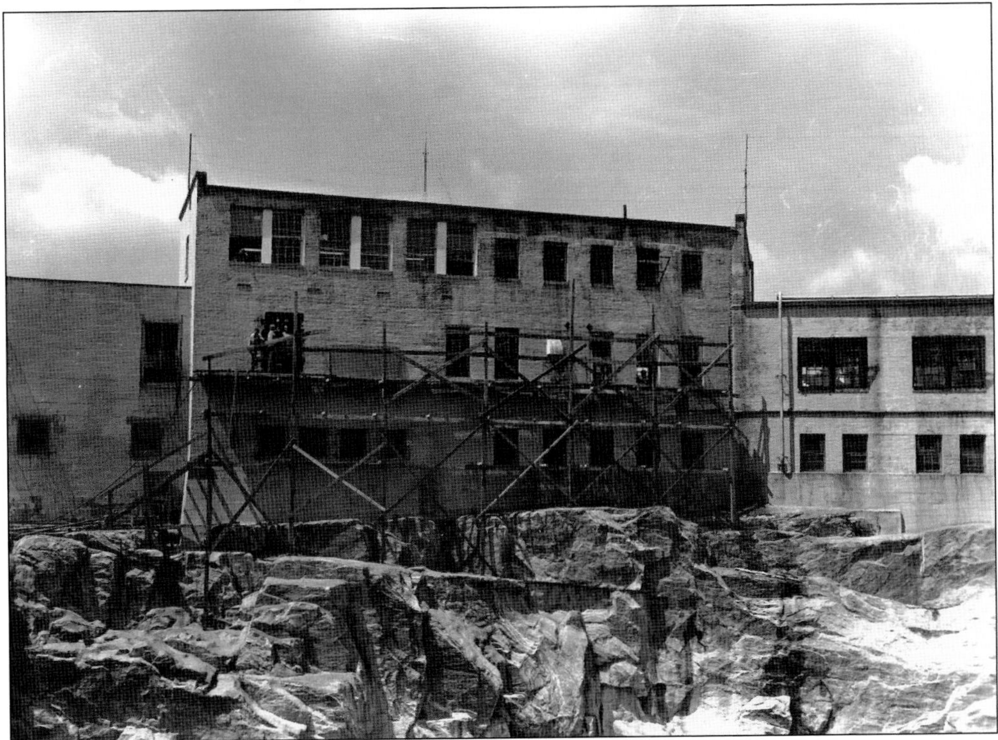

This photograph was taken in the 1980s and shows workers putting stucco on the outside of the industries building that was built above the quarry.

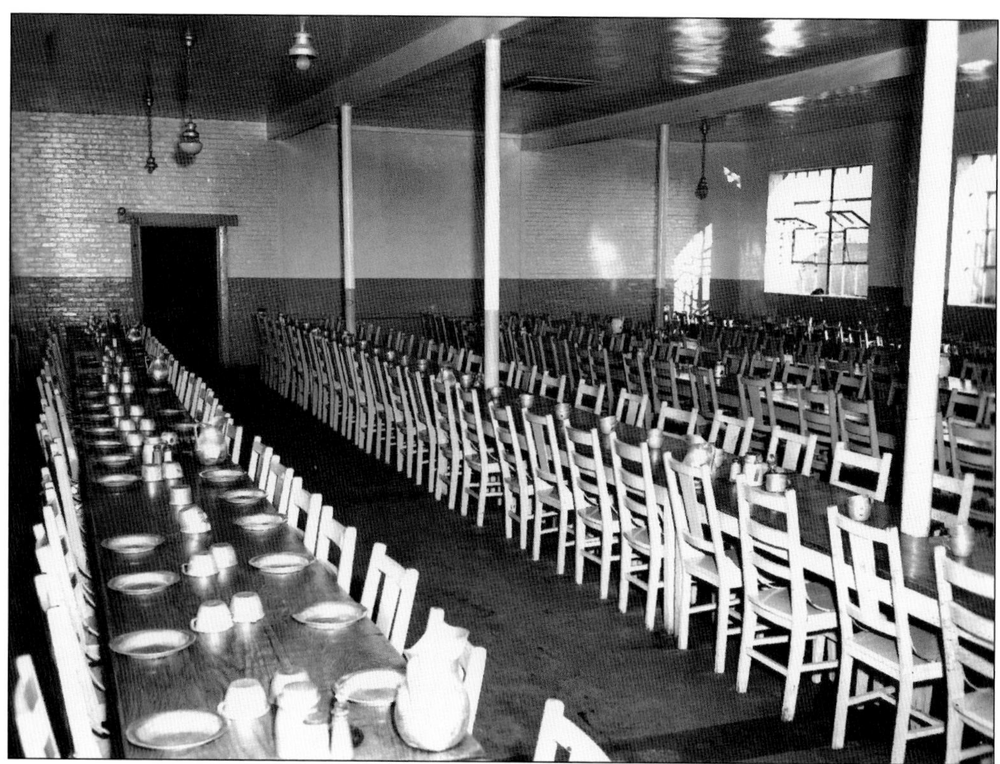

Early convicts were not allowed to converse. At the dedication of the rebuilt prison in 1924, Board of Prison Commissioners member Charles S. Hichborn informed the convicts of the following major change, "Man is essentially a social being. Unsocial conditions are unnatural and unwholesome. If carried to extreme, they are demoralizing and brutalizing. After being seated at tables in the Dining Room, conversation will be allowed."

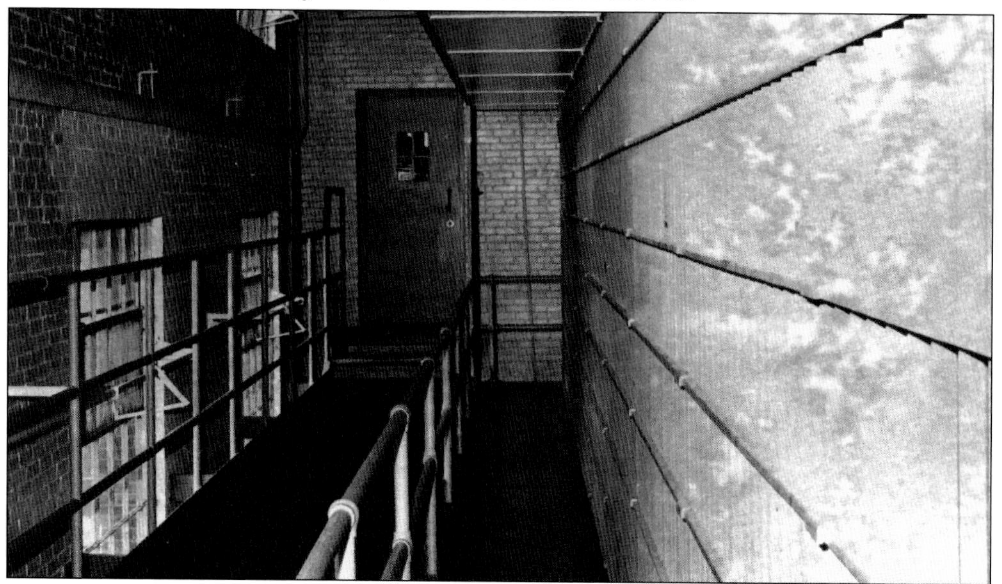

This photograph is an early-1960s view of the door leading from the west block housing to the dormitories and on to the segregation unit.

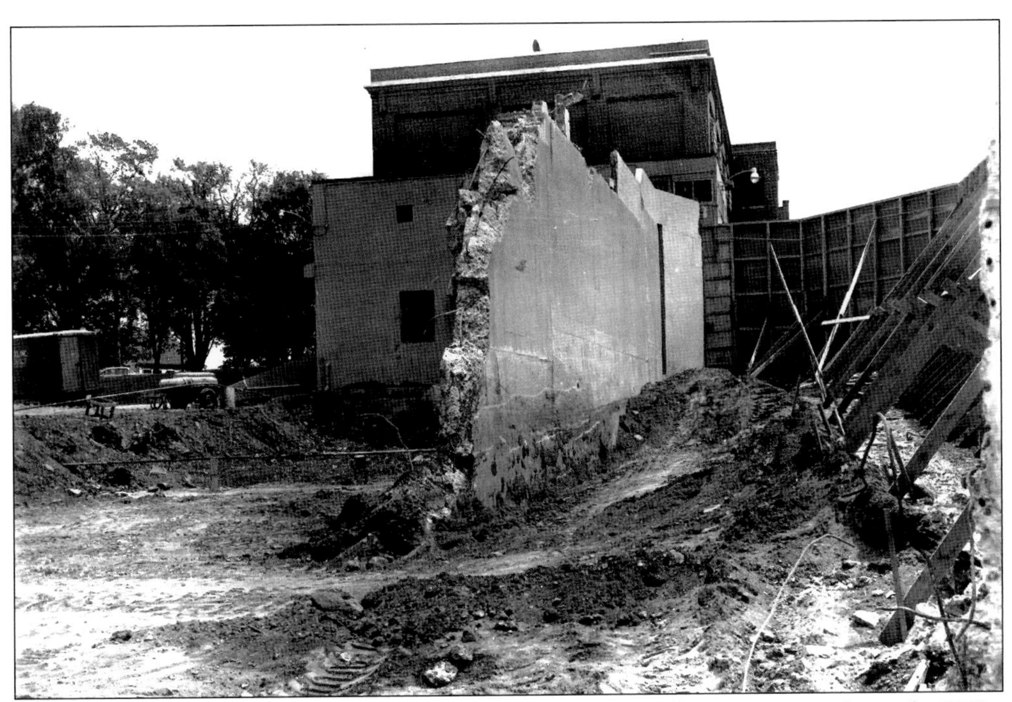

Progressive reform led to the improvement of the prison's infrastructure in the early 1960s. Pictured above is the demolition of a section of the west wall in preparation for a new housing unit that would contain segregation, the dormitories, and the commissary. Shown below is a temporary plywood barrier used in place of the concrete wall during construction.

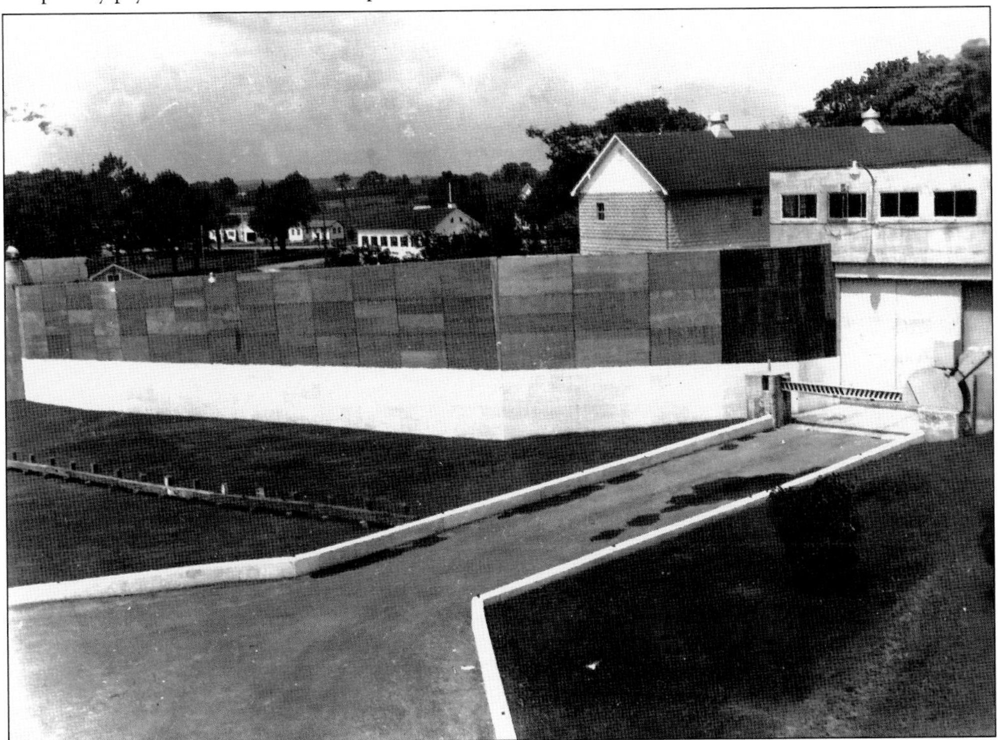

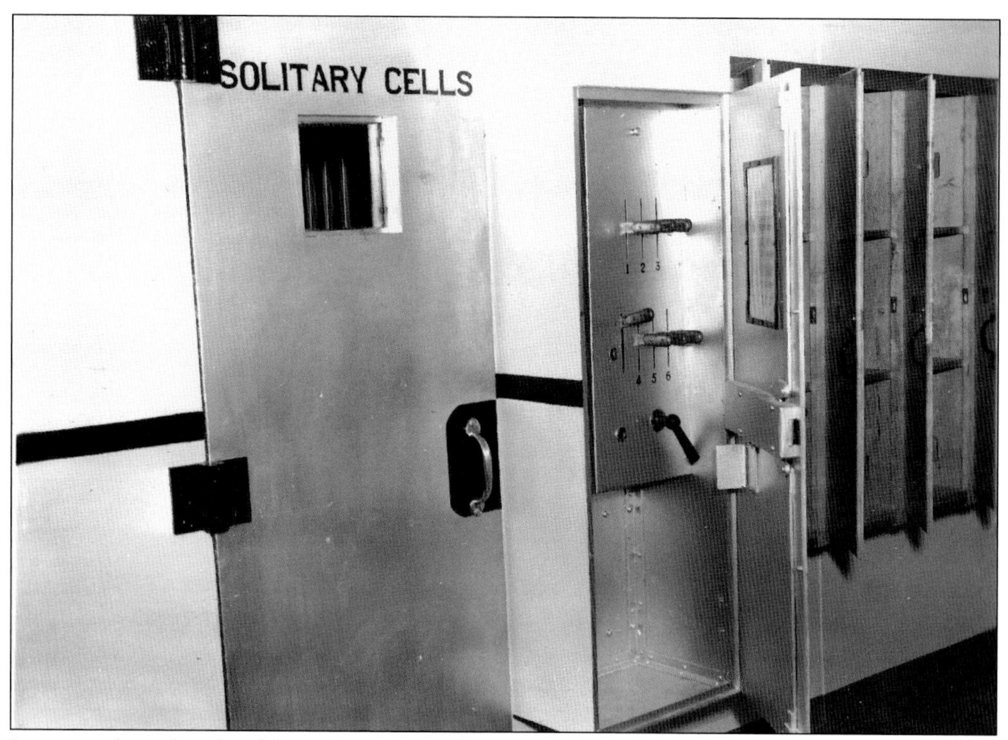

Inmates who refused to follow the prison rules were segregated from the general population and lost their privileges for a period of time. Each cell had an inner door, a small entrance, and an outer solid door with an observation window.

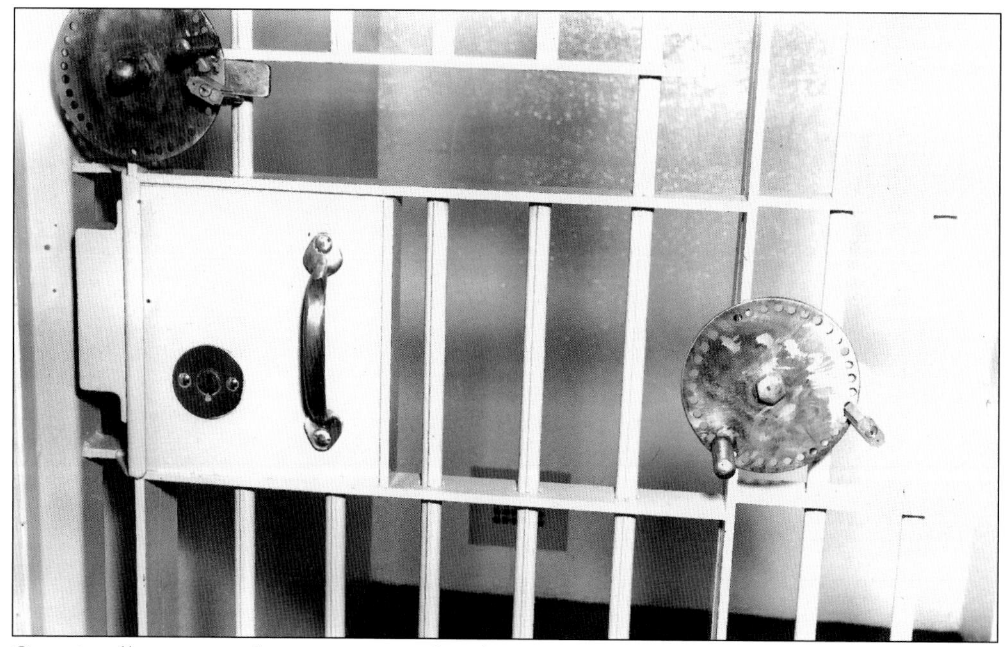

Occasionally, segregated inmates engaged in disruptive and loud behavior, such as rattling their cell doors. The "cell wheel" pictured above was attached to the cell frame and door, preventing doors from rattling.

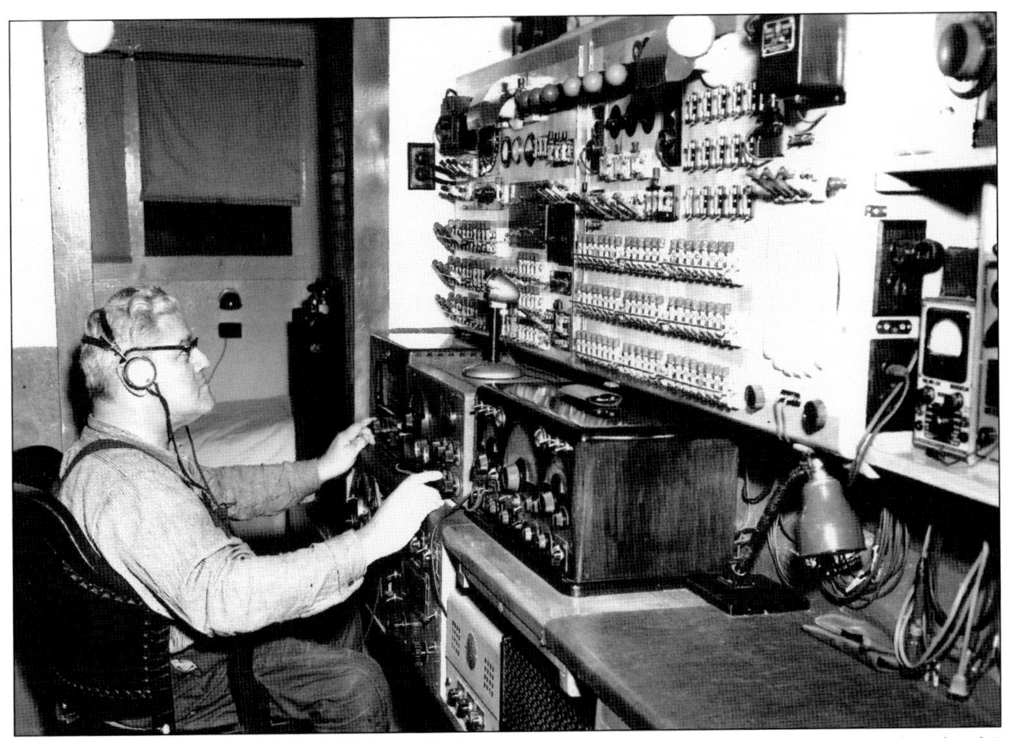

An inmate is shown in the above picture working in what was known as the "radio shack" where a limited selection of radio stations and programs were provided to inmates in their cells. Inmates could purchase headphones to listen to these programs.

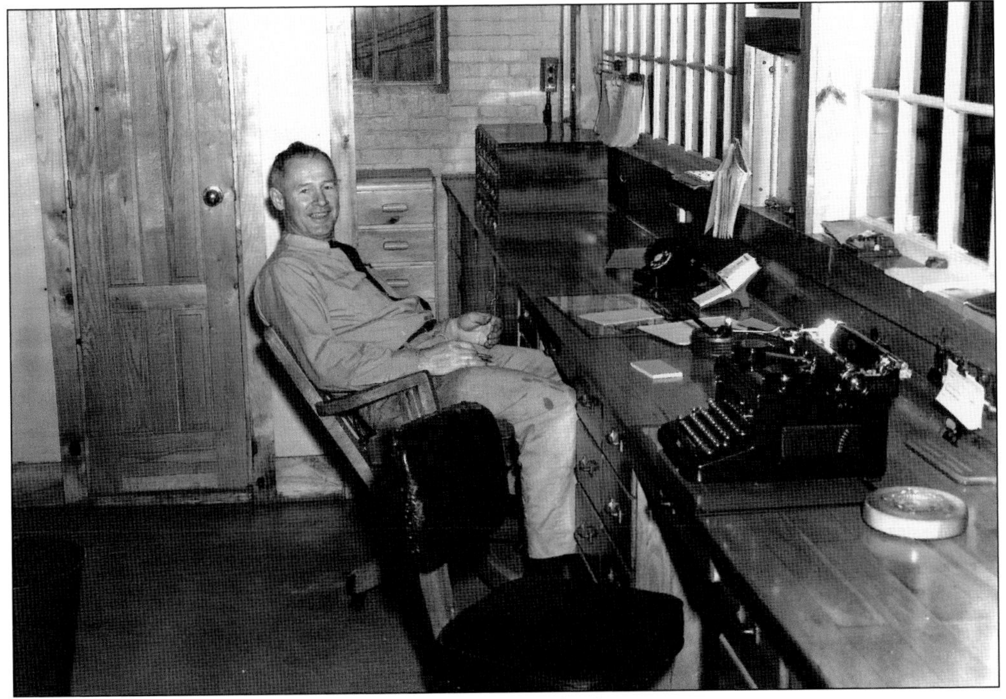

A prison guard is seen here working in an office inside the prison.

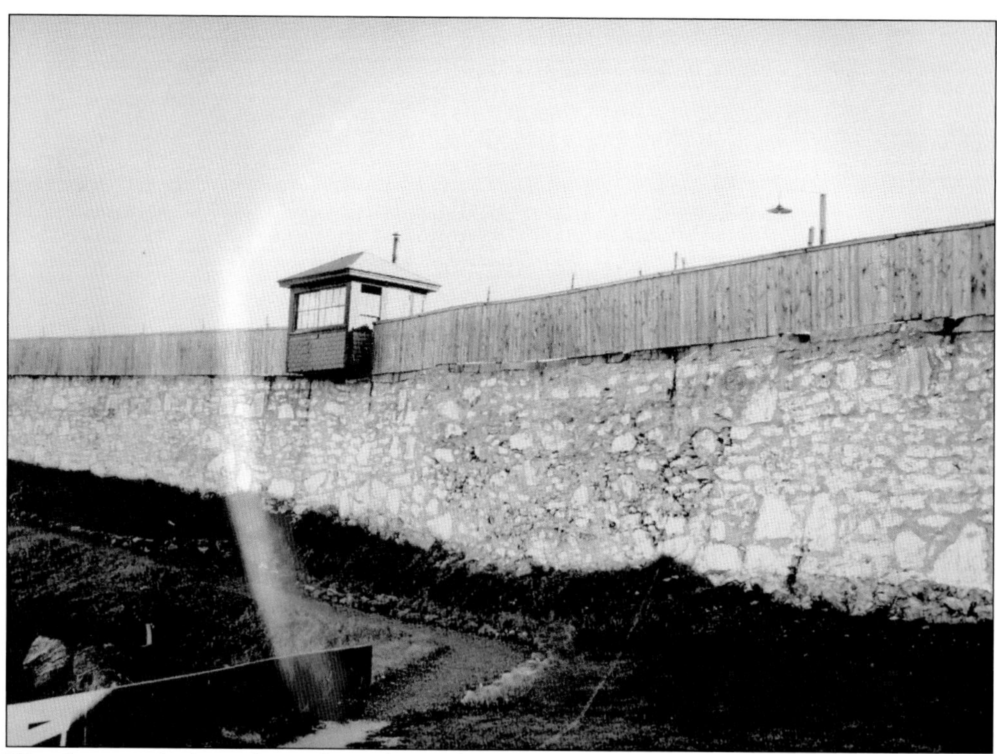

The photograph above shows the early watchtower yard post above the original stone wall with wood fencing on top. The photograph below is of the same tower post on a replacement cement wall. Although there were significant technological advances over time, the mission of the wall posts never really changed. (Below, courtesy of Michael Lokuta.)

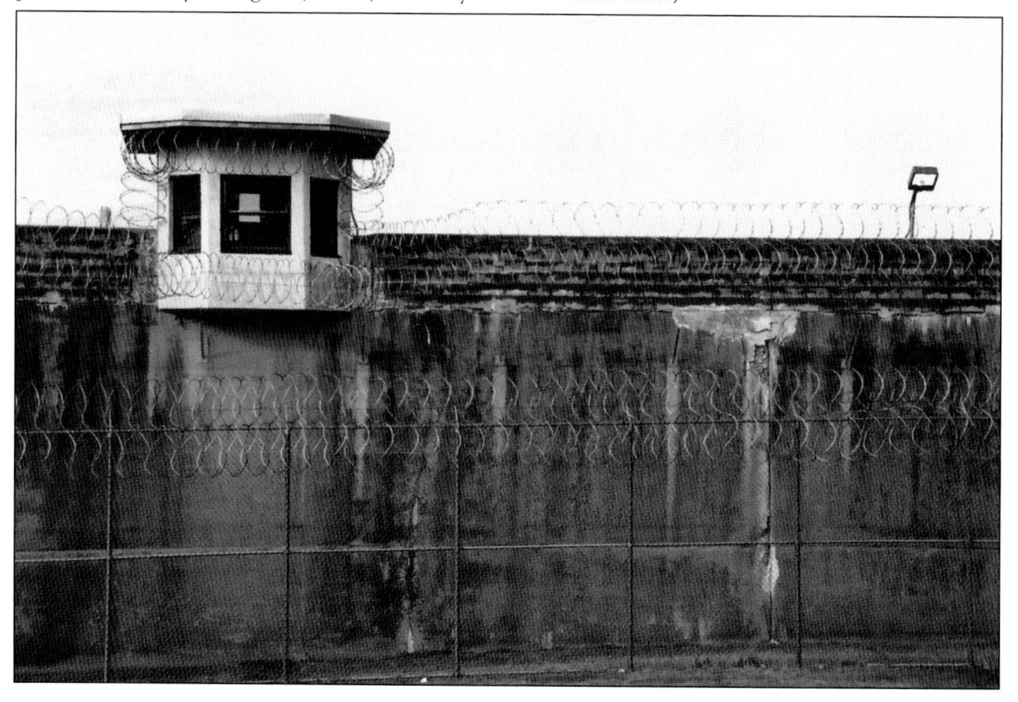

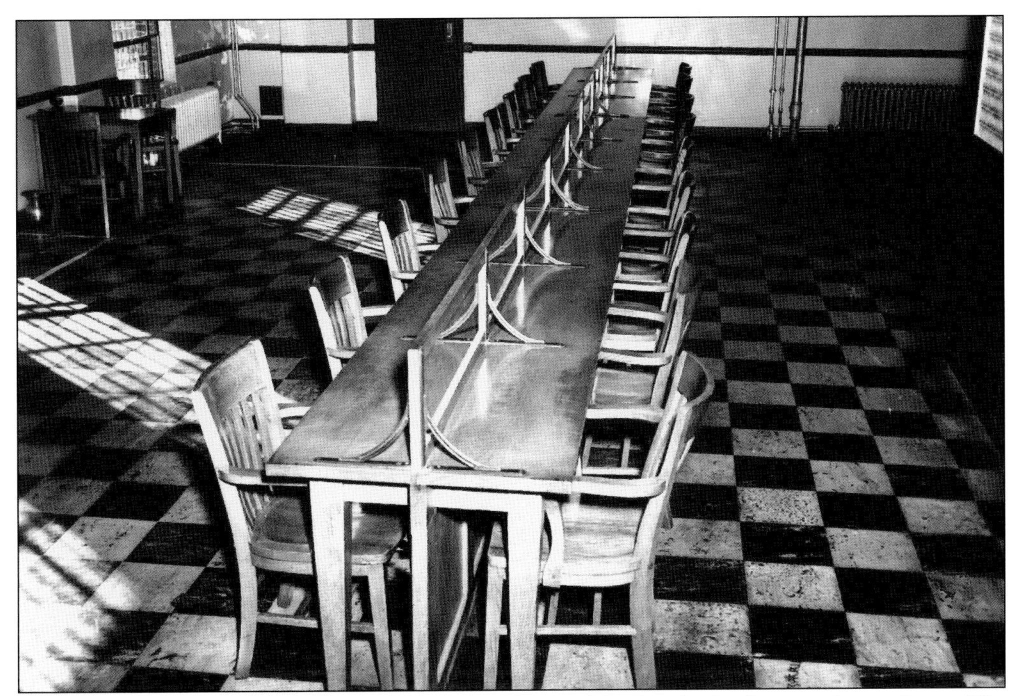

Inmate visitation took place in a room with a long table that had a barrier down the middle to prevent inmates from being able to touch their visitors. Over the years, the visit room was changed to individual tables and chairs and limited physical contact between visitors and inmates was allowed.

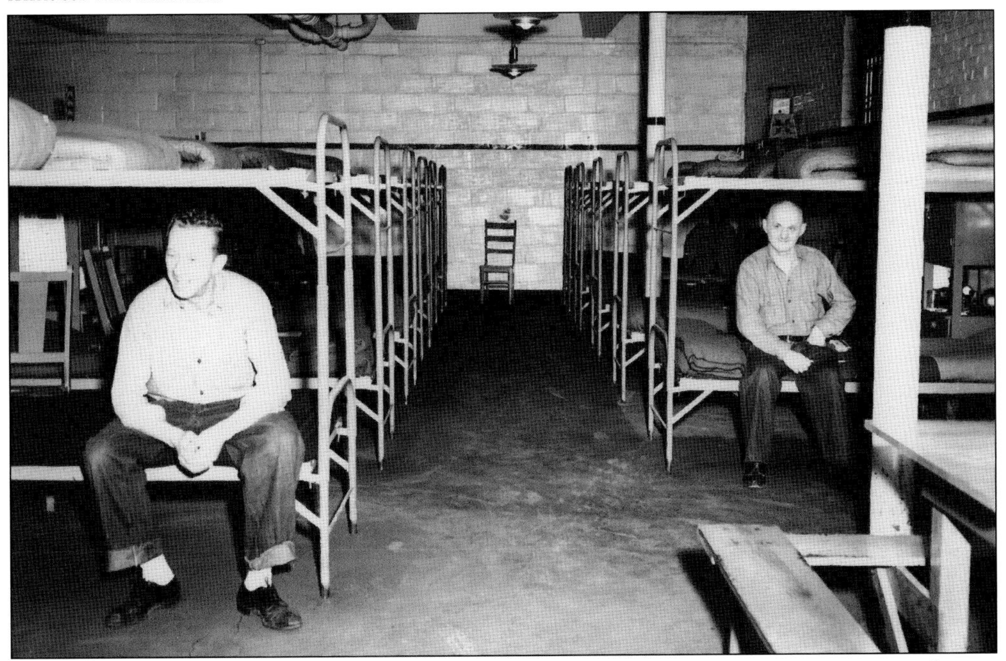

Dormitory-style living for eligible inmates increased the housing space for a growing population. Changes in national prison standards eventually led to double celling in housing areas where inmates were classified as appropriate for this housing assignment.

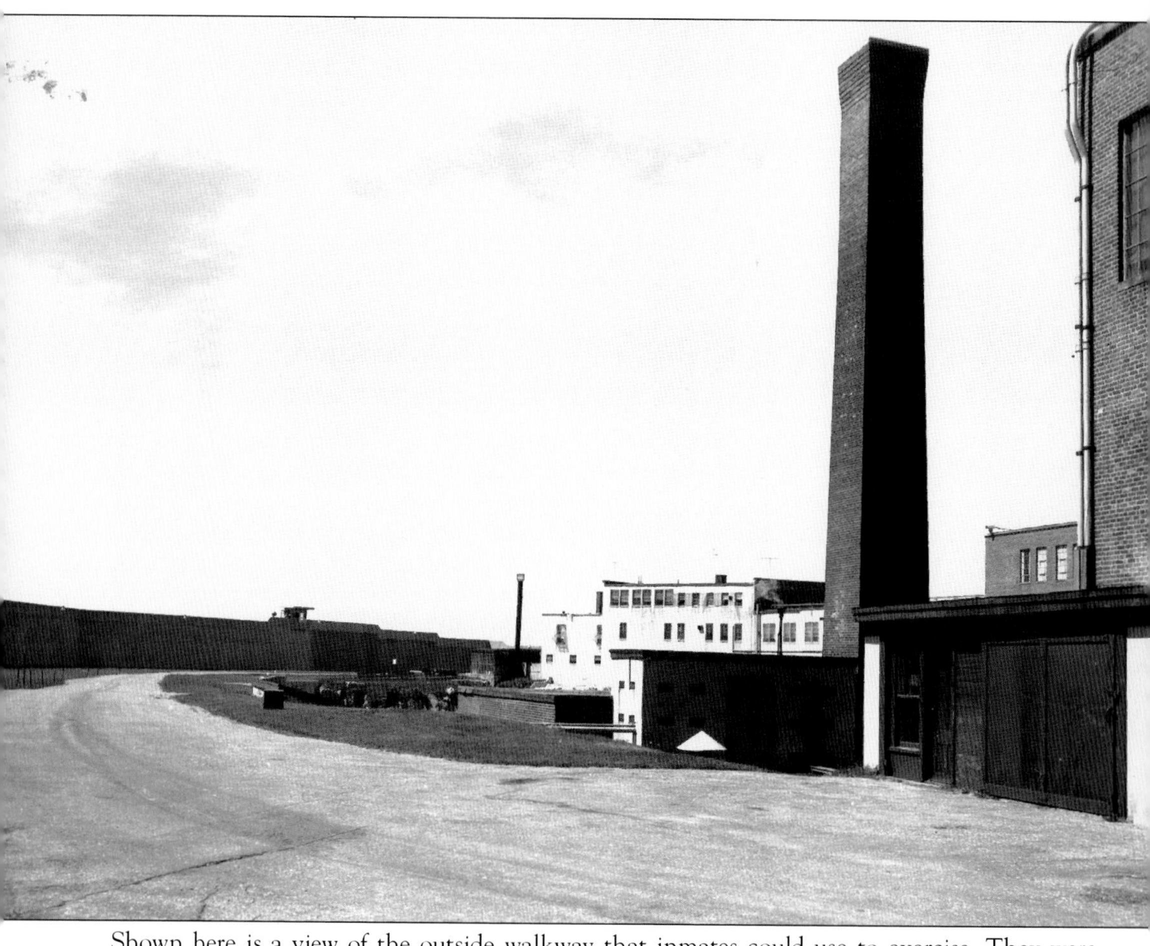

Shown here is a view of the outside walkway that inmates could use to exercise. They were required to wear belts with brightly colored cloth flags attached that signified to the wall post that they had permission from the recreation department to be walking up there.

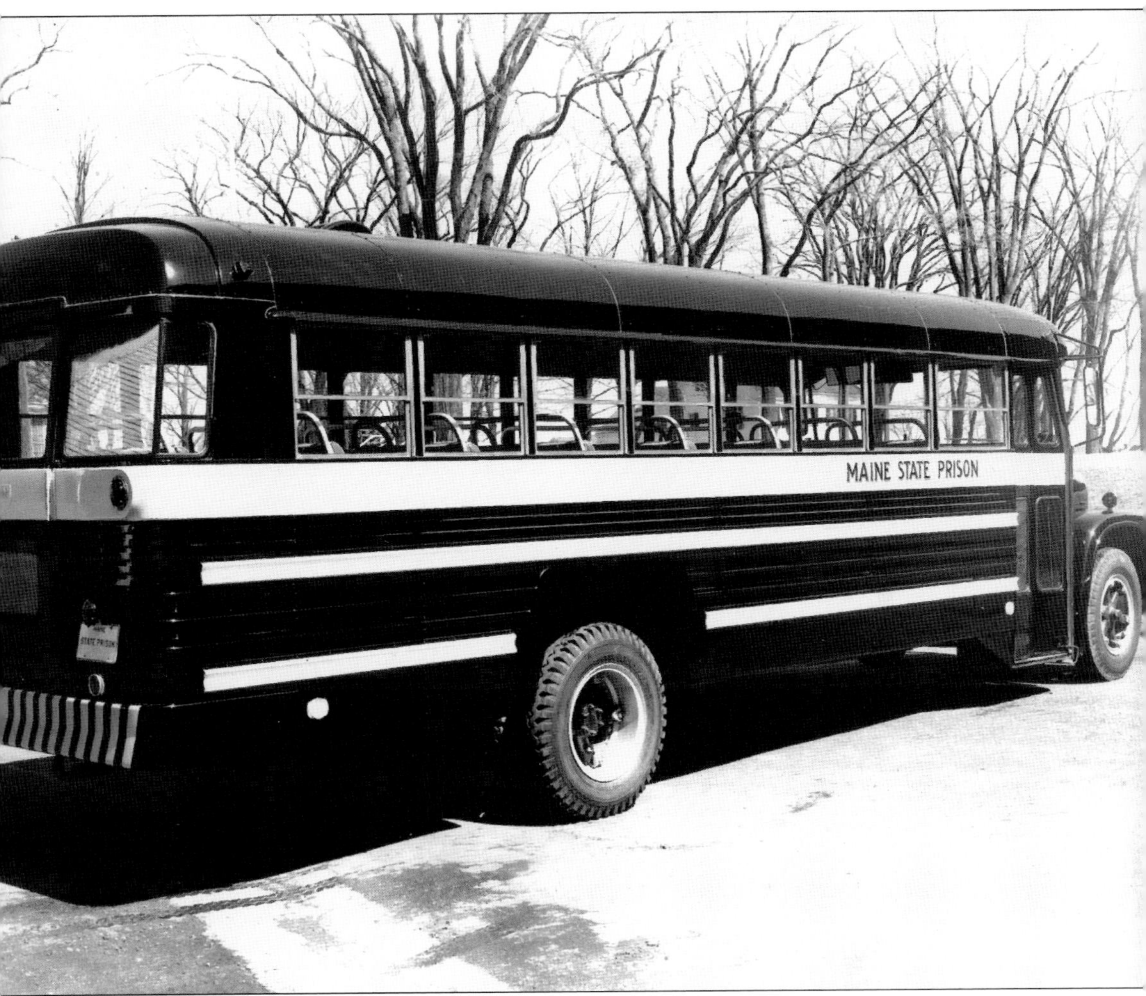

This prison bus was used to transfer inmates from Thomaston to the new facility in nearby Warren in 2002. It was refurbished with a sally port attached to the back emergency door to walk inmates in four-point restraints from the commissary loading docks onto the bus. It took three days round-the-clock to move 400 inmates to the new facility.

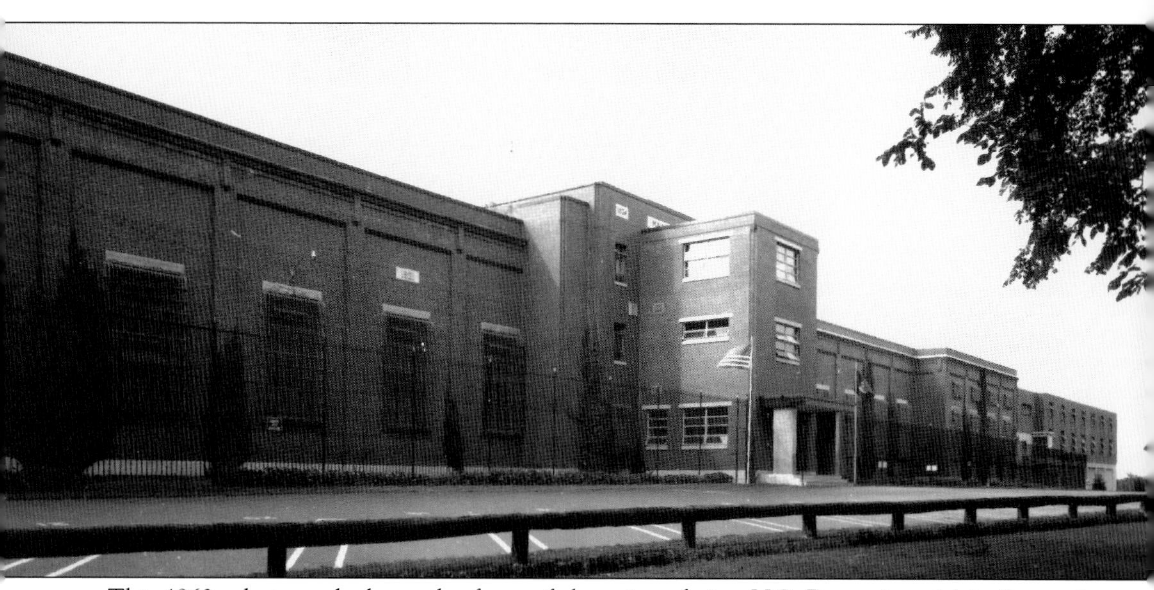

This 1960s photograph shows the front of the prison facing U.S. Route 1, or Main Street. It shows the east wing on the left, administration in the middle, and the center and west blocks on the right. The exterior changed little over the years.

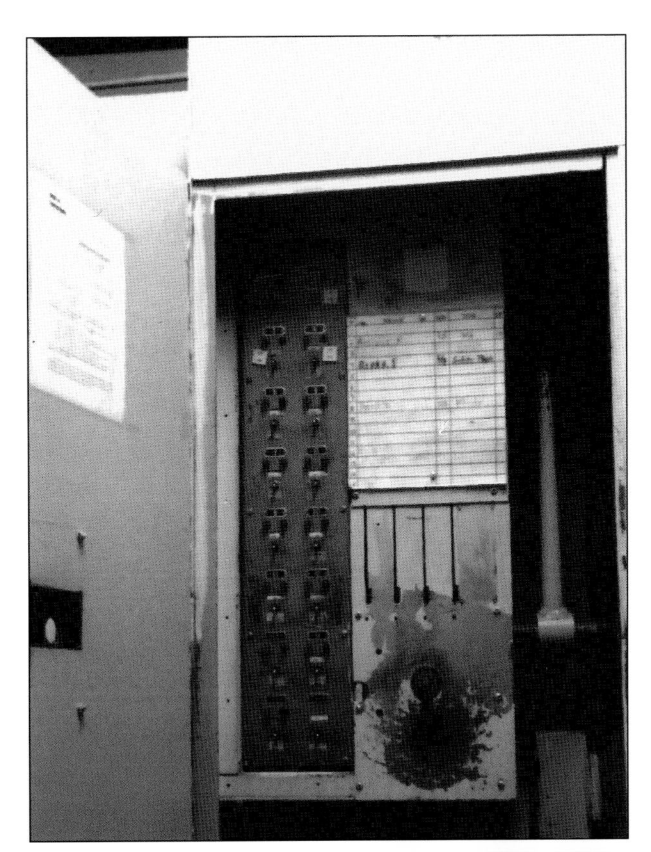

Until the 1980s, officers released inmates from their cellblocks by manually pulling a lever in lock boxes located at the ends of cellblocks. It was common to hear an officer yell out "rolling the corridor," which warned inmates to enter their cells. The officer would then pull a lever in the lock box that would roll and lock the cell doors shut. Later electric mechanisms were installed in the east wing lock boxes.

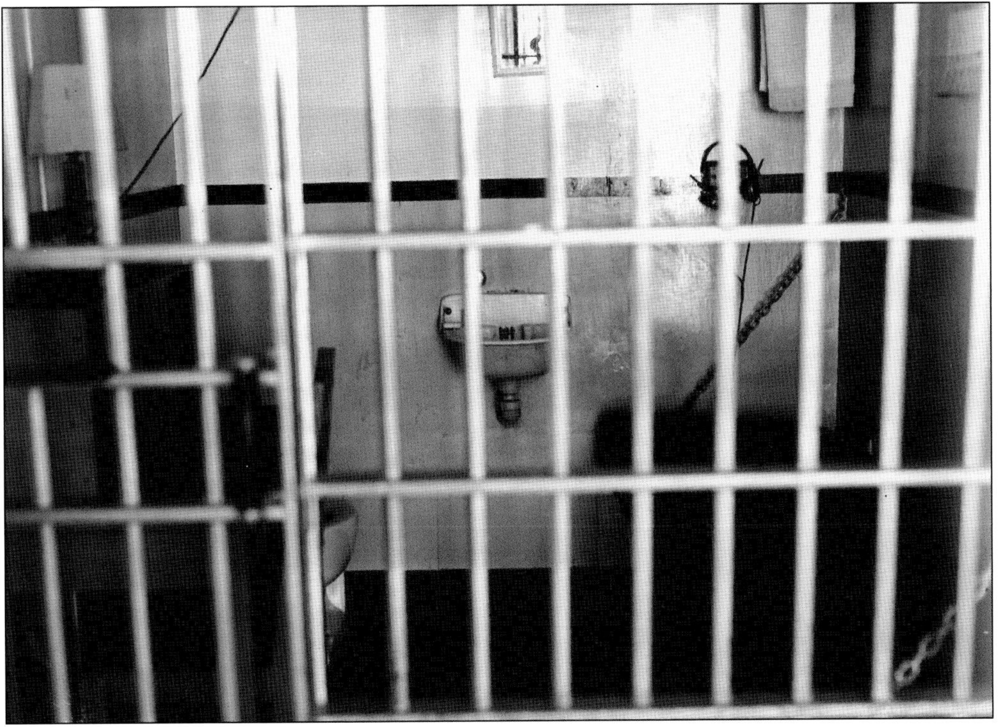

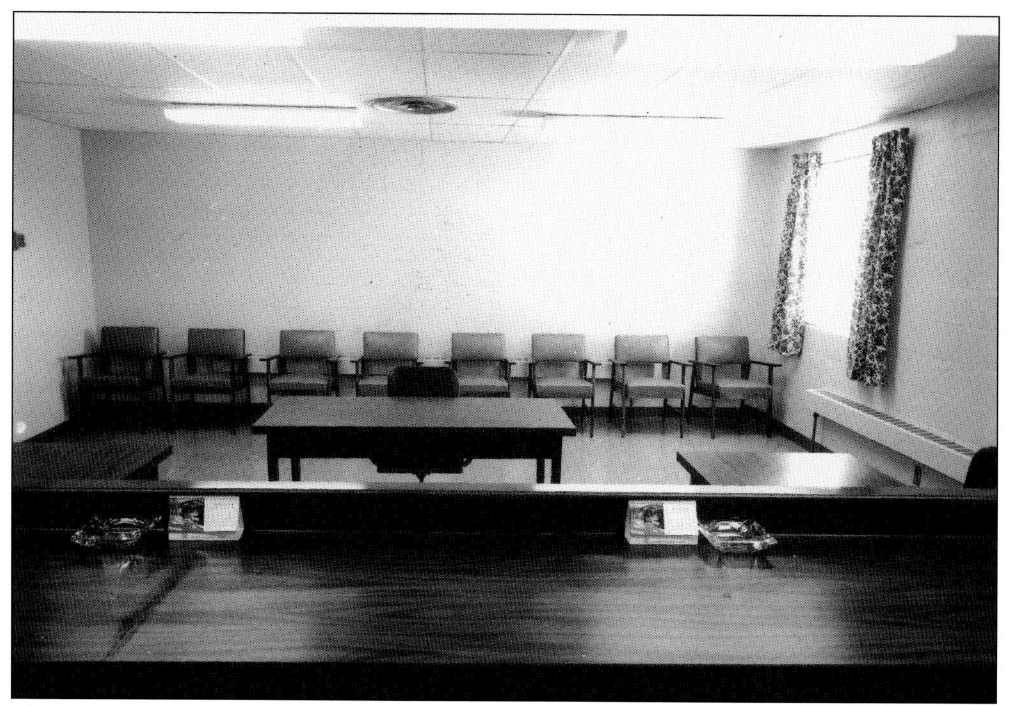

The parole board room, as it was generally known, was used for parole and other hearings. Maine abolished parole in 1976, and only a handful of inmates who were sentenced prior to 1976 remain on parole status. Some victims of an inmate's crime attended parole hearings in order to provide input into the parole decision process.

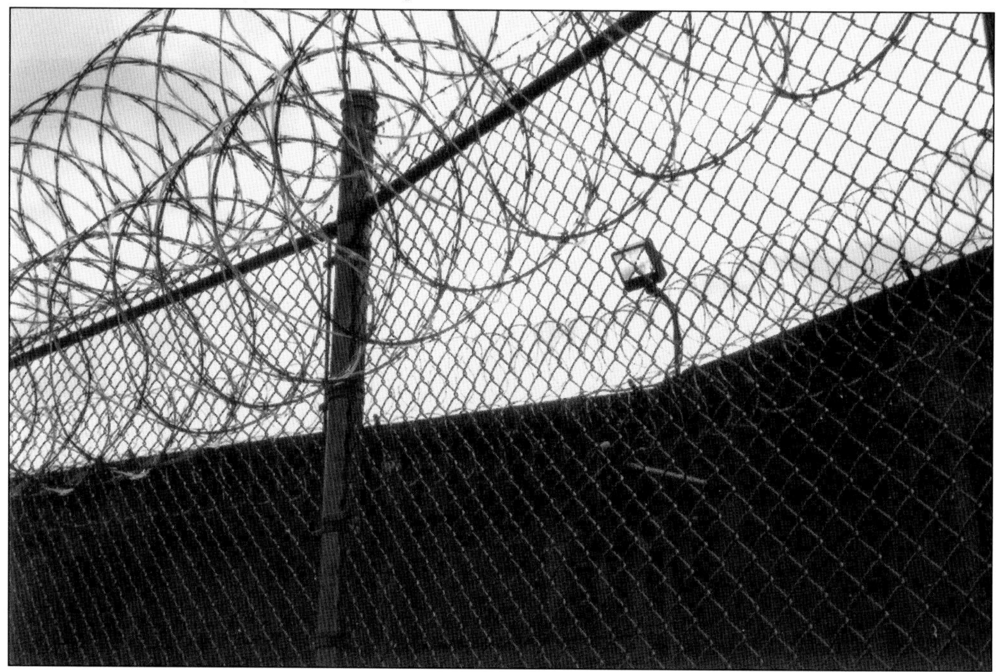

This photograph is of an evening view of the razor wire on top of the wall. In the late 1980s, razor wire and a taut wire system were added to wall security. (Courtesy of Michael Lokuta.)

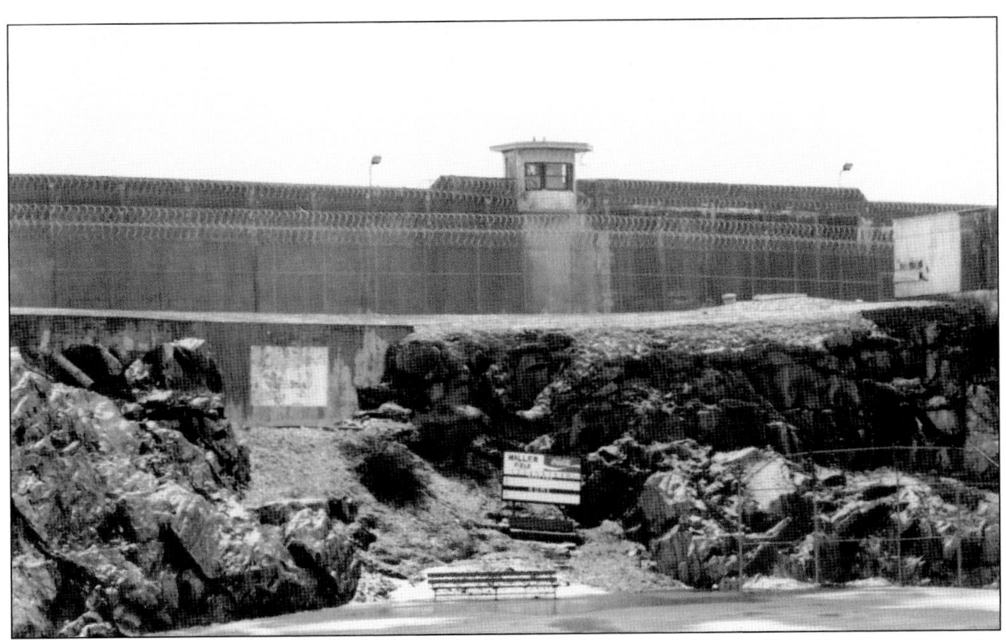

Shown here are two photographs of an early spring 2002 view of the baseball diamond in the former quarry, following the move to Warren. (Courtesy of Michael Lokuta.)

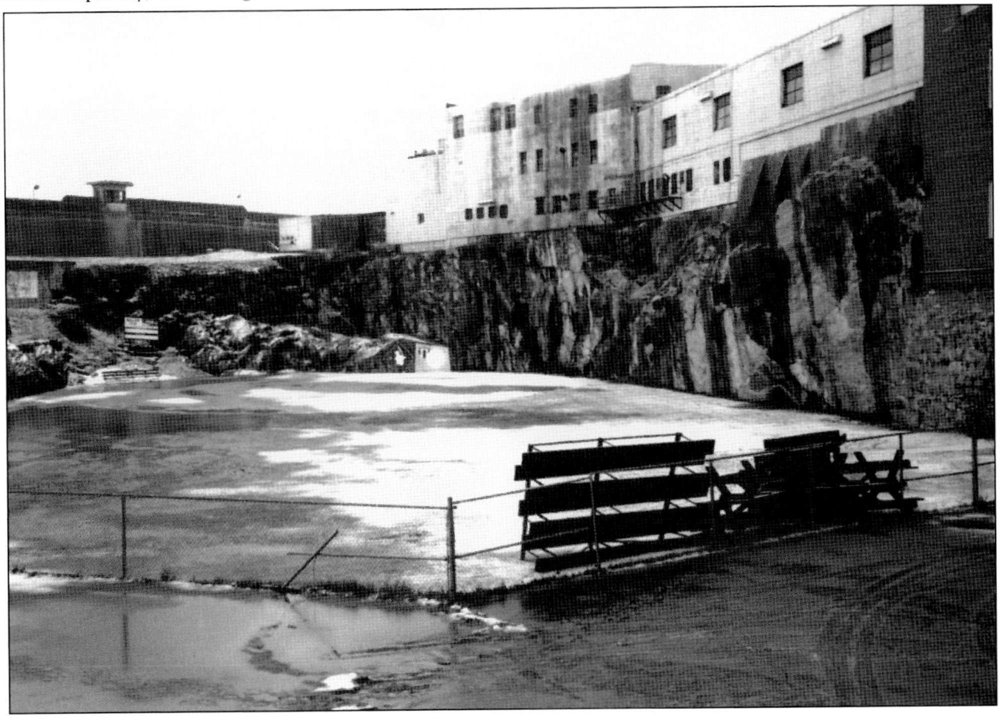

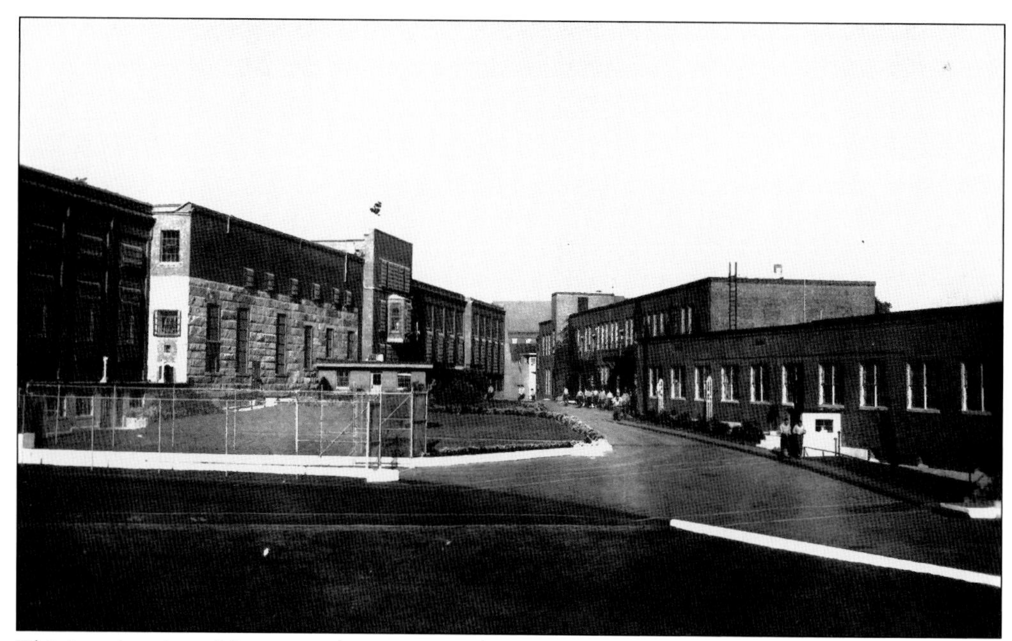

This interior view of the prison shows inmates leaving the dining hall. The education department, library, and chapel were beyond the kitchen on the right. In April 1988, a small group of Pagan inmates staged a standoff demonstration on the rooftop of the chaplain's area protesting that they should have greater latitude to practice their faith. Although a tense situation, it ended after seven hours with no injuries.

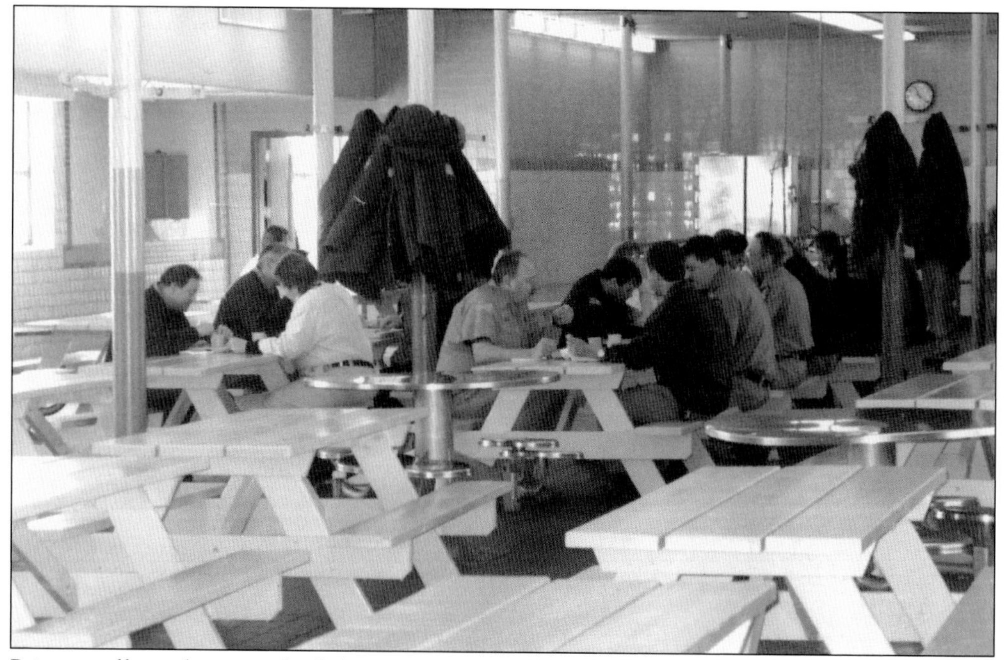

Prison staff ate the same food that was served to the inmates, and in the same mess hall, as shown here. Since inmates prepared and served the meals for both staff and fellow inmates, there was little contamination of food because the inmates did not want to risk angering one another.

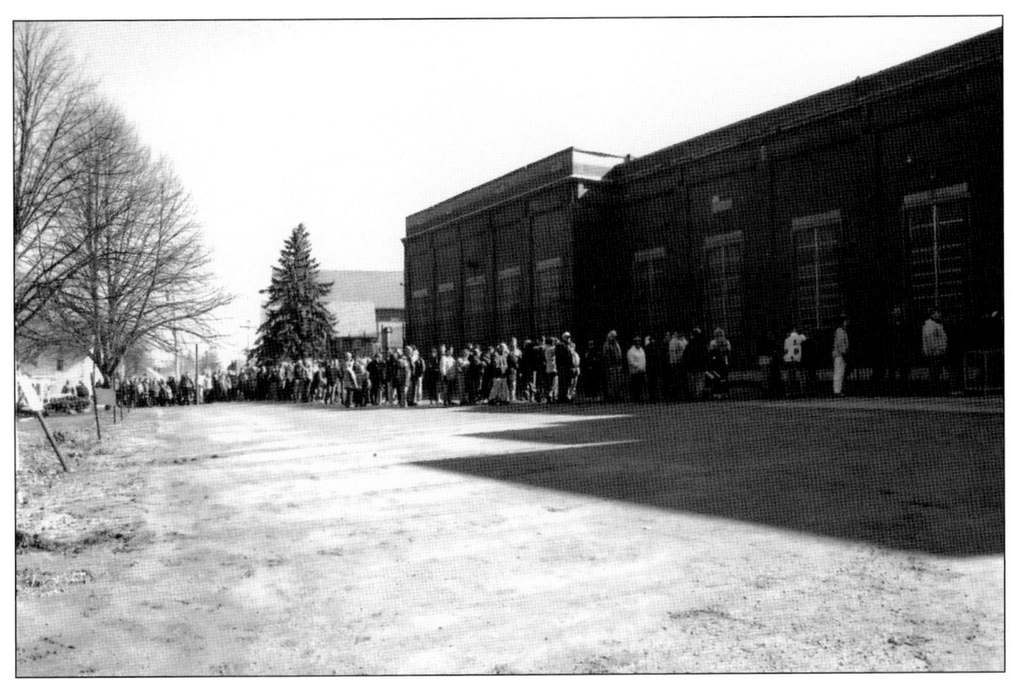

Shortly after closing the prison, the public was allowed to tour the facility, and 14,000 people lined up for the opportunity. The line of people extended down the road for a half mile. For most, this was the first time they had ever seen what lay beyond the prison walls. (Courtesy of Michael Lokuta.)

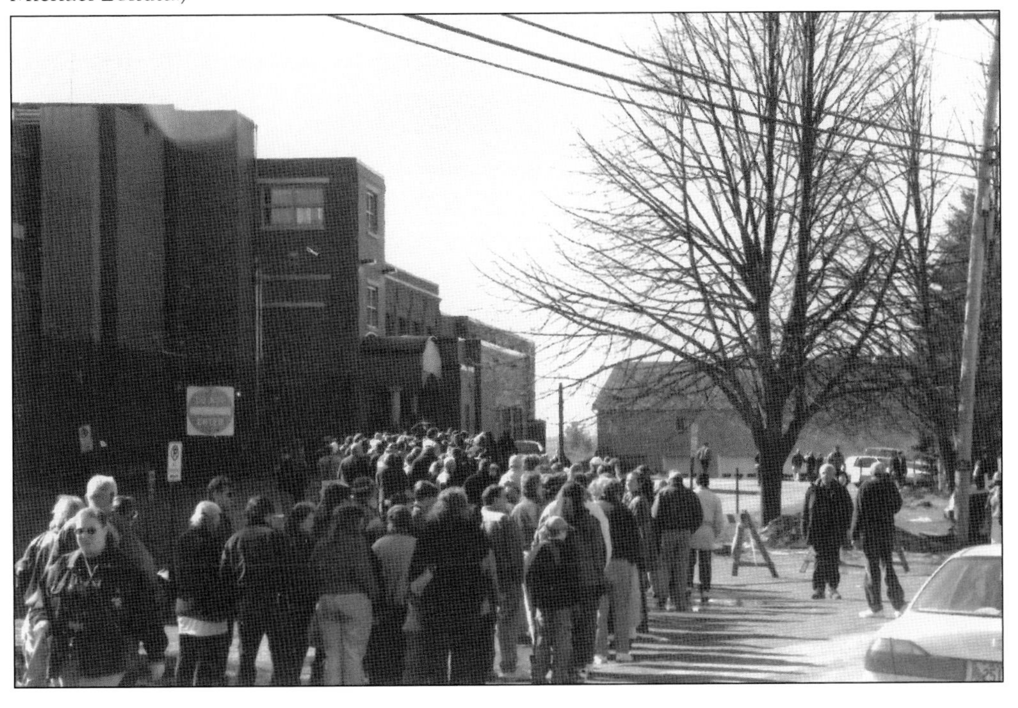

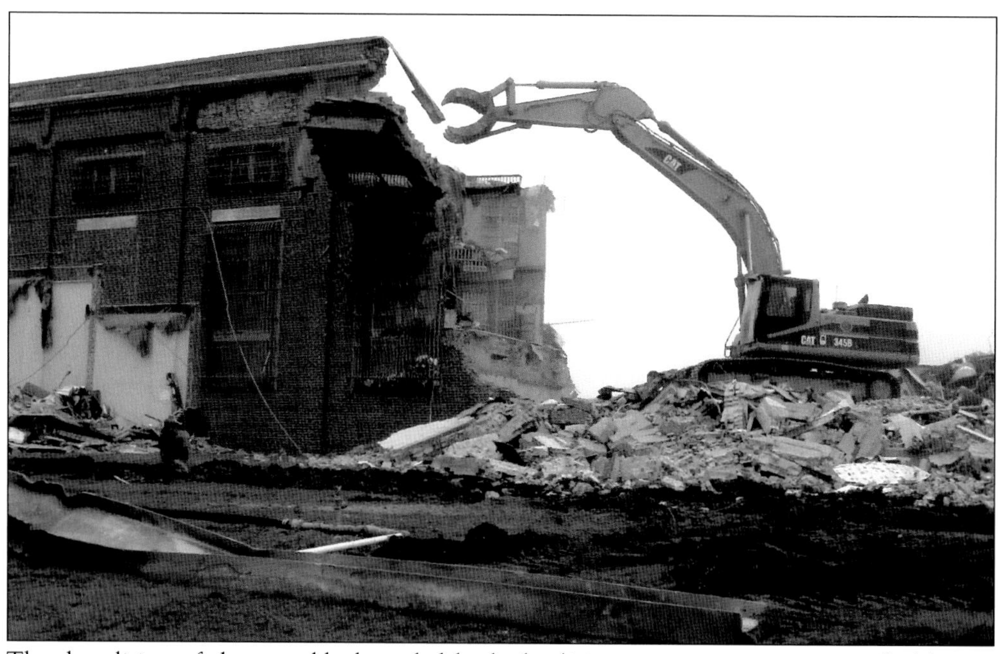

The demolition of the west block peeled back the living space many inmates called home. (Courtesy of Gilco Corporation.)

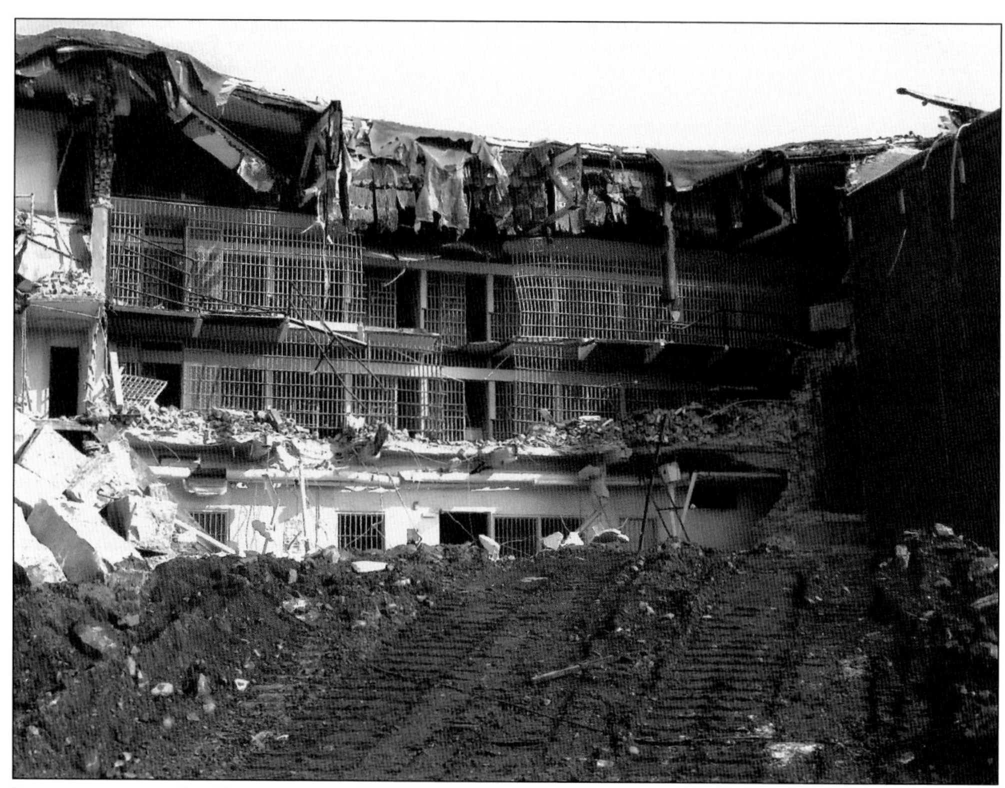

Row upon row of cells were exposed to the sun as the demolition continued.

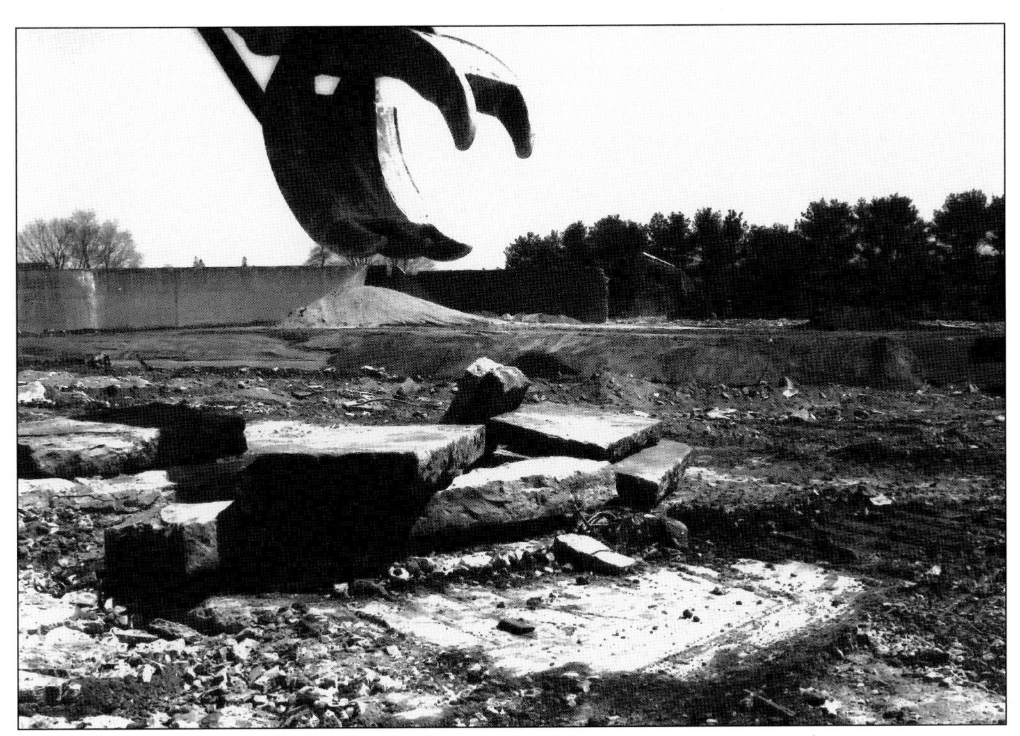

An excavator broke up large slabs of concrete. (Courtesy Gilco Corporation.)

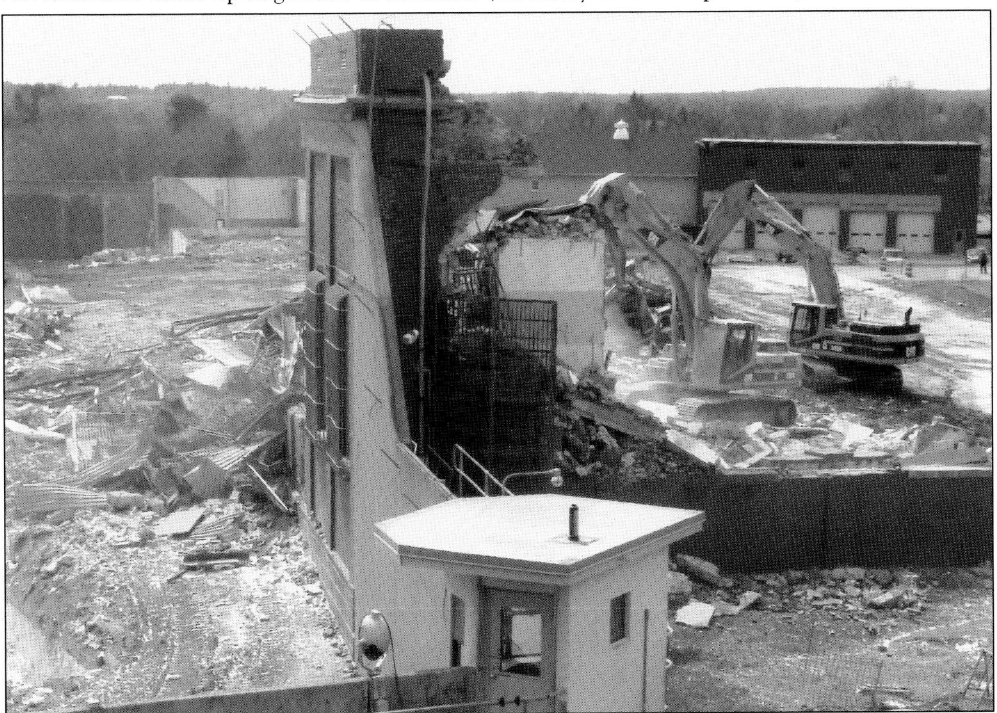

This was the last section of the Maine State Prison to be demolished, with two H. E. Sargent Inc. excavators finishing the job. Many bystanders were amazed at how fast the prison came down. (Courtesy Gilco Corporation.)

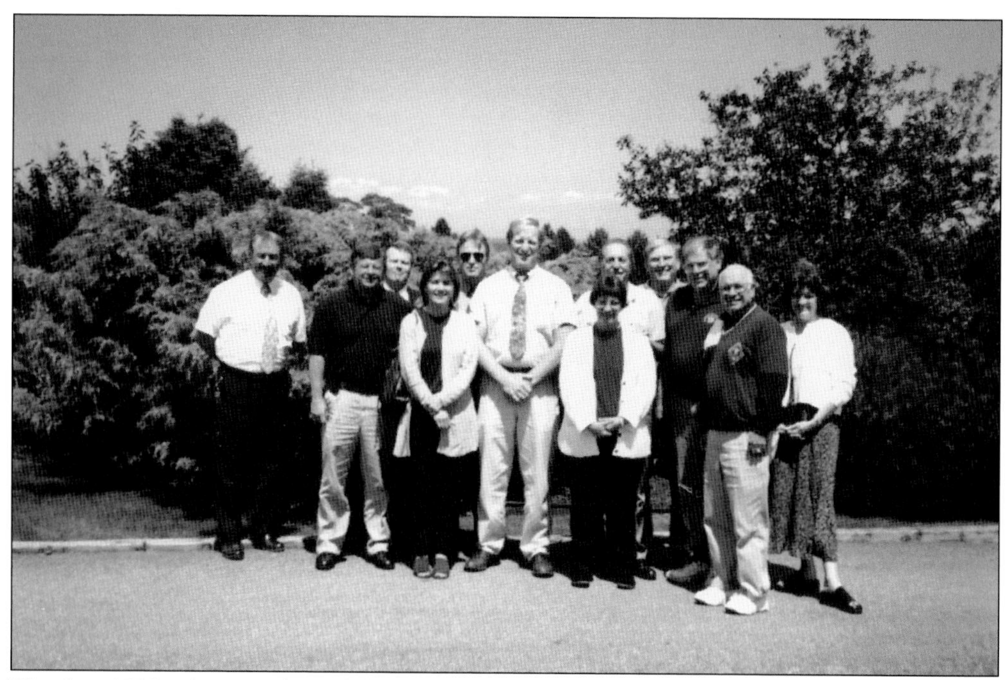

This late 1990s photograph is of the Department of Corrections and Maine State Prison staff. From left to right are Deputy Warden Harold Doughty, Deputy Warden Nelson Riley, personnel manager David Rankin, director of support services Karen Carroll, assistant director Albert Barlow, Warden Jeffrey Merrill, prison administrative coordinator Esther Riley, Deputy Warden Bruce Wentworth, principal David MacMillan, associate commissioner Martin Magnusson, director of classification Frank Westrack, and the warden's secretary Diane Lugar.

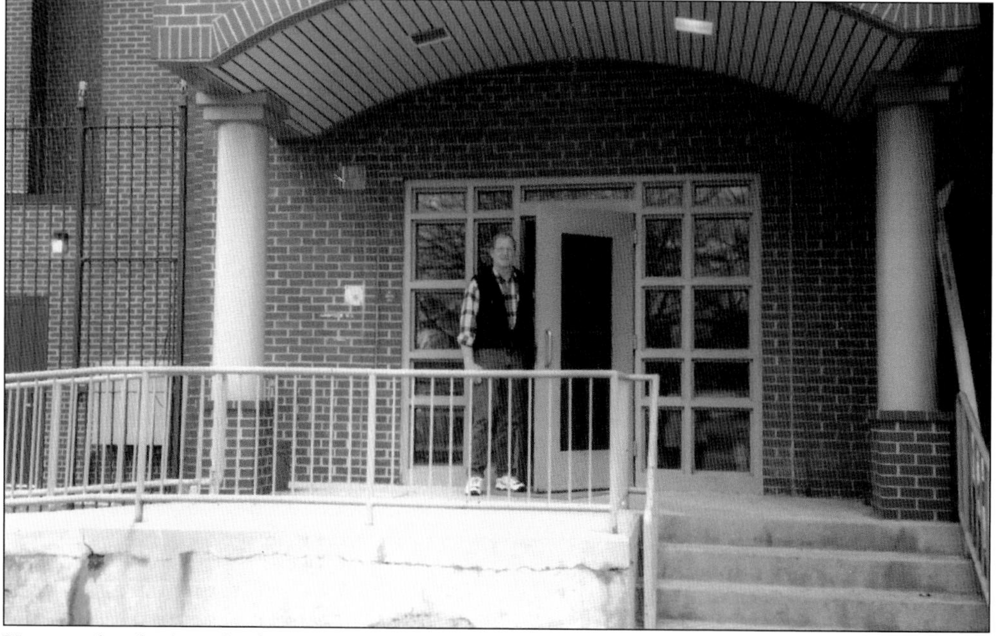

Here is a last look at the front entrance as Warden Jeffrey D. Merrill locks the front door, closing the chapter on 178 years of history.

Two

Programs, Services, and Activities

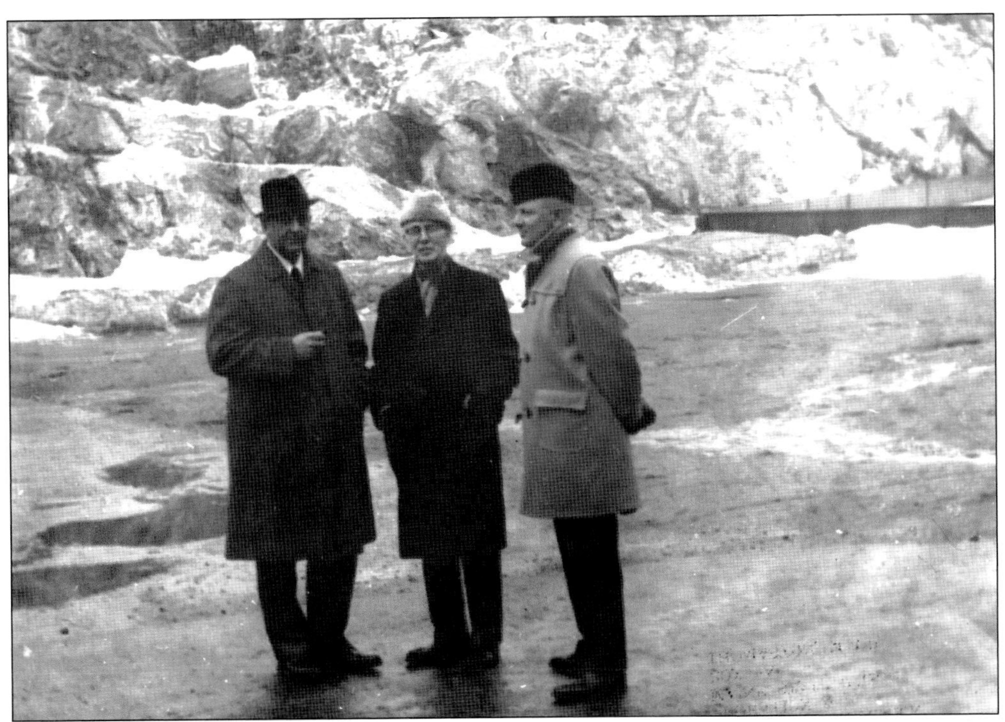

In 1915, Austin "Spike" MacCormick, one of the nation's leading prison reformers, began his career as a penologist in an unusual way as an occupant of cell 67 in the Maine State Prison where he spent a week as an undercover convict. During a visit in 1969, he was photographed standing in the yard (center) talking with Warden Allan L. Robbins and son James MacCormick, probation and parole officer. (Courtesy of the MacCormick family.)

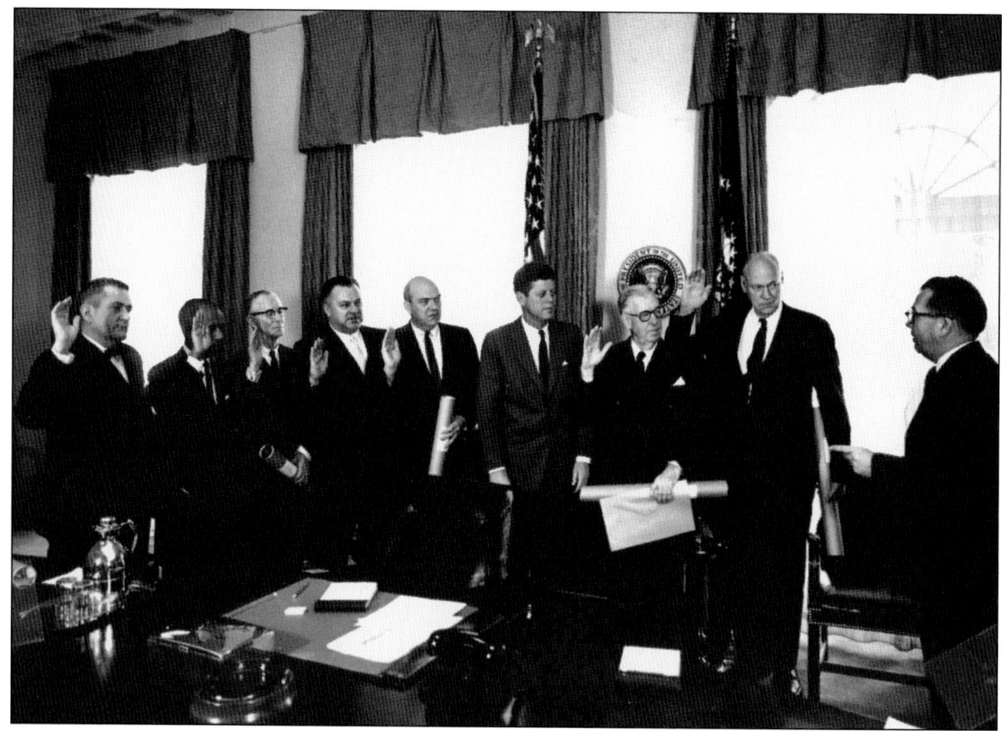

During his four years in the U.S. Bureau of Prisons, Austin MacCormick was one of the major forces behind the transformation of the federal system that raised it from one of the worst prison systems in the country to one of recognized leadership. He also served on federal commissions under Pres. John F. Kennedy and Pres. Lyndon B. Johnson. (Courtesy of the MacCormick family.)

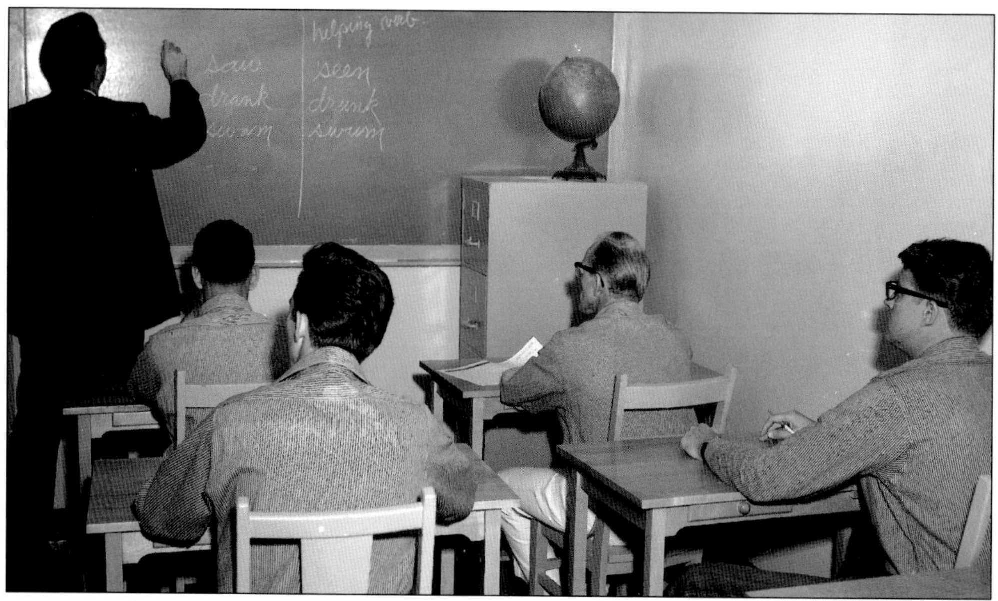

MacCormick's commitment to prisoner education reform culminated in his 1929 book *The Education of Adult Prisoners* that later became a hallmark work on correctional teaching and learning. In this photograph, a staff instructor is teaching inmates in a prison classroom.

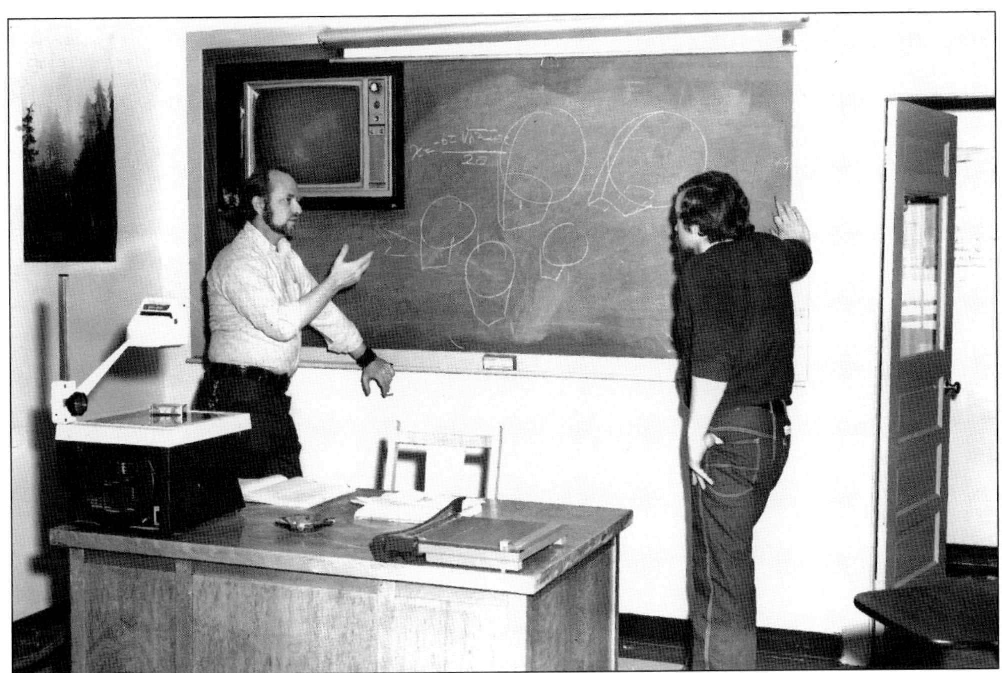

Inmates could work on their basic education up through high school equivalency. Trusties eligible to transfer to the prison farm could take an innovative driver-training course started by Warden Allan L. Robbins. Others could spend time in the library to study state statutes in the hope of discovering a point of law that would result in their sentence reduction. (Courtesy Portland Sunday Telegram.)

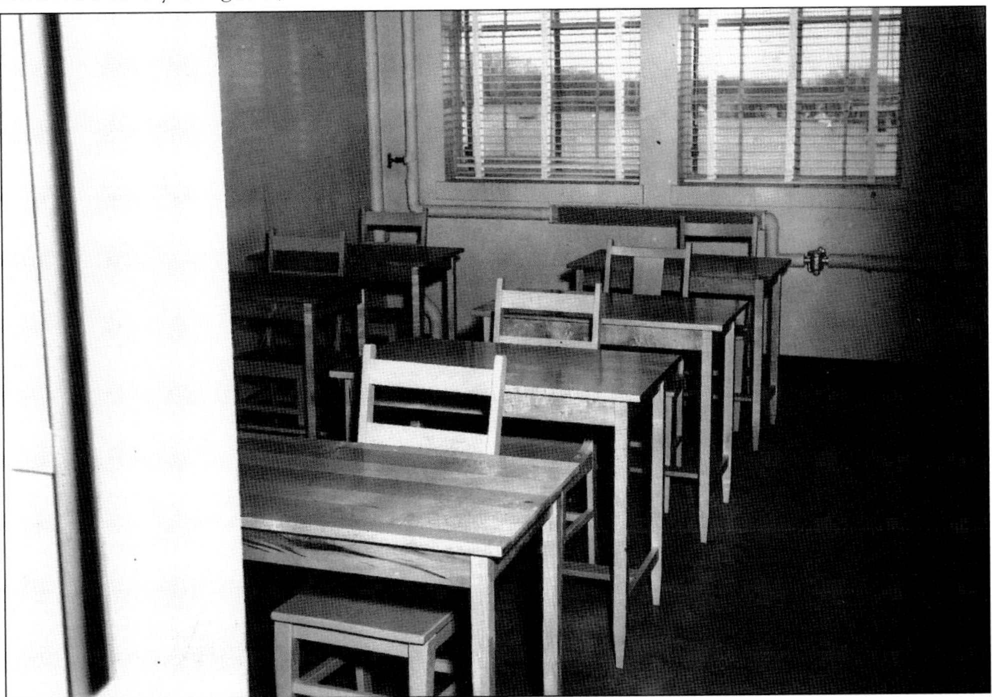

This is another view of a classroom showing the inmate-made wooden tables and chairs.

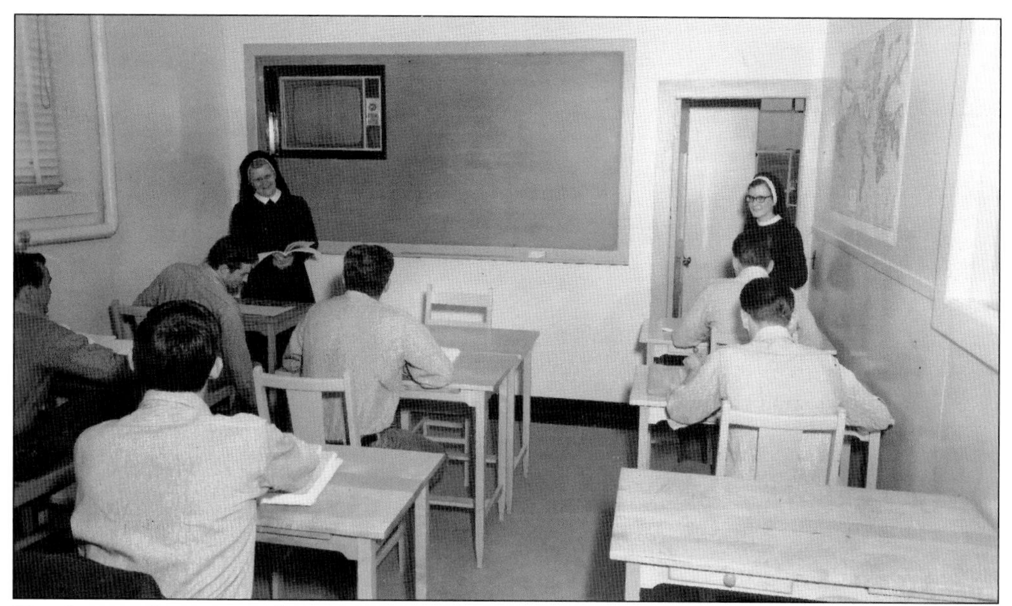

Two Sisters of Mercy taught a braille class to inmates who aspired to become certified braillists, qualified to transcribe books for the blind. They visited the prison biweekly to teach a dozen interested inmates.

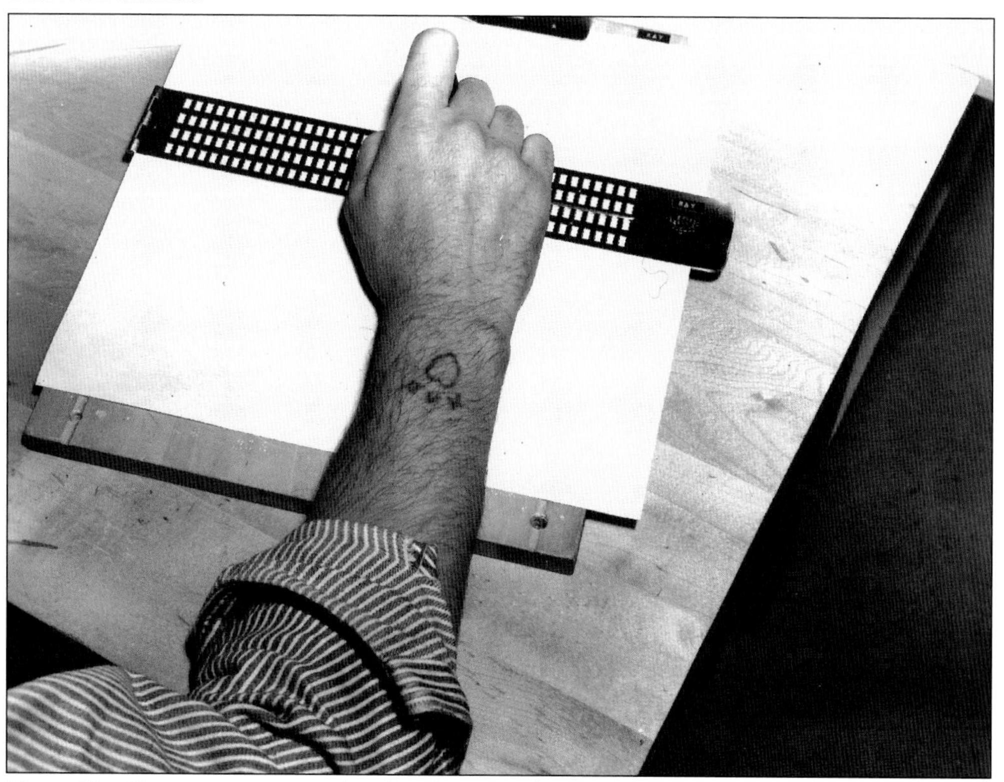

Manual braille projects were undertaken by trained inmates for the Blind Children's Resource Center, a Portland community organization. The braille project began in the late 1960s by the Jaycee prison chapter.

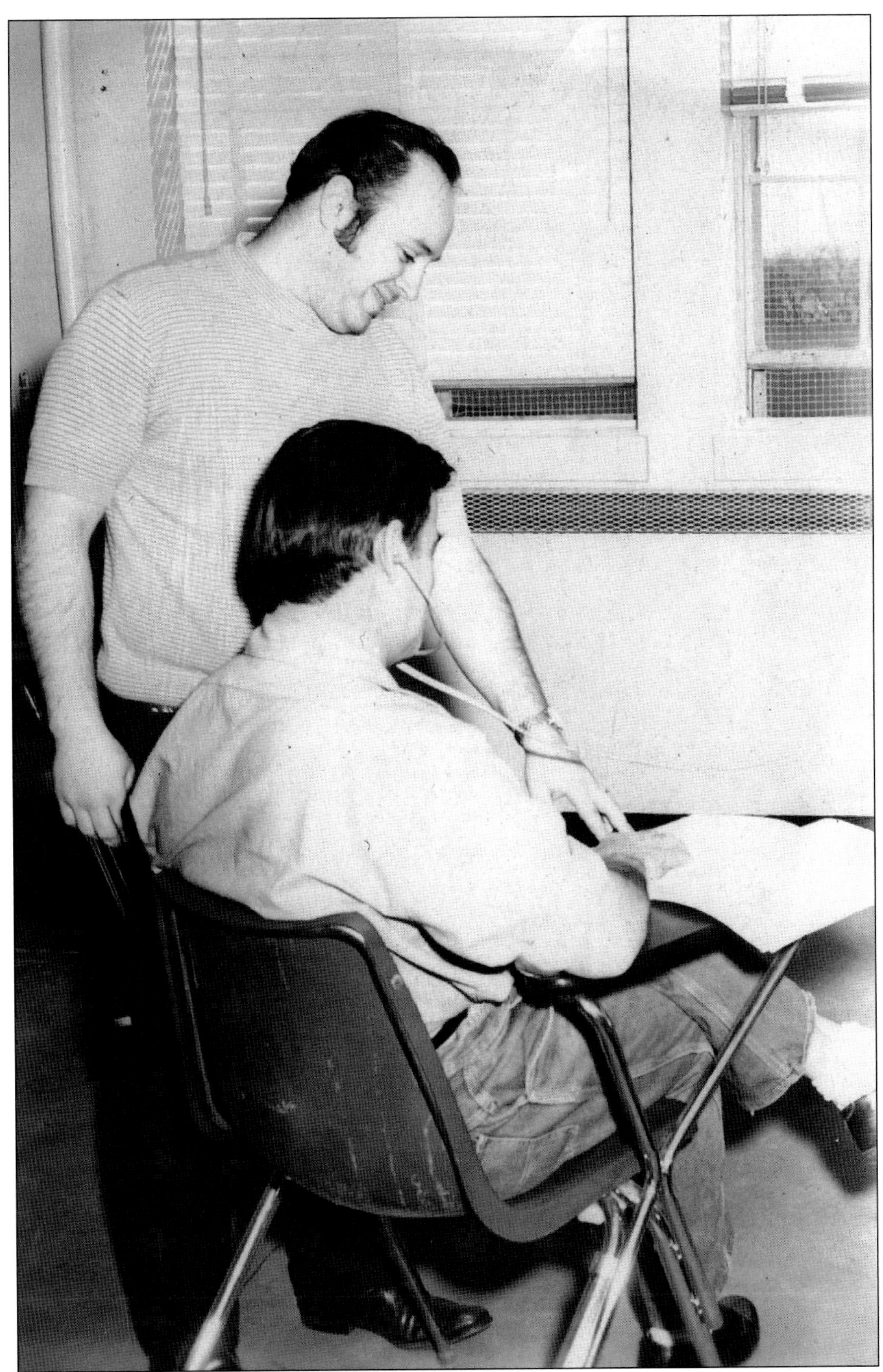

Inmate tutors provided literacy help to others. They also taught music, art, math skills, and assisted with GED preparation under the direction of education staff. In addition, community volunteers worked with inmates to improve their literacy levels. An Instructional Television (ITV) college program was offered at a fee to inmates and occasionally professors visited to teach classes.

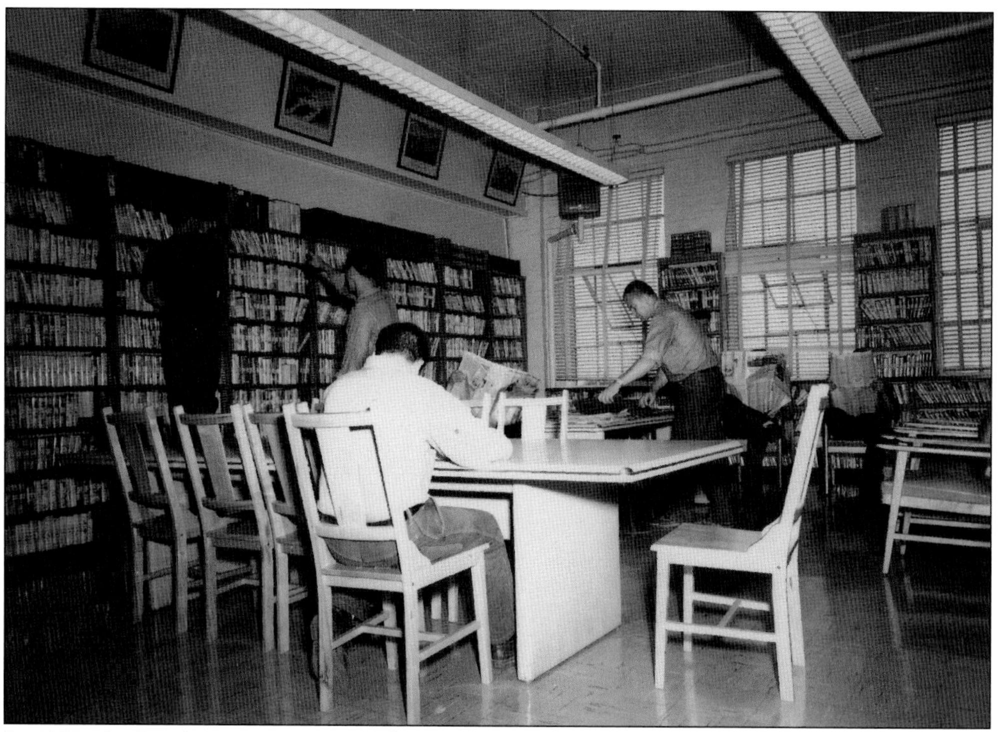

In 1830, the legislature appropriated $75 to purchase religious books for the convicts. By 1953, Warden Allan L. Robbins reported that the library contained 4,500 volumes, and by the mid-1960s, it contained over 7,800 volumes. He encouraged staff to donate their unwanted books.

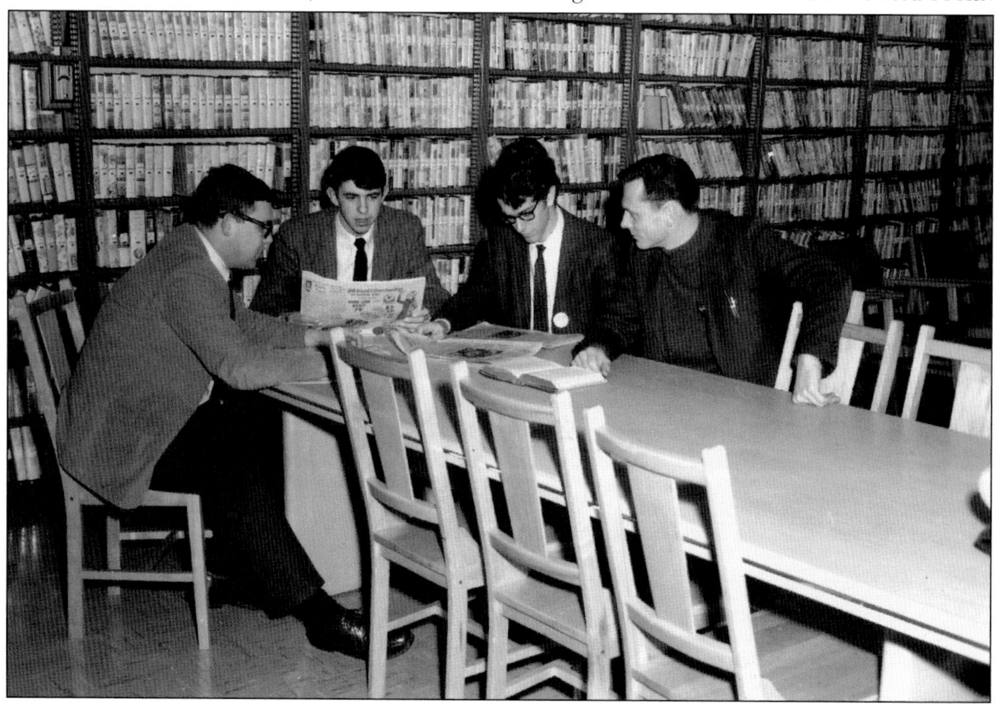

The library was a popular place to spend time reading newspapers.

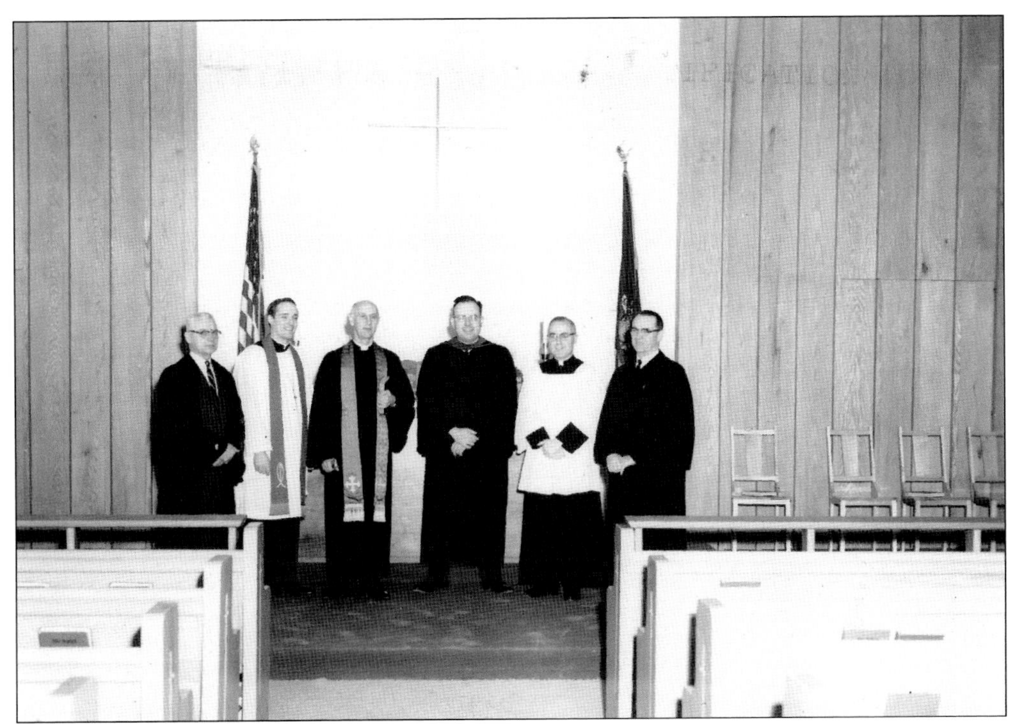

Religious services and visits by community chaplains and priests were considered important for inmate rehabilitation.

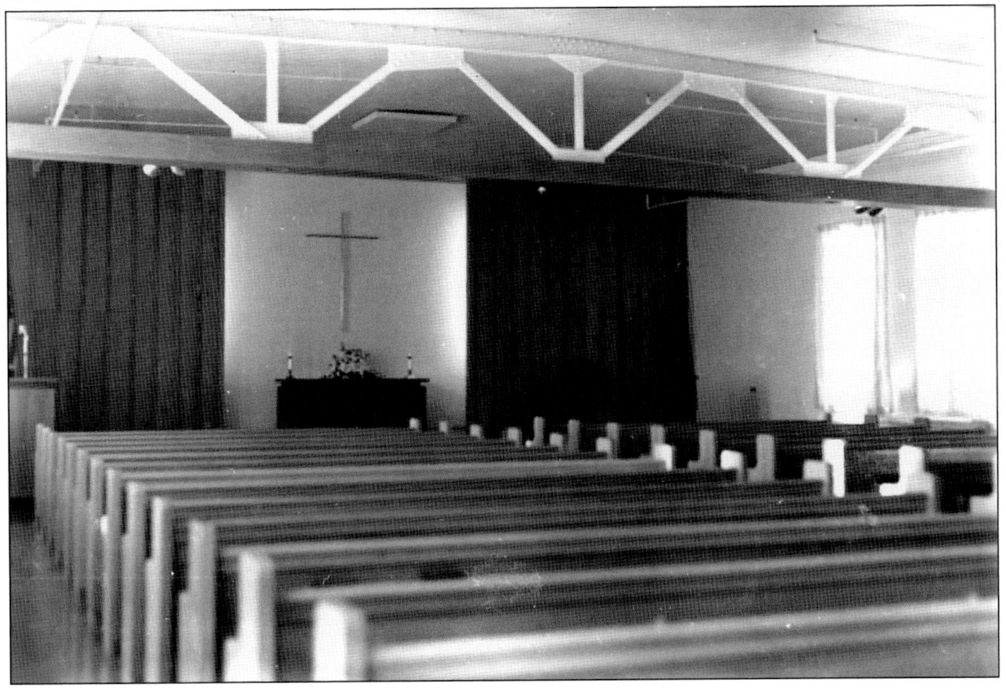

The chapel was a large room with wooden pews made by inmates in the industries program. Under Warden Allan L. Robbins, the chapel was redesigned and modernized to seat up to 250 people.

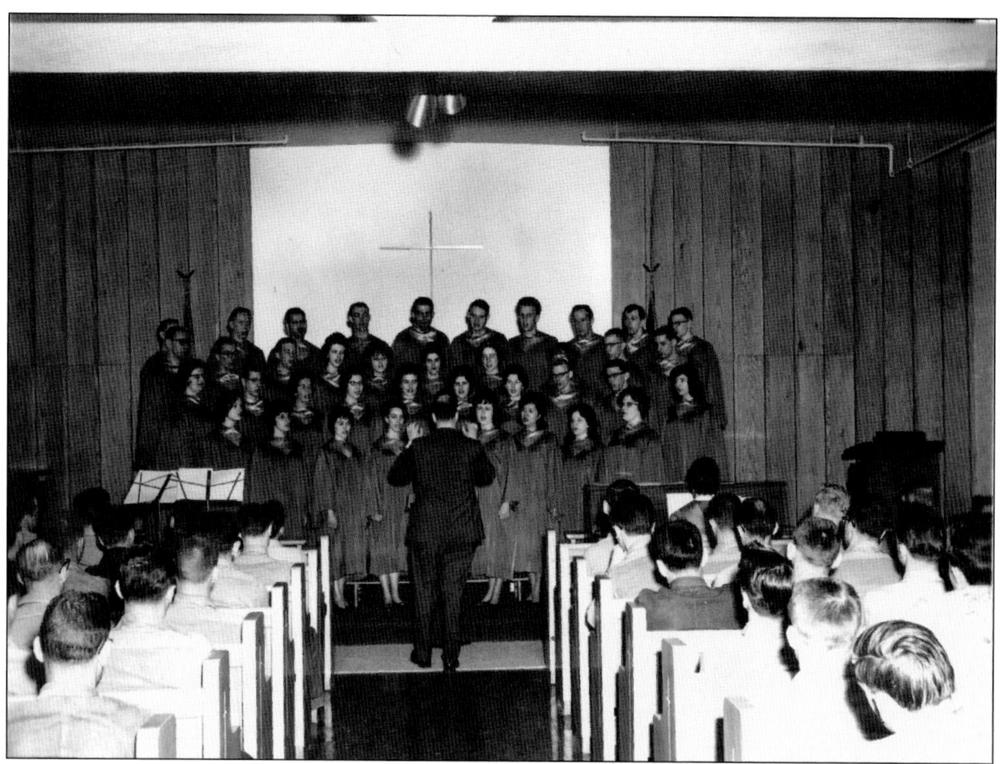

Community church choirs visited the prison on occasion.

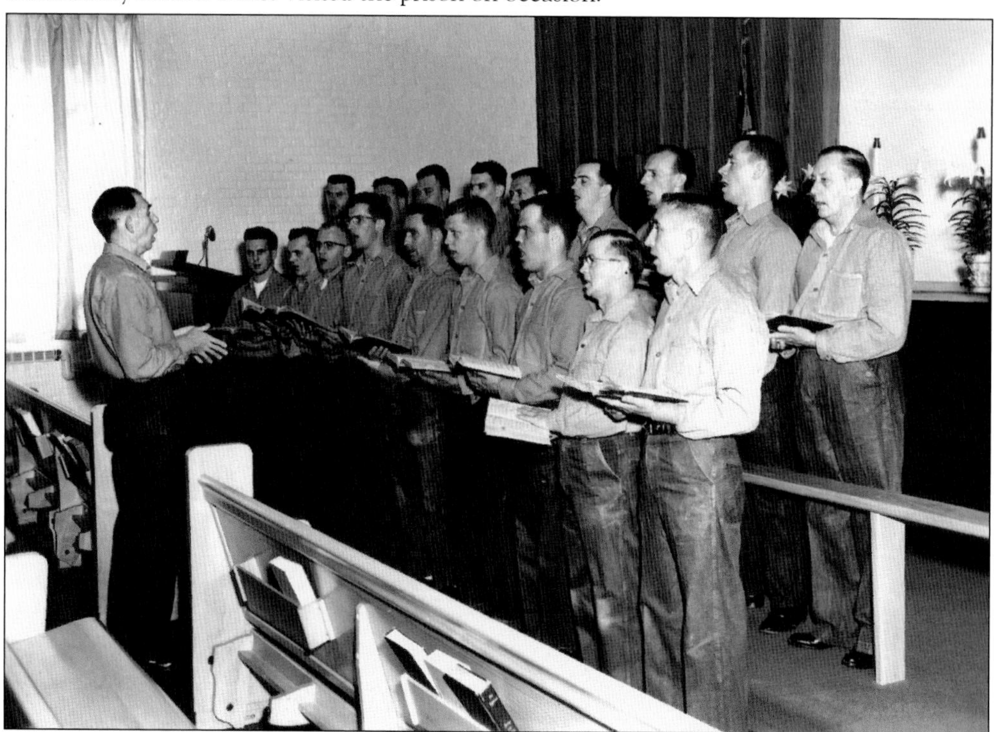

An inmate choir sang hymns at many of the services.

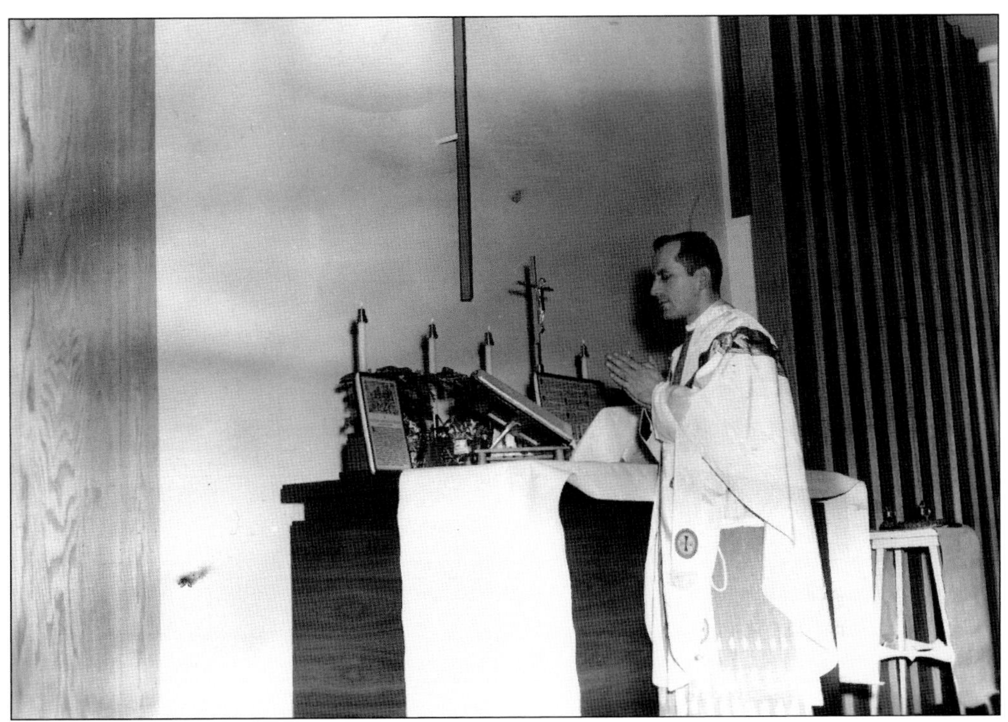

A visiting priest holds mass. Although a full-time Protestant chaplain was employed during the 1960s, it was difficult to find a full-time Catholic priest.

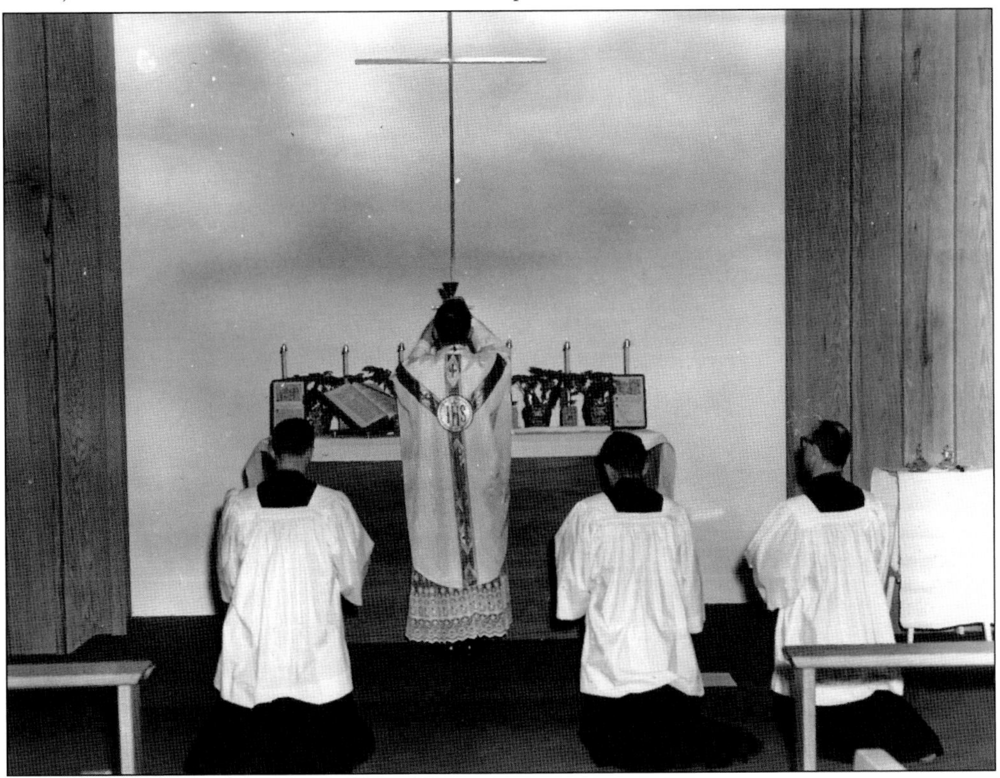

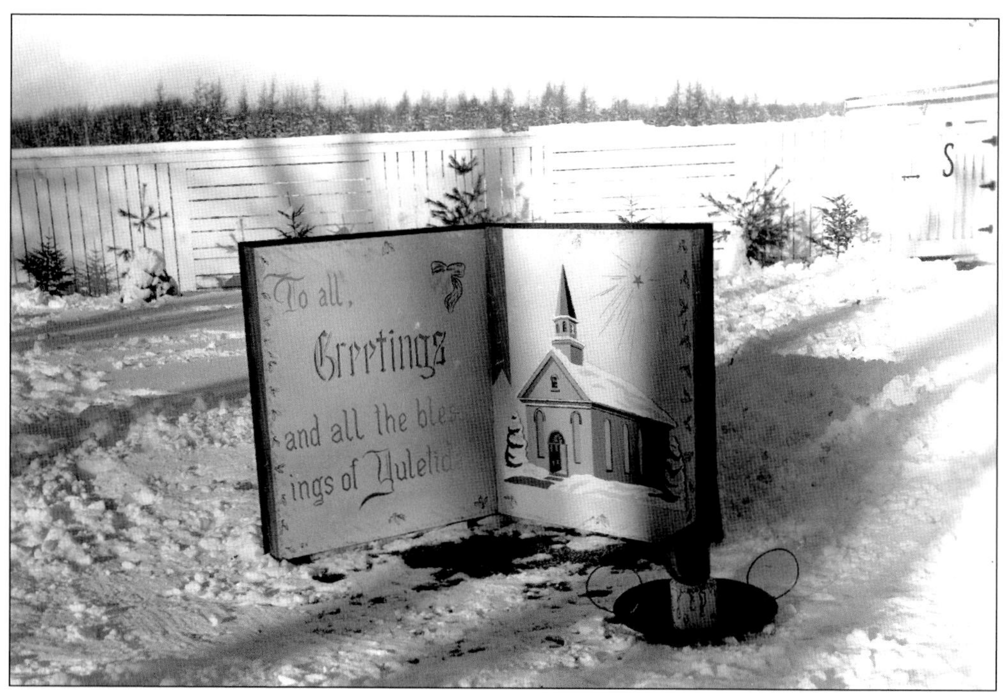

This inmate-crafted holiday and Nativity scene was on display at Christmastime in front of the prison entrance.

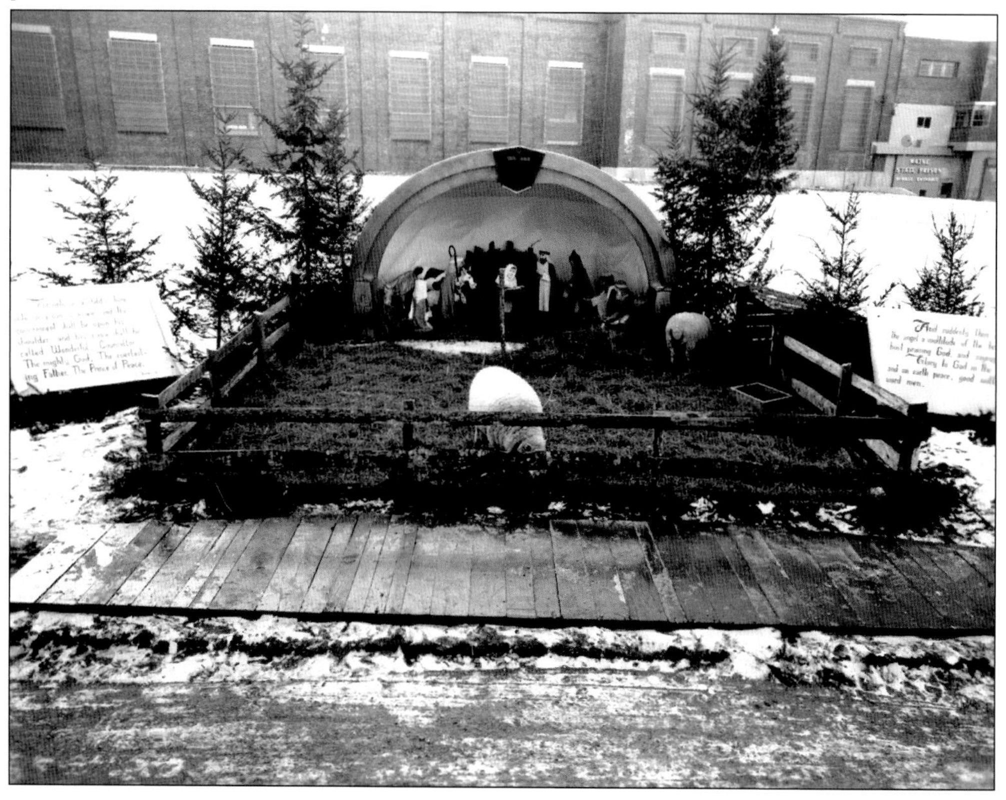

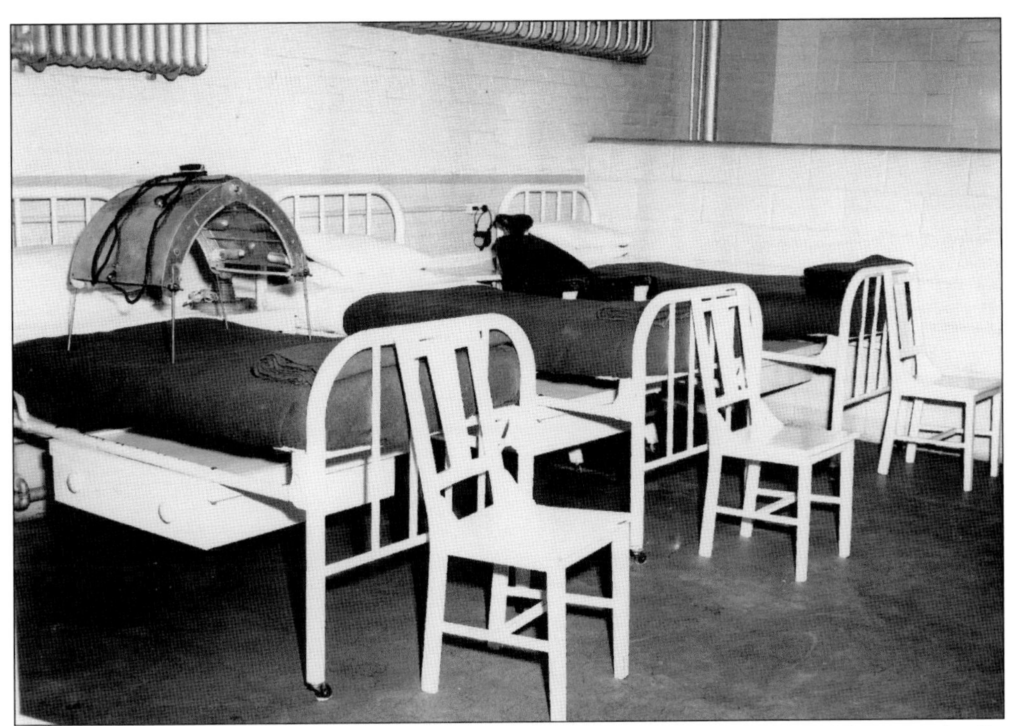

Within 24 hours of an inmate being received at the prison, he was assessed by a medically trained officer who would refer physical problems to the prison physician. Tuberculosis and blood tests were part of the initial screening. From 1950 to 1951, the medical department received over 9,000 inmate requests for medical treatment. In 1952, a 15-bed prison hospital was completed, and by the end of 1953, the hospital had its own x-ray machine and operating room where surgeries were performed by the prison physician or outside doctors.

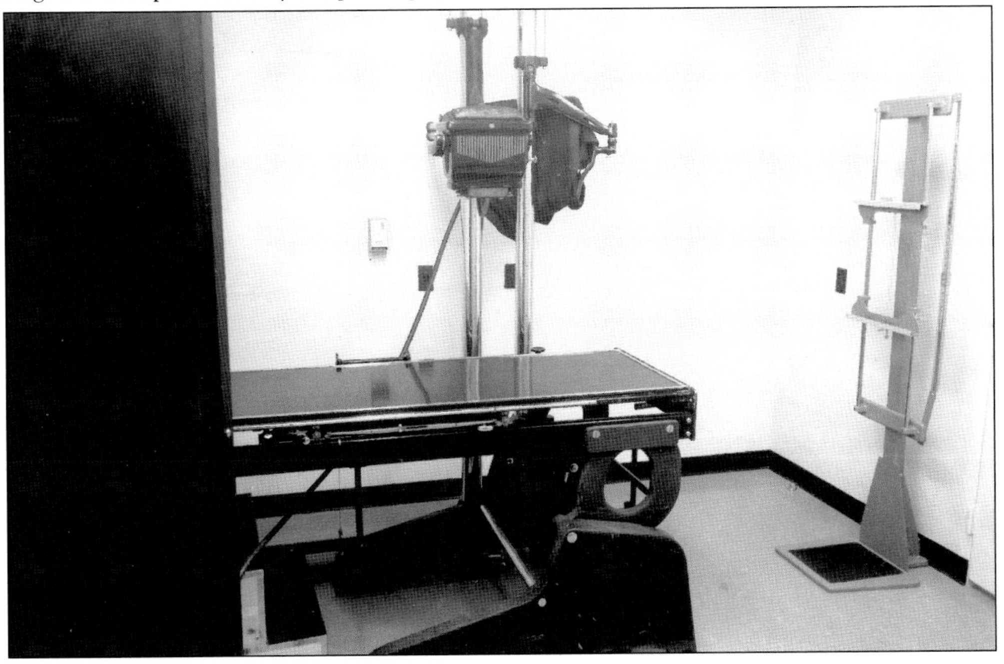

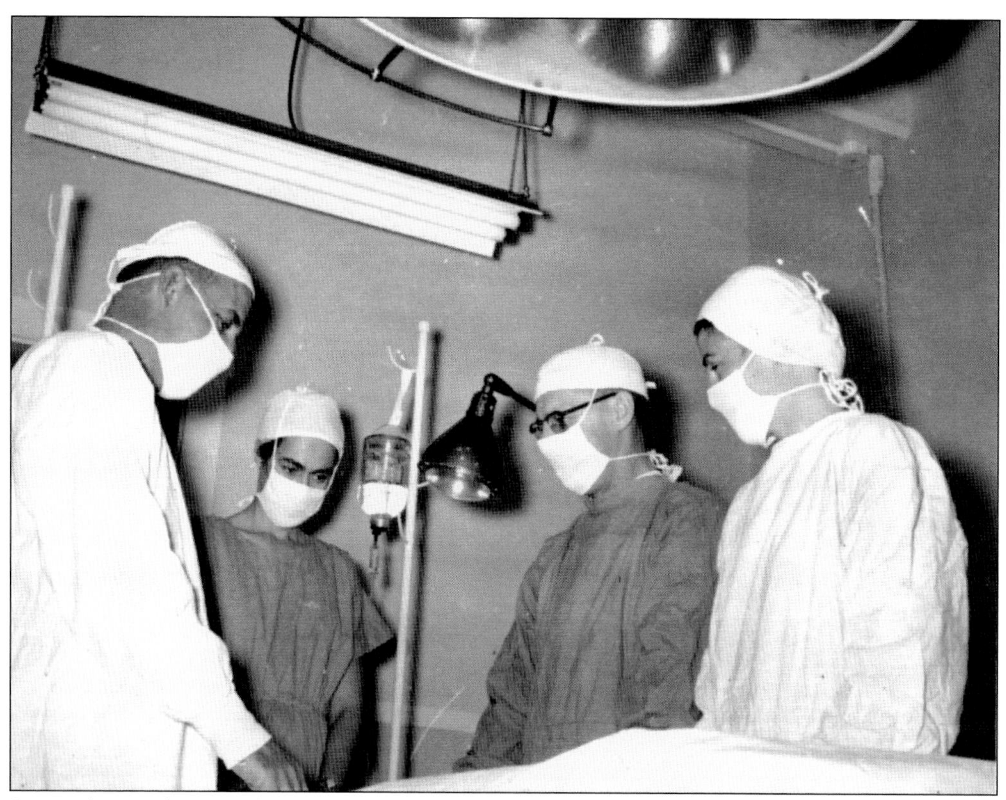

Surgical procedures in the operating room ranged from appendectomies to limb amputations.

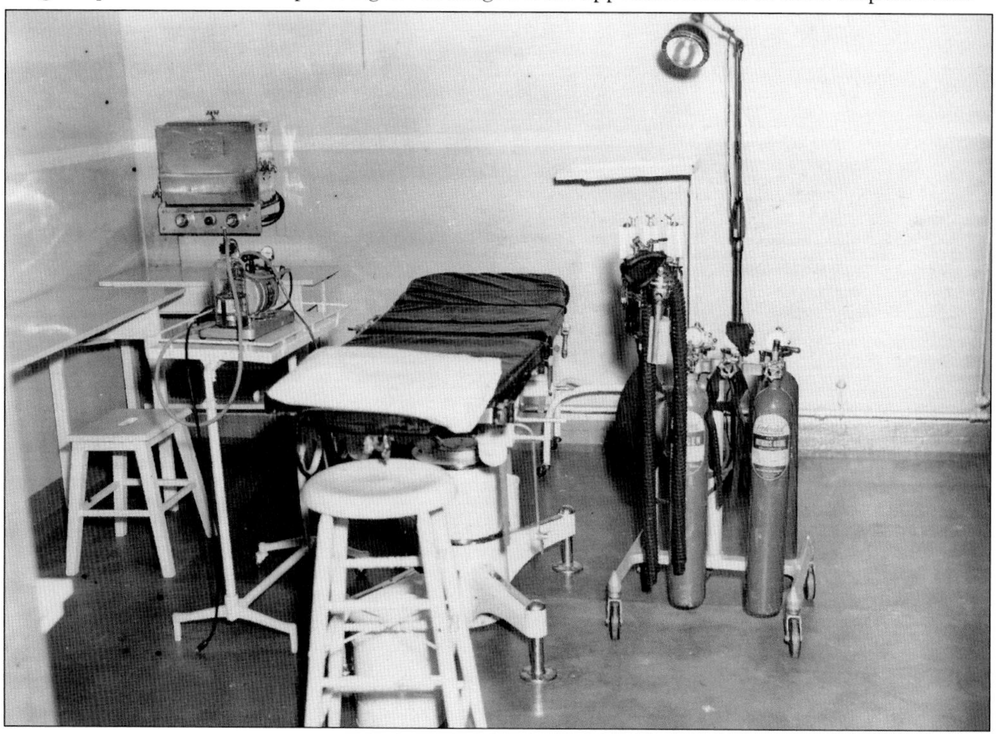

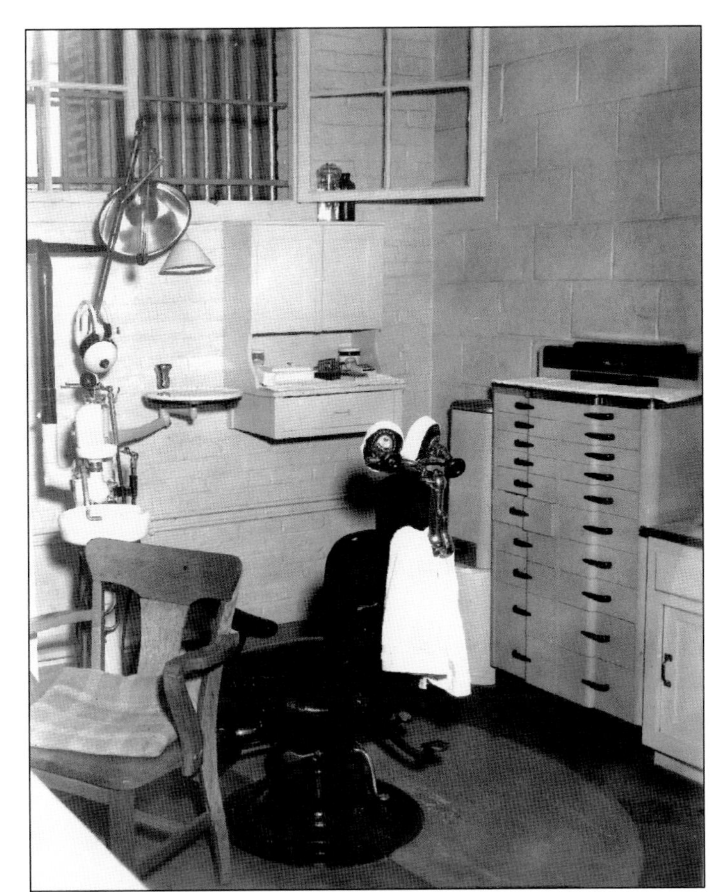

Dental care was provided in a modest dental clinic used by the dentist, who performed extractions, fillings, and denture work. It was later upgraded with modern equipment as seen in the photograph below.

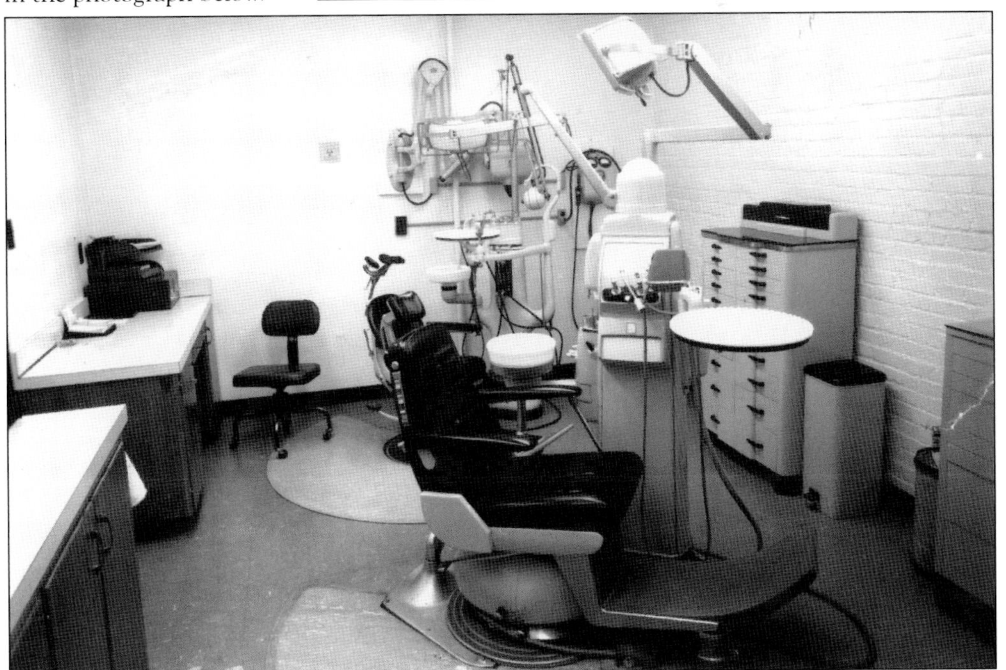

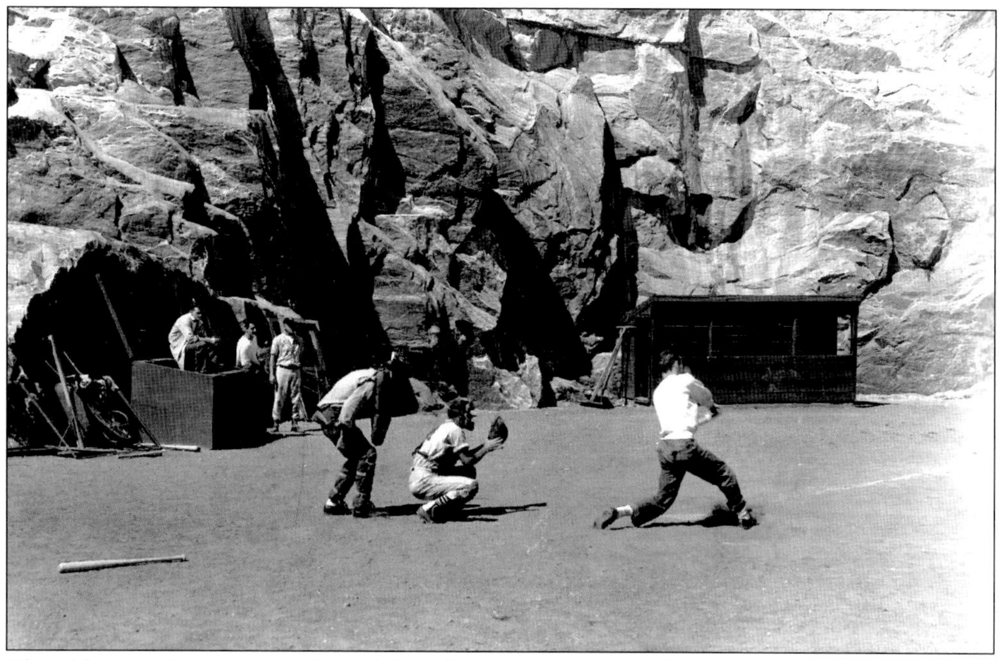

The old quarry became a stark backdrop for many recreational activities such as baseball, ice hockey, donkey baseball, tennis, basketball, visiting marching bands, and concerts. In winter months, the hockey rink provided outside entertainment. Indoor recreational activities included the television room, card tables, Ping Pong, chess, and checkers.

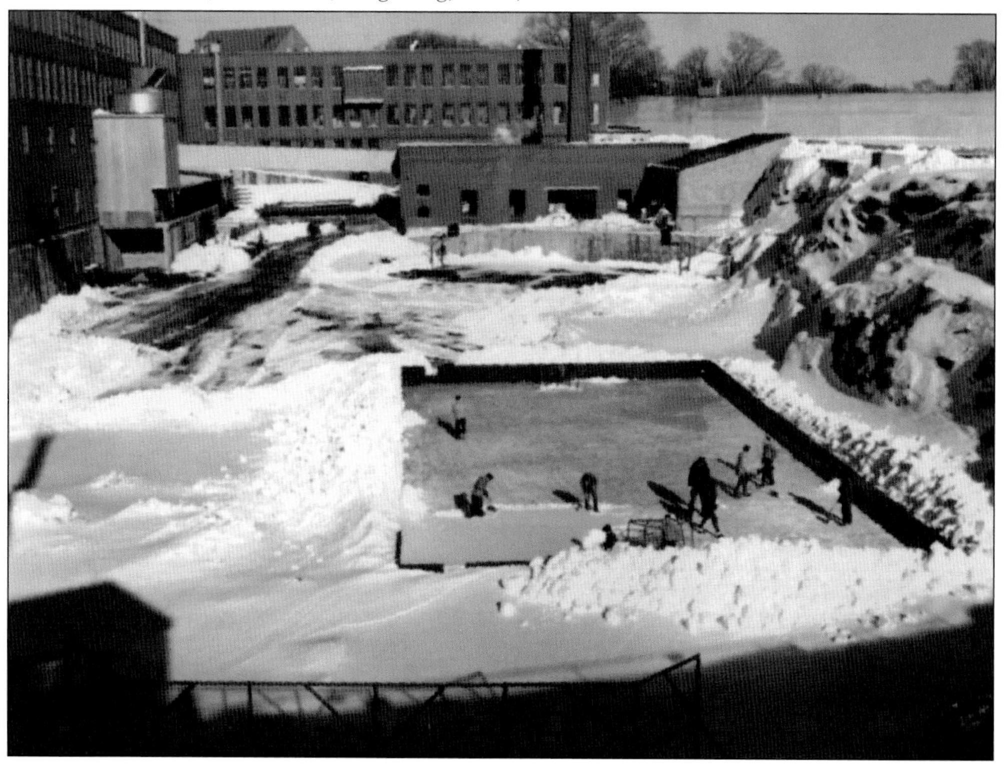

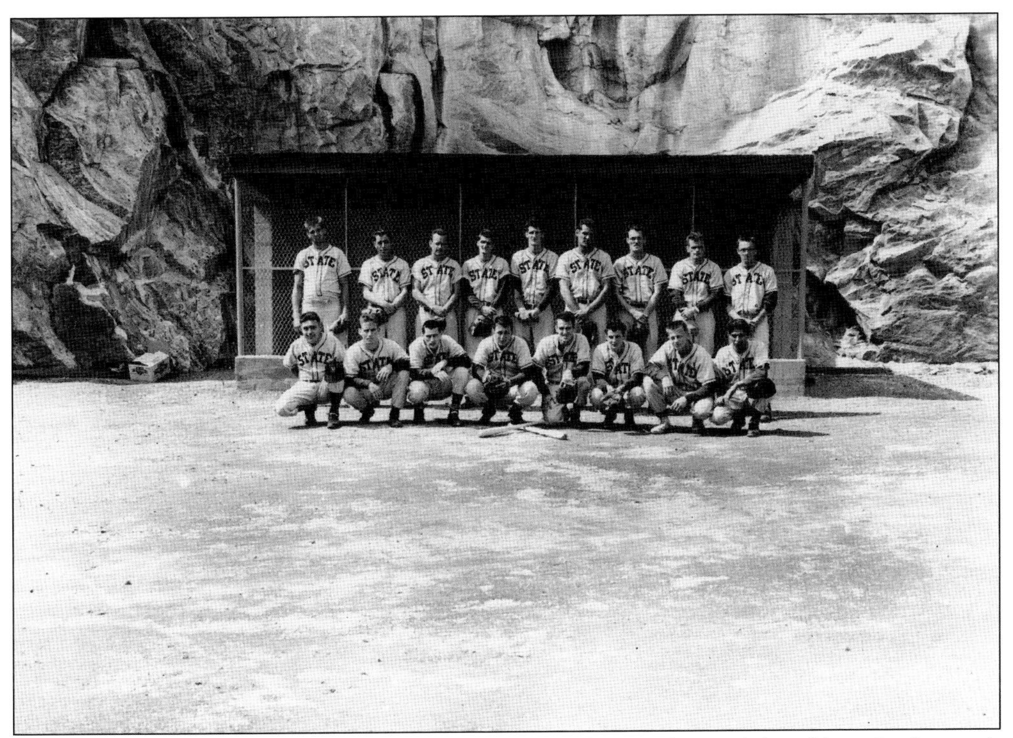

This 1960s picture of the prison baseball team was taken in front of the old ice hockey rink fence. Inmates played against semiprofessional teams in coastal Maine in the 1950s and 1960s. They played in the quarry until the early 1970s.

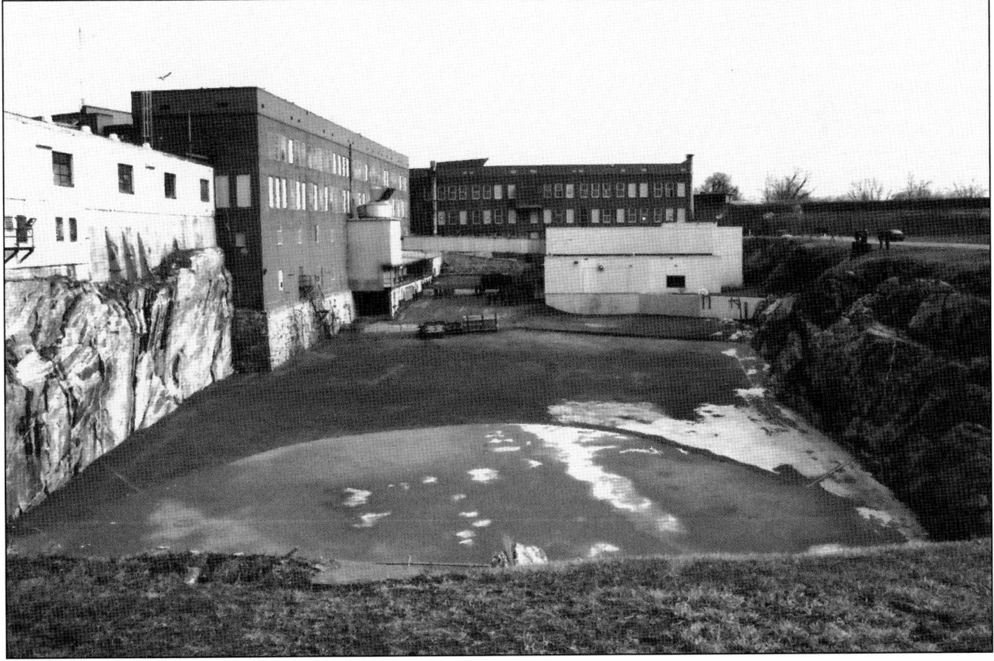

This photograph taken in the 1990s shows the new location of the baseball diamond. (Courtesy of Michael Lokuta.)

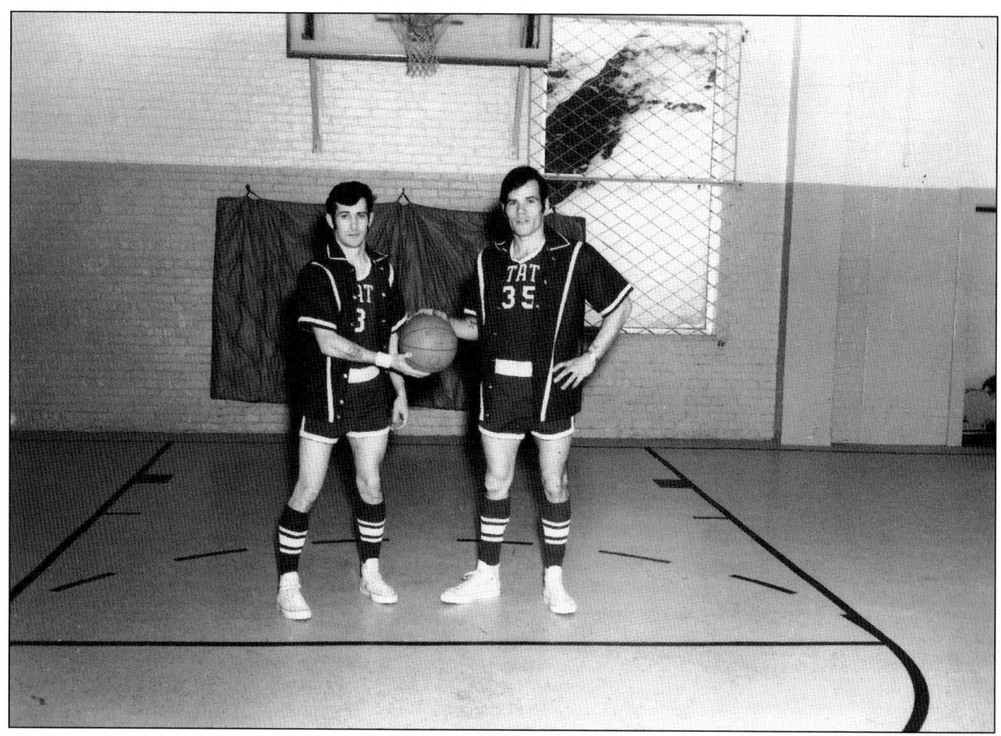

This photograph taken in the late 1960s shows the prison's basketball team captains in the renovated gymnasium, which had been the old boiler room. Prior to the renovation, the basketball courts were located outside.

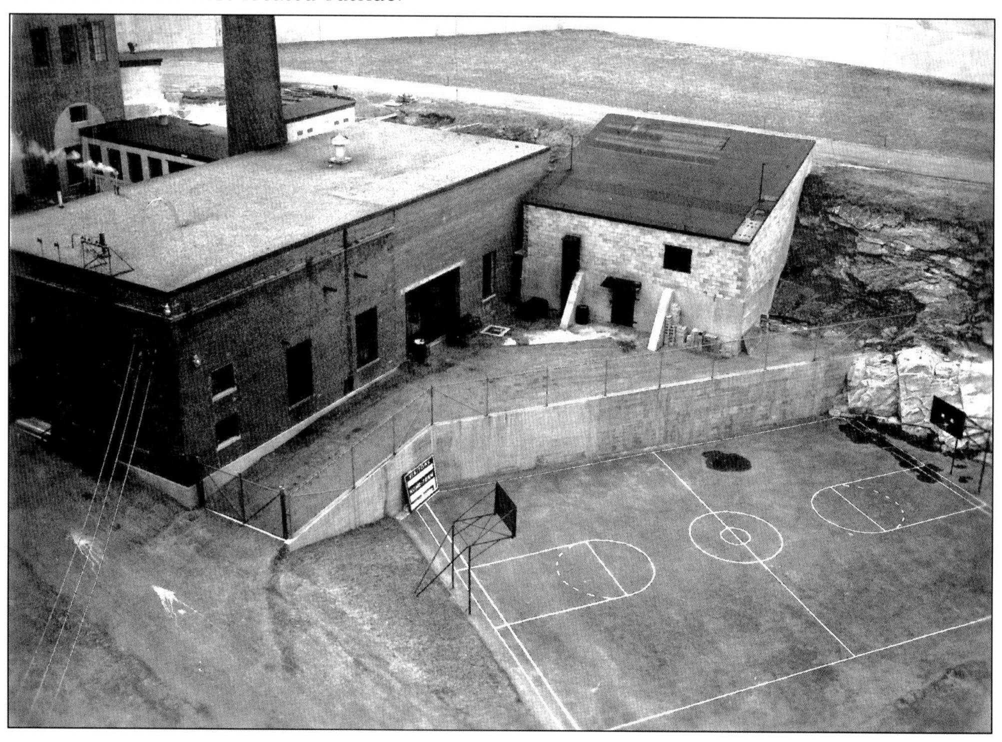

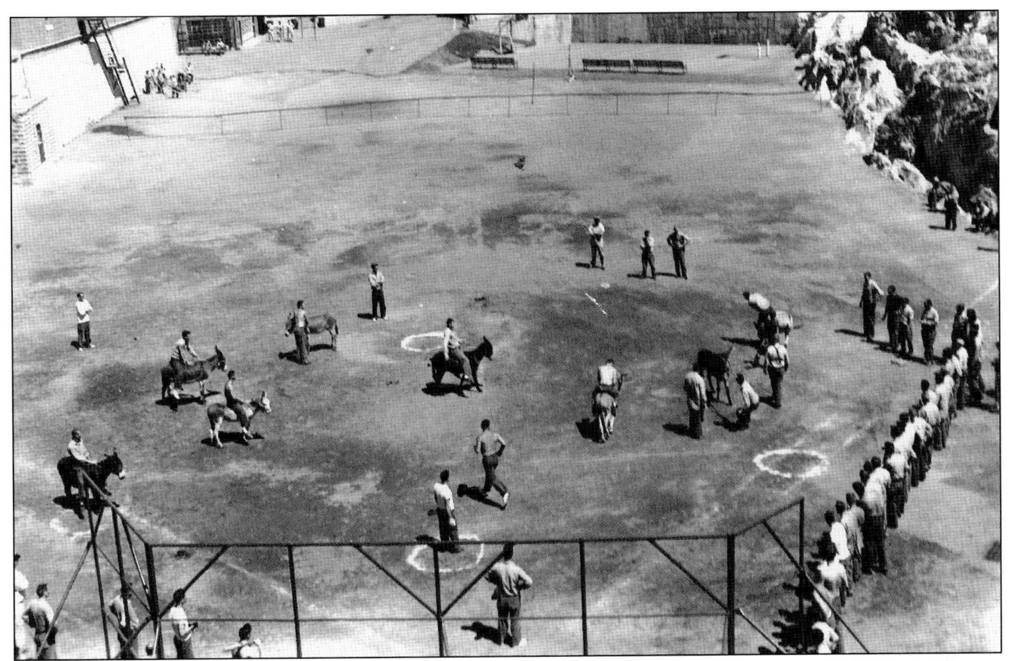

Donkey baseball was a unique event inside the prison. Imagine playing a baseball game riding a donkey around the bases. All the players except the pitcher and catcher had their own donkey. Running, throwing, and catching while on a donkey must have been a challenge and amusing to watch.

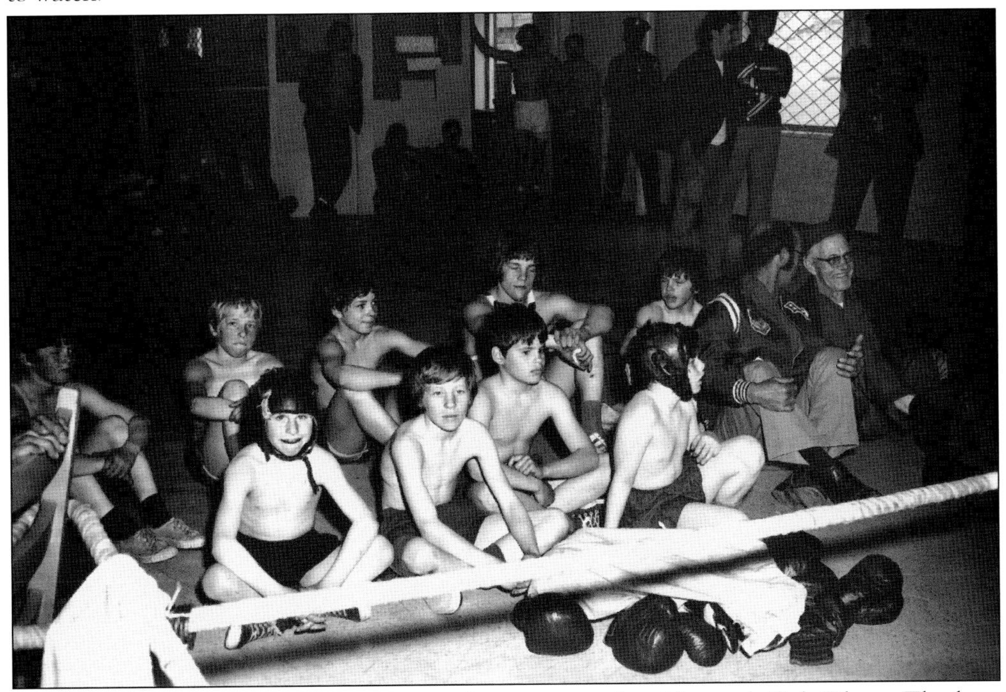

A Canadian youth boxing team came to the prison yearly with coach Bob Edgett. The boys sparred with each other, and some boxed against the inmates. This was a popular event that generated a large turnout.

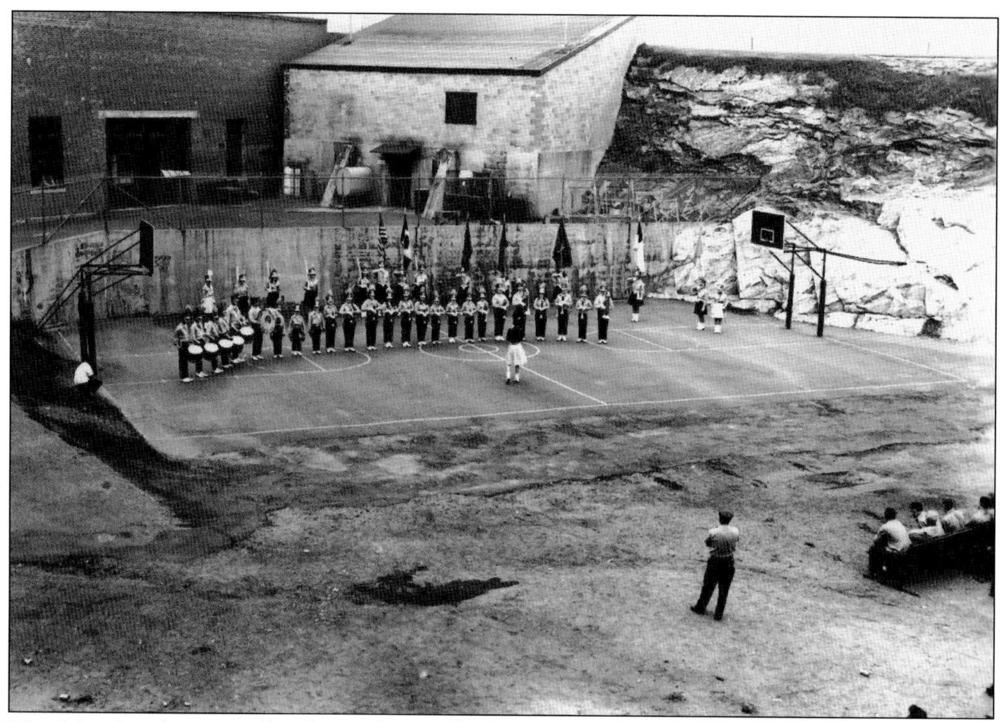

Marching bands were a familiar sight inside the prison, as were concerts provided by notable Maine performers.

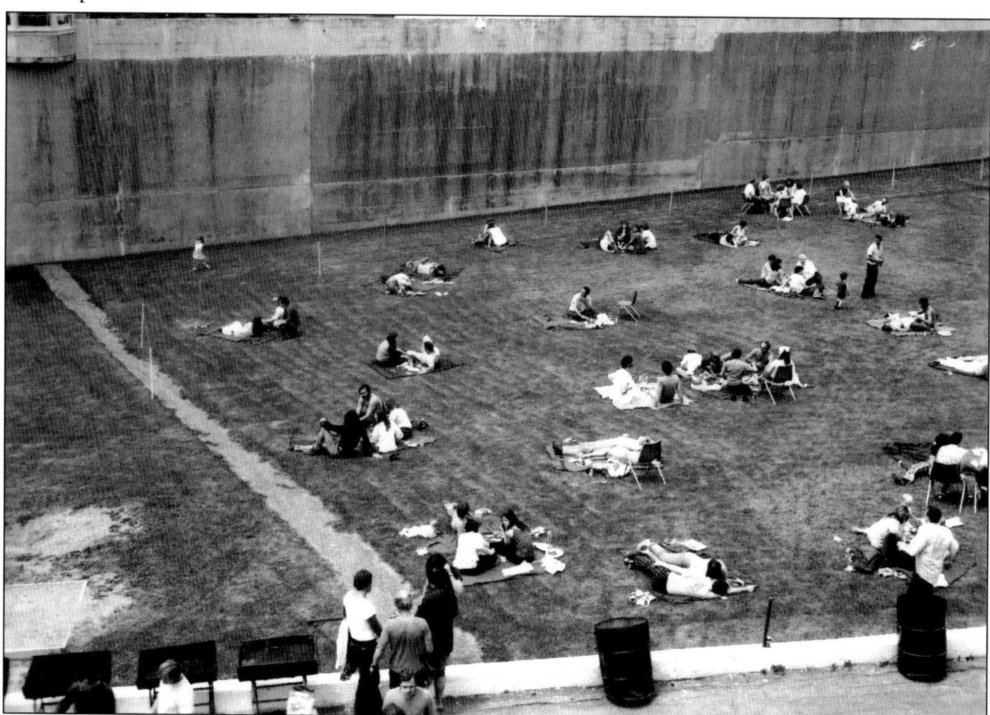

Family picnics and barbecues were a regular event in the 1970s where wives and children visited inside the prison. Similar activities occurred in other prisons around the country.

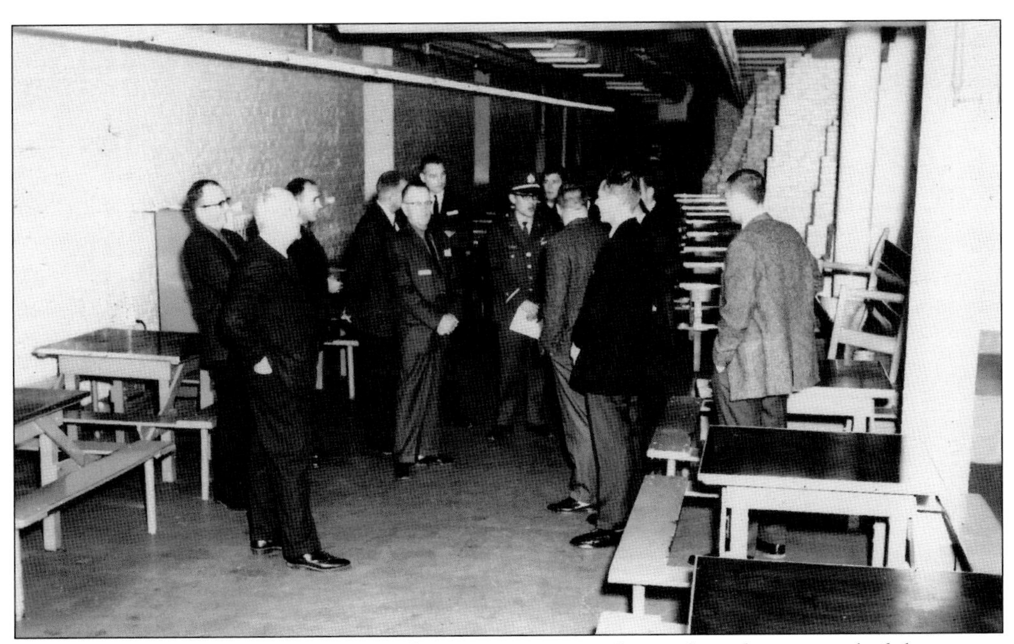

Known as the "Monte Carlo Room," this game room was located on the east end of the quarry below the industries woodshop. The back wall of the room shows a granite ledge remnant from the quarry. Ping Pong, board games, cards, and other social activities were permitted during recreation periods. In this photograph, prison officials are touring the area.

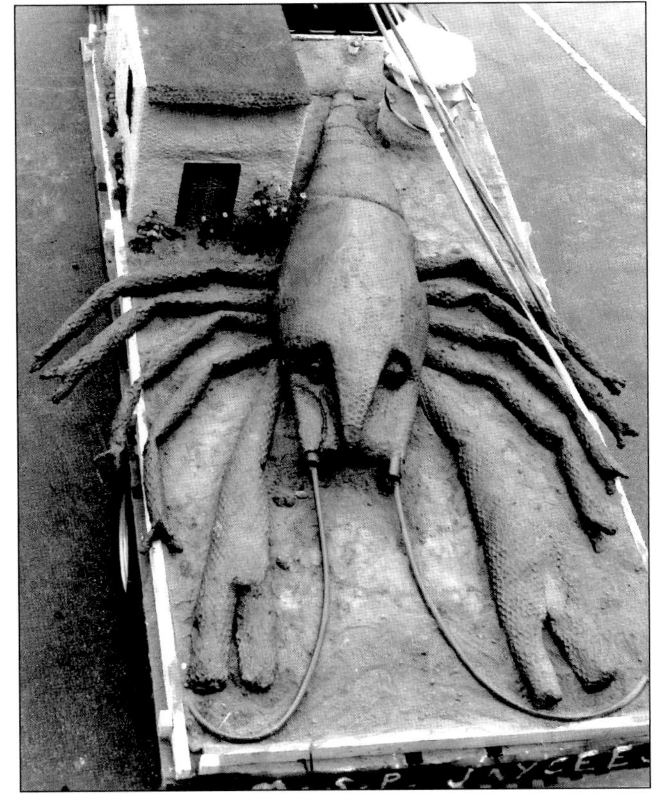

In this 1960s photograph, a large-scale model of a lobster was constructed by inmates for a local parade. Lobster bakes were a popular inmate group fund-raising opportunity in the 1980s. In *Consider the Lobster*, author David Foster Wallace wrote, "some early American colonies had laws against feeding lobsters to inmates more than once a week because it was thought to be cruel and unusual, like making people eat rats."

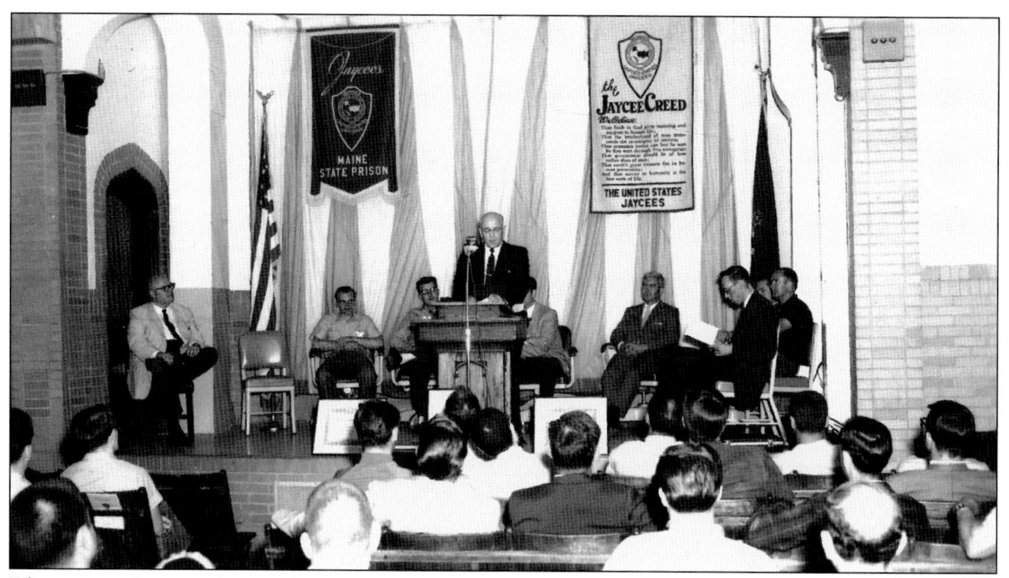

The prison Jaycee chapter has been an active service club since the 1960s, raising money for various charities over the decades.

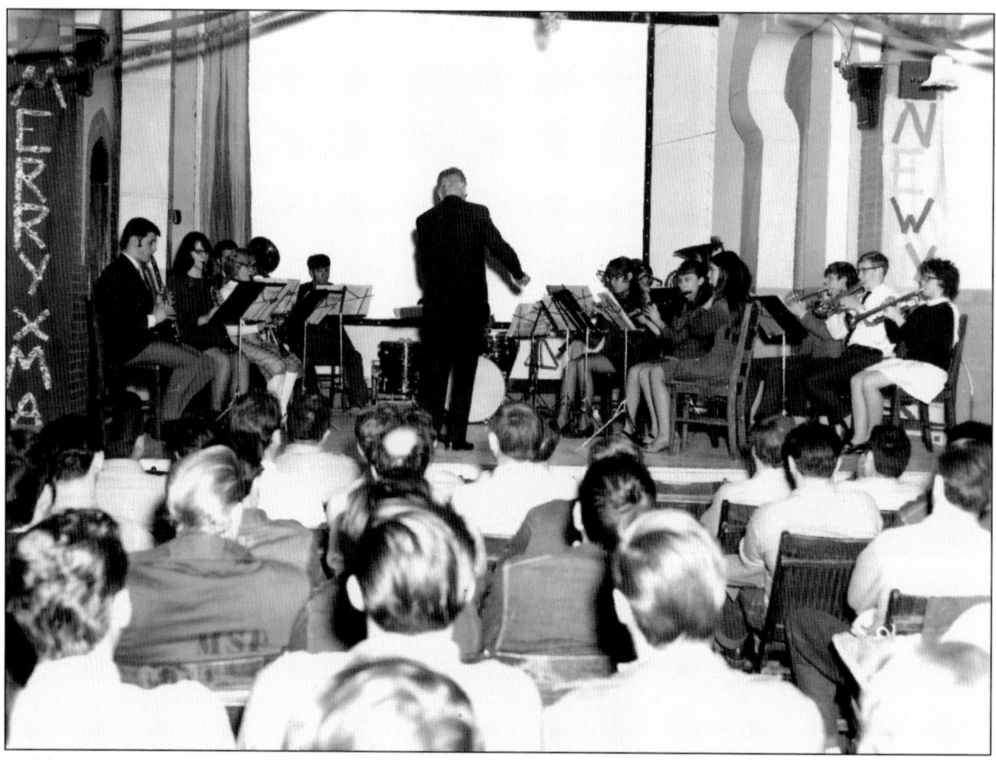

A Christmas concert was provided by school students. One Christmas, Warden Allan L. Robbins purchased ice cream for the inmates out of his own pocket.

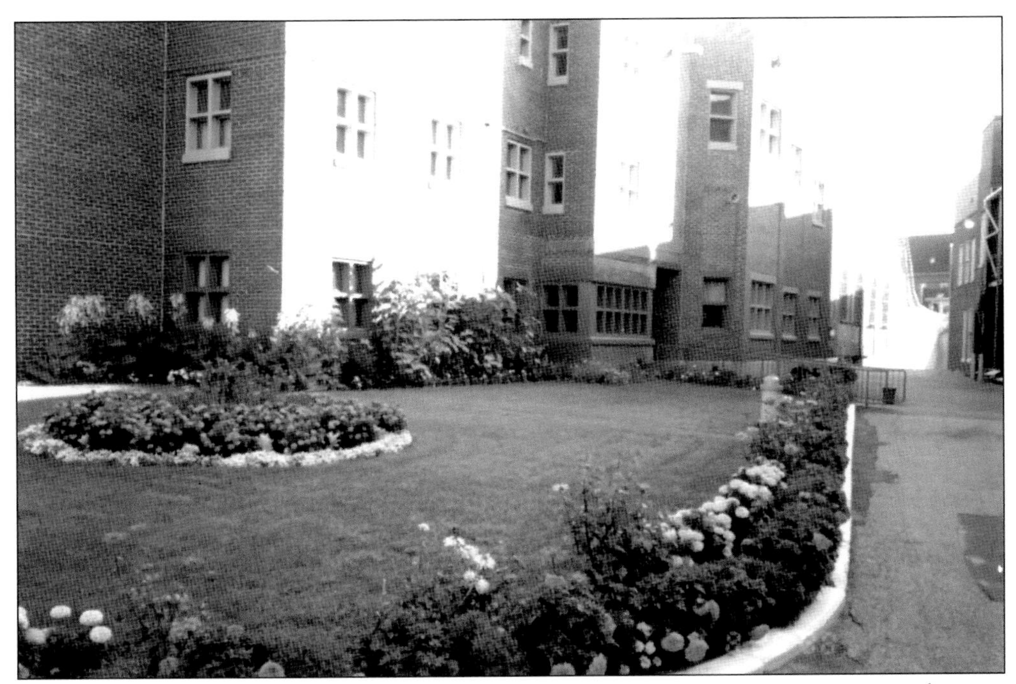

The prison gardens were a tradition for many years, increasing in size as more prisoners became interested in working in the flower beds. Many of the flowers were started in the garden shack. One season in the 1990s, a giant pumpkin was nurtured inside the compound and put on display in the lobby. (Courtesy of Michael Lokuta.)

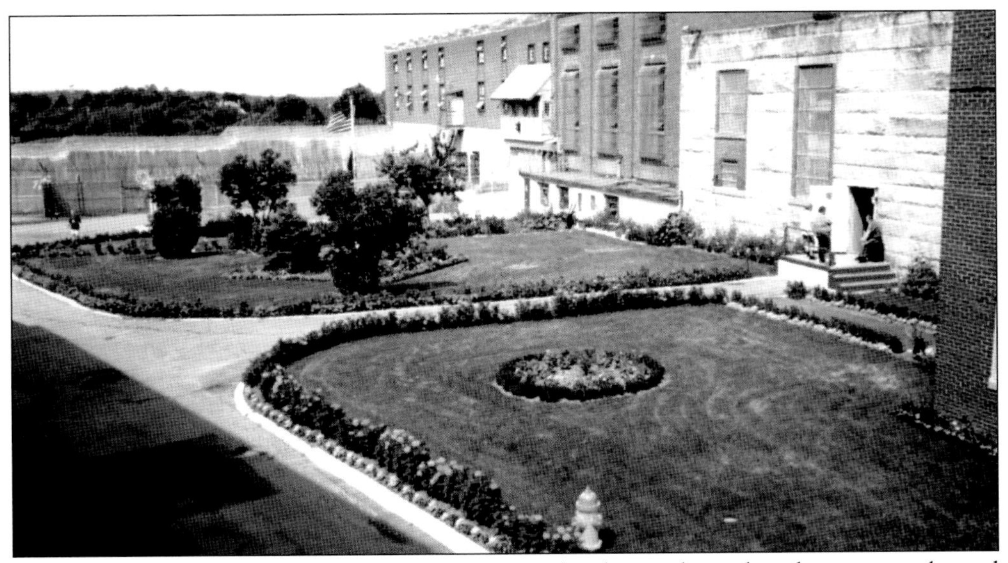

The University of Maine Cooperative Extension taught a horticulture class that was popular and provided a foundation for inmates to pursue landscaping jobs in the community when released.

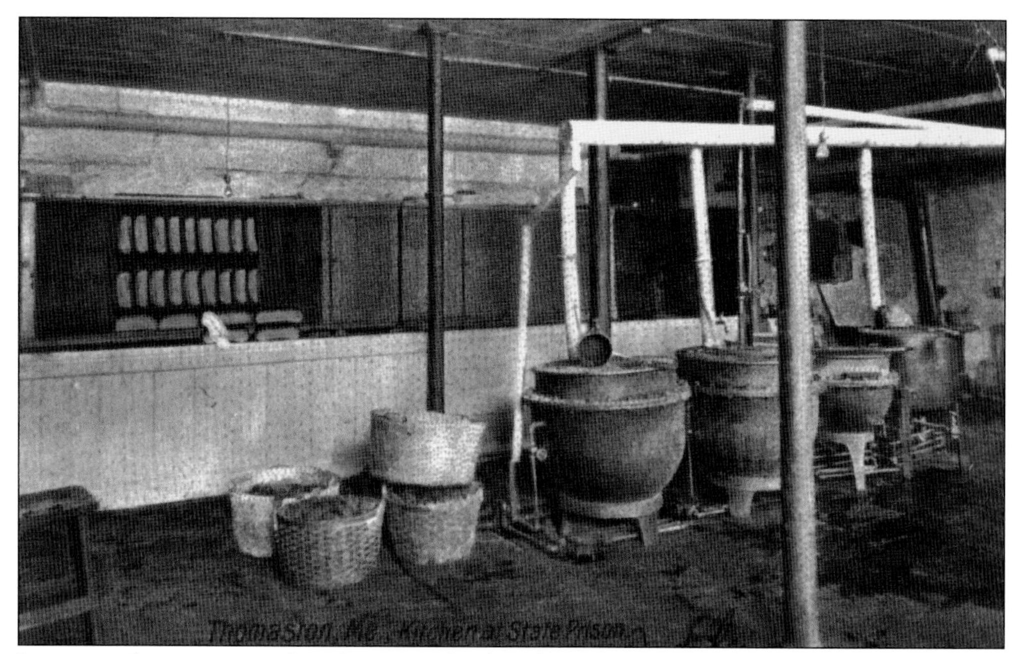

Large metal vats were used in the prison kitchen for preparing food for inmates. In later years, the vats were discarded and used by the local boatyard to heat pitch for filling deck plank cracks on seagoing vessels. A brick encasement was built to contain fire for the heating.

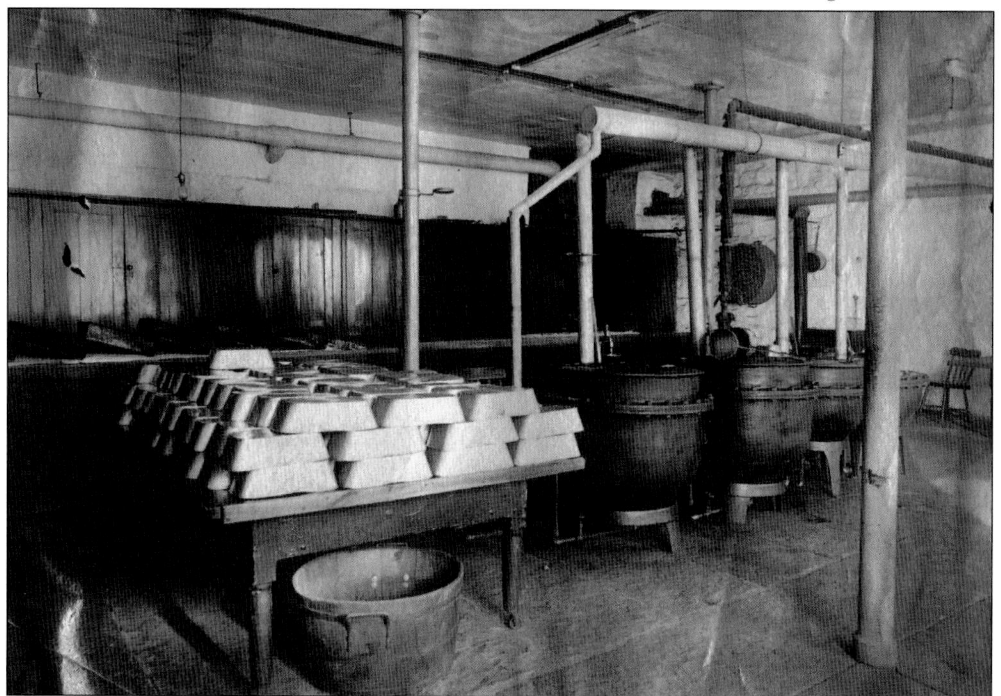

In 1824, breakfast and supper consisted of three gills of Indian meal pudding, or a half pound of bread and a half gill of molasses. Dinner was a generous serving of beef, a half pound of dry fish, or a pound of fresh fish with hog's lard or butter, a half pound of bread, and a half pint of potatoes. Drink was water, or when allowed, spruce or hop beer.

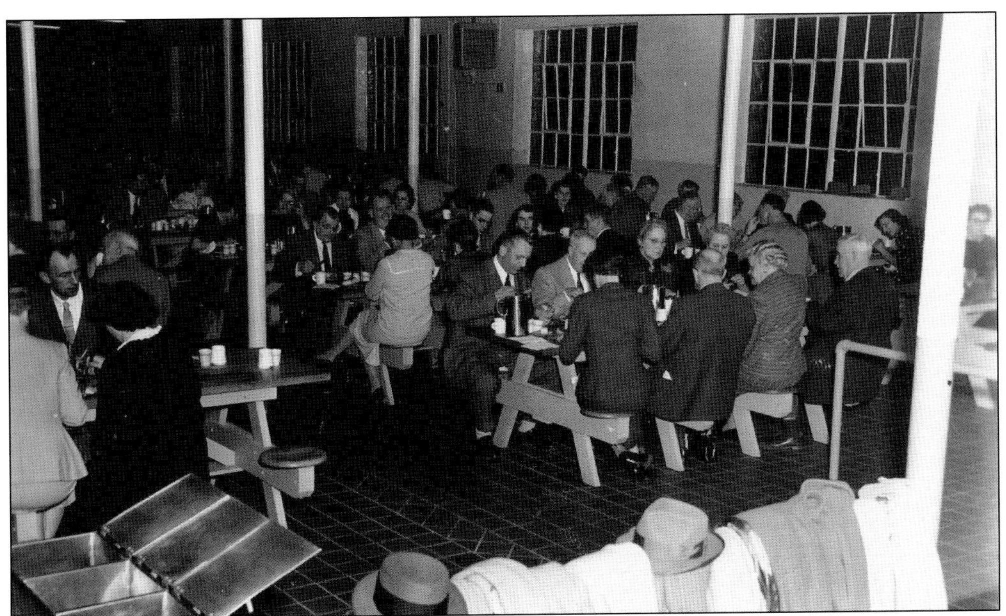

In 1907, congregate eating replaced serving meals in convicts' cells. In this 1950s photograph, prison staff and their families are seen eating in the dining hall probably before a special event or play.

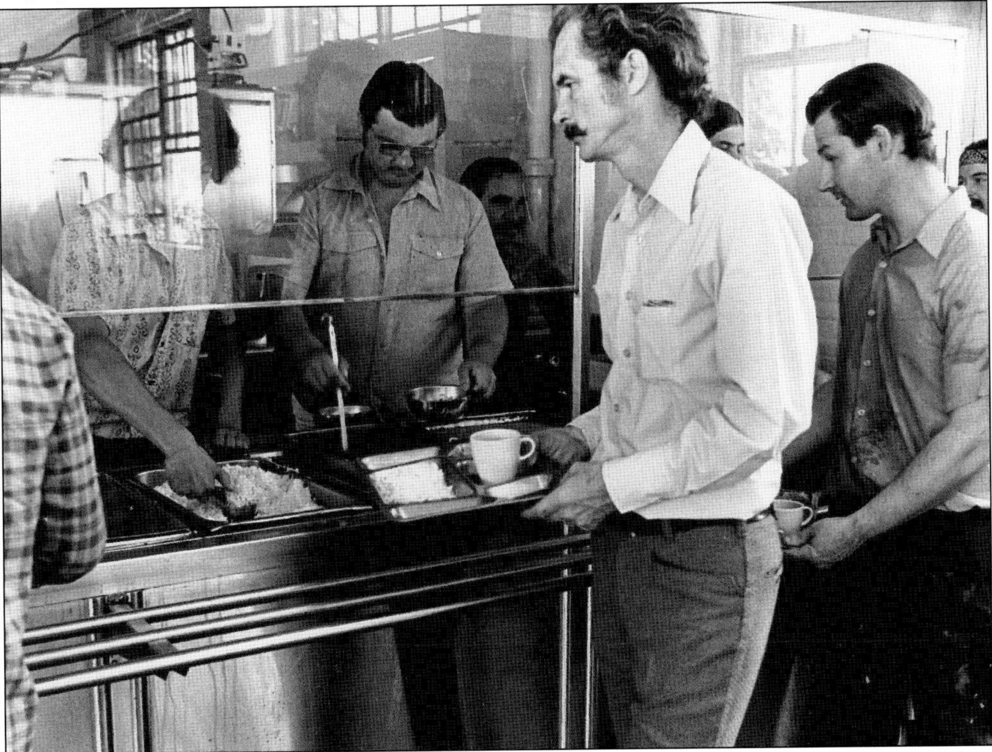

This 1960s photograph shows inmates serving a meal to other inmates in line. Four hundred inmates were served cafeteria style in less than a half hour for each meal and the average per capita food cost was 87¢ per inmate per day in the mid-1960s.

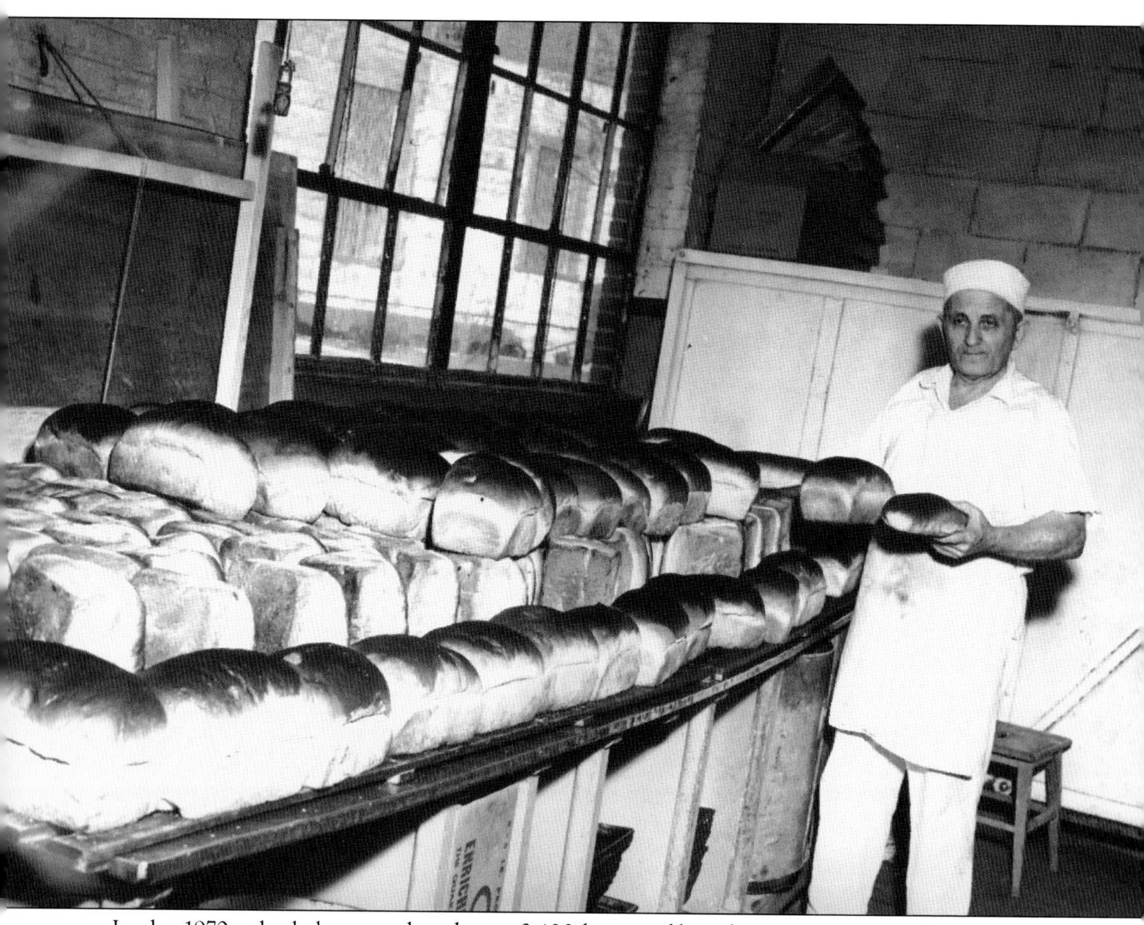

In the 1970s, the bakery produced over 3,400 loaves of bread every month. Sufficient beef, pork, poultry, eggs, milk, and cream were supplied to the prison from the prison farm in South Warren.

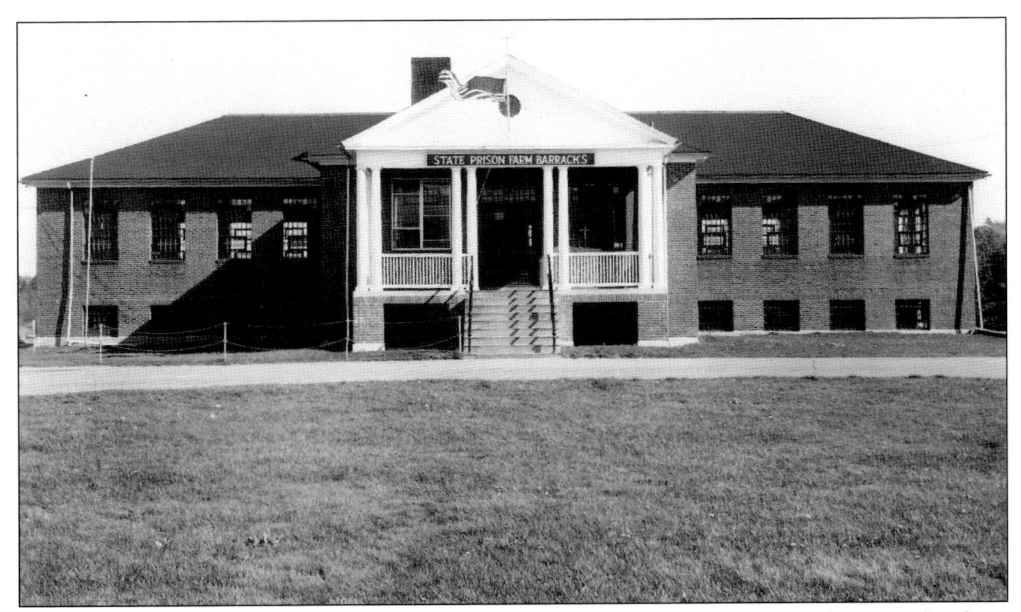

In the 1930s, a farm barracks for the Maine State Prison was constructed two miles from Thomaston. It consisted of the barracks, three farms including a hennery, turkey barn, piggery, cannery, slaughterhouse, and dairy, and a pasteurization plant. In the words of Warden Allan L. Robbins in the 1950s, "The Prison Farm represents one of the more advanced stages of penological development in the Maine prison system."

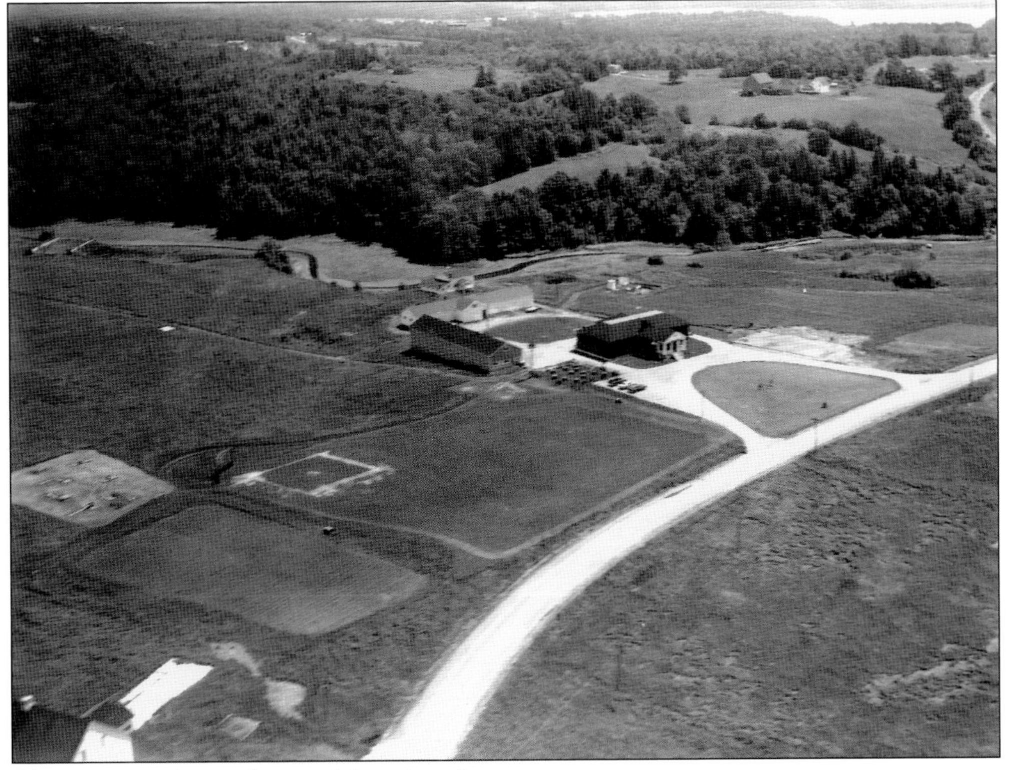

Above is an early aerial view of the prison farm.

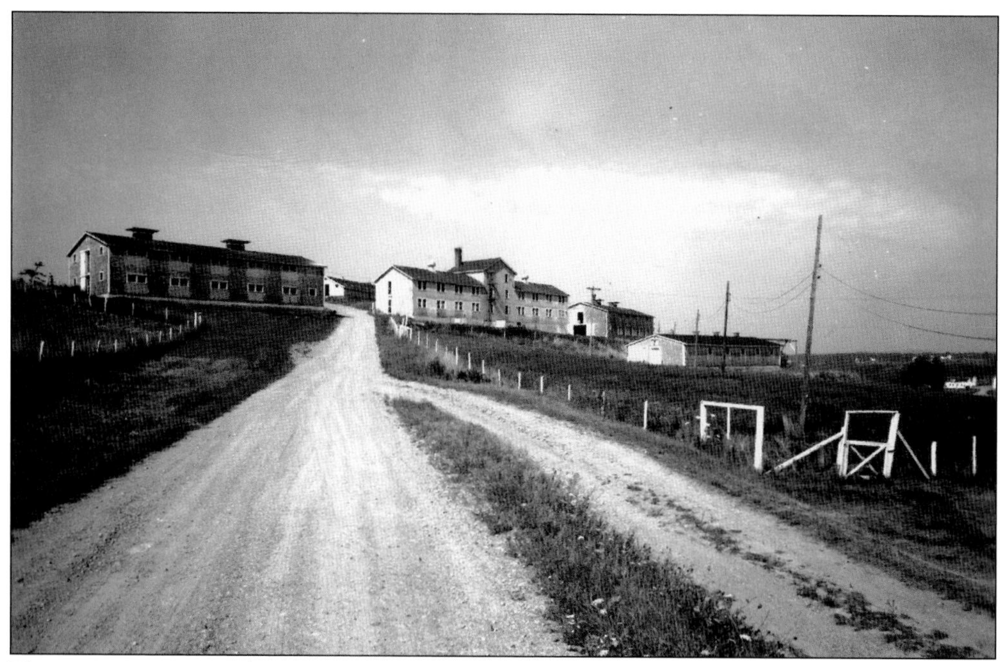

The massive two-story hennery is pictured on the right. It could hold 8,000 chickens. Today it is used for storage.

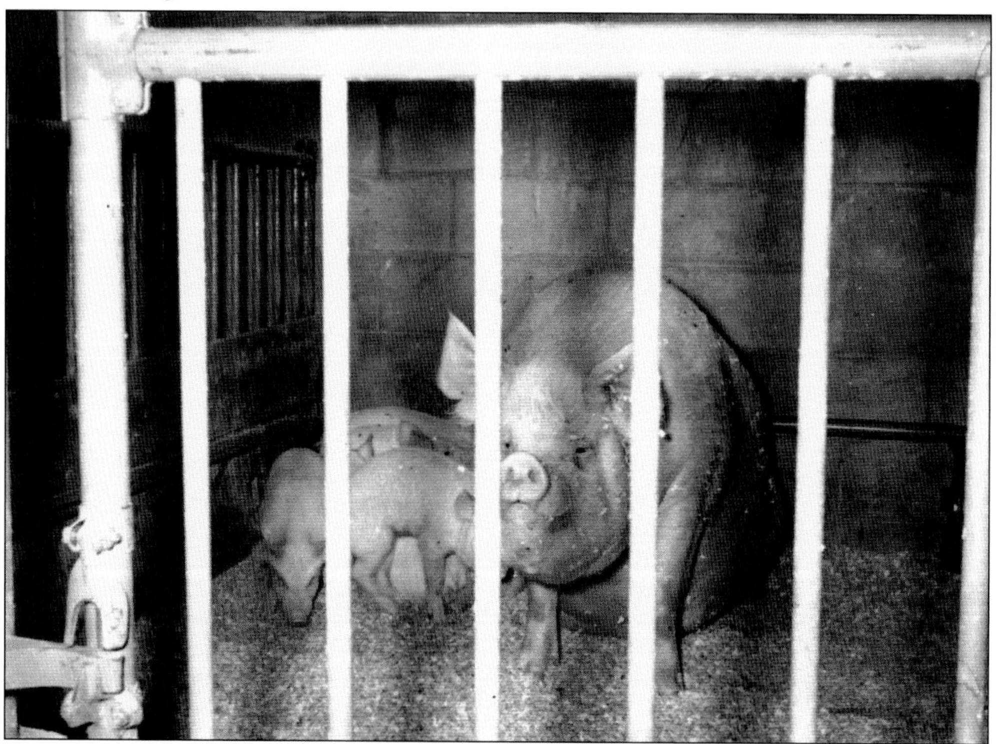

The piggery sat at the top of a hill that is still called Pig Hill today. It could hold 250 pigs. After slaughter, meat from the chickens, turkeys, beef cattle, and pigs was used to feed the inmates in the prison and at other institutions.

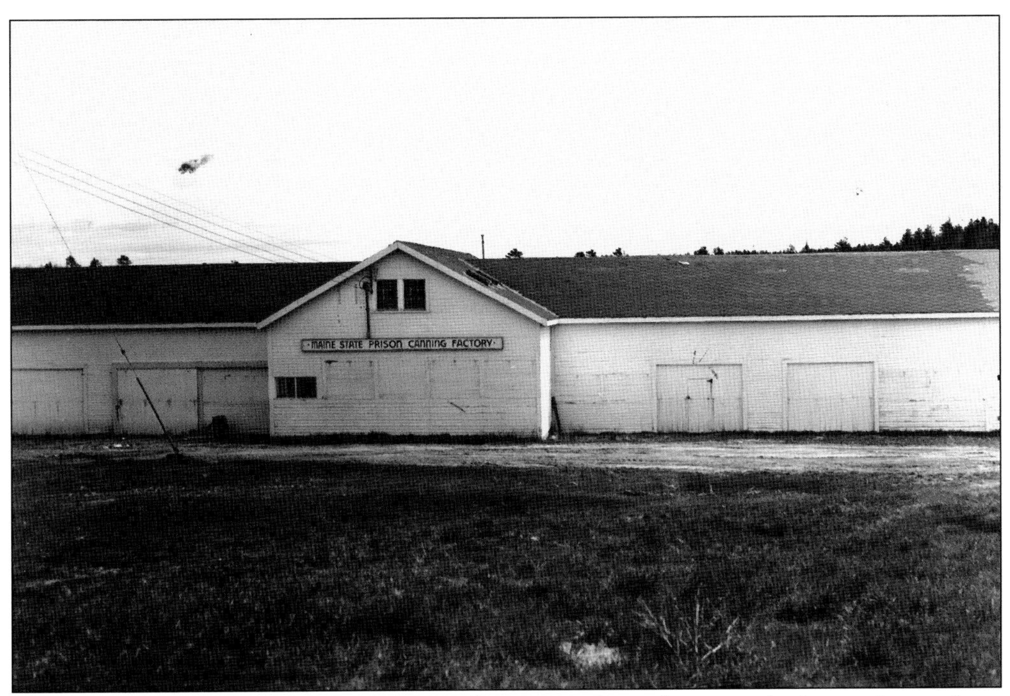

In 1971, the cannery produced 25,000 cans of peas, corn, beets, beans, and other garden products for the prison and over 12,000 cans for other institutions. The cannery had a gross business of over $20,000 in that year.

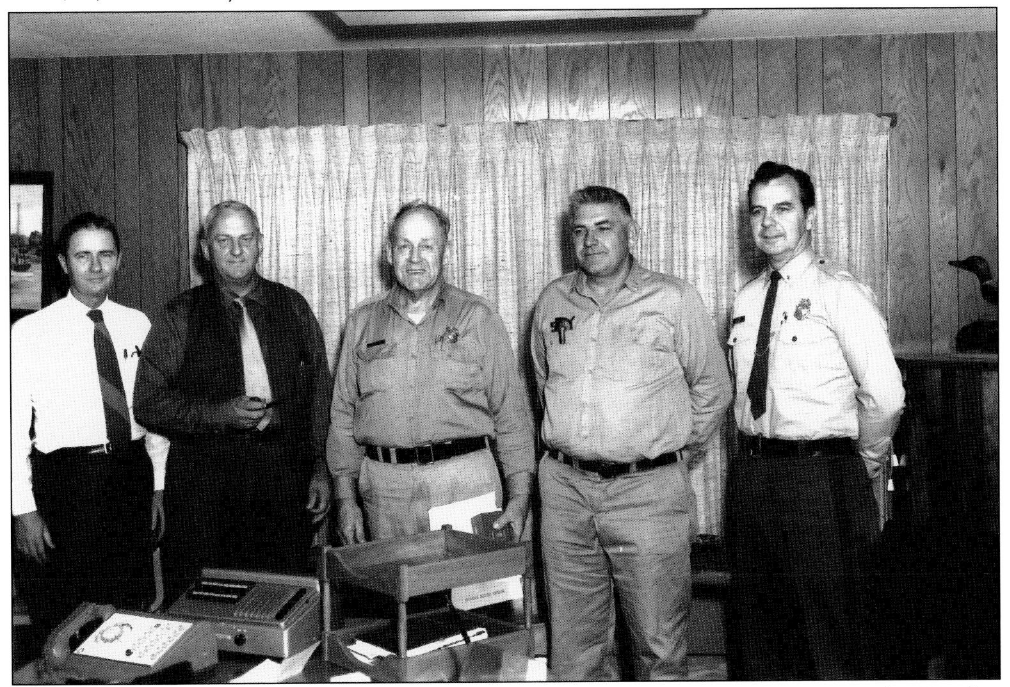

In this early-1970s picture, from left to right, are Deputy Warden Robert Kennedy, Warden Allan L. Robbins, an unidentified staff member, Lt. Lesley Fleck, and Inspector Kenneth Jacobson. Lieutenant Fleck was the last employee to hold the title of farm superintendent.

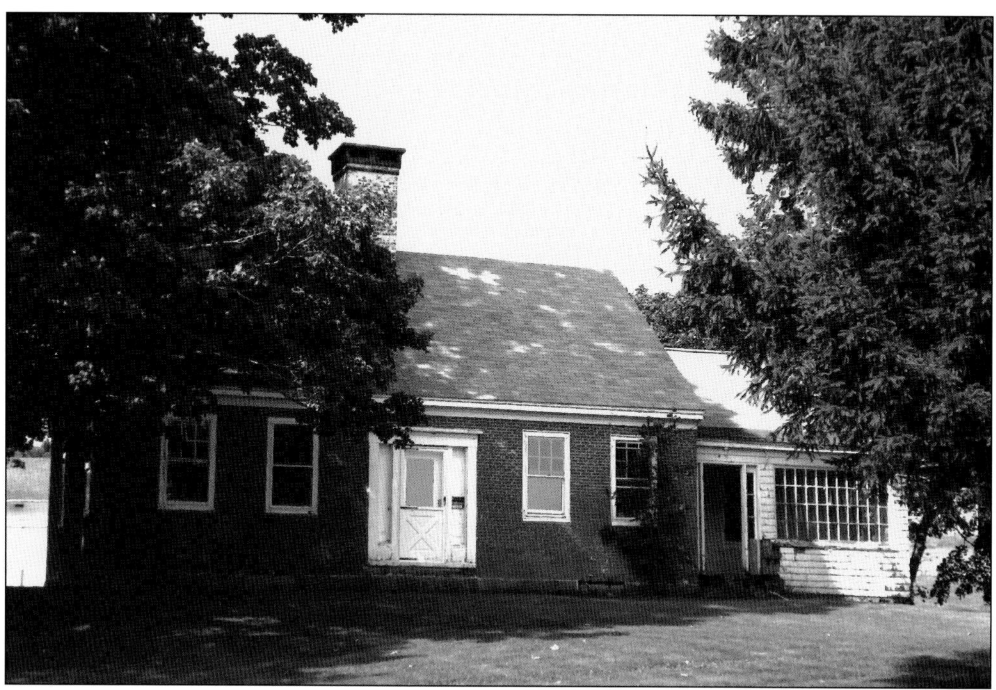

The Barrett Farm was purchased in 1919 as part of the prison farm program and was the home of the farm superintendent for many years.

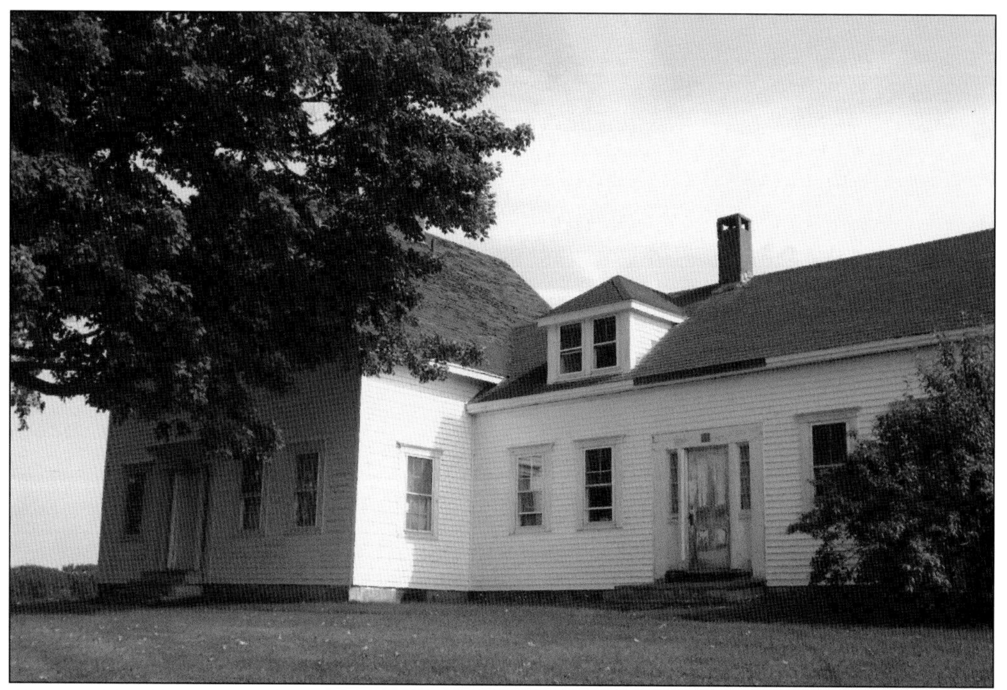

The Bucklin Farm was also purchased as part of the prison farm program and was used as housing for supervisory staff working at the farm or prison.

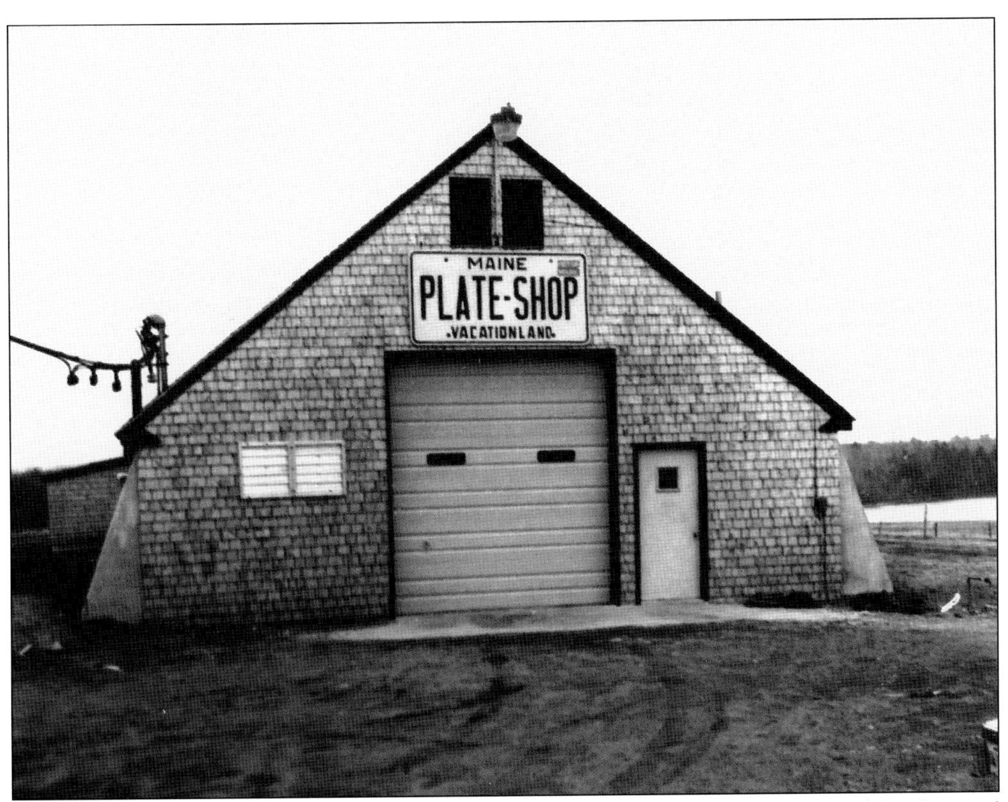

In 1980, the license plate shop moved from the prison to the Bolduc Correctional Facility and has provided steady employment for eligible inmates.

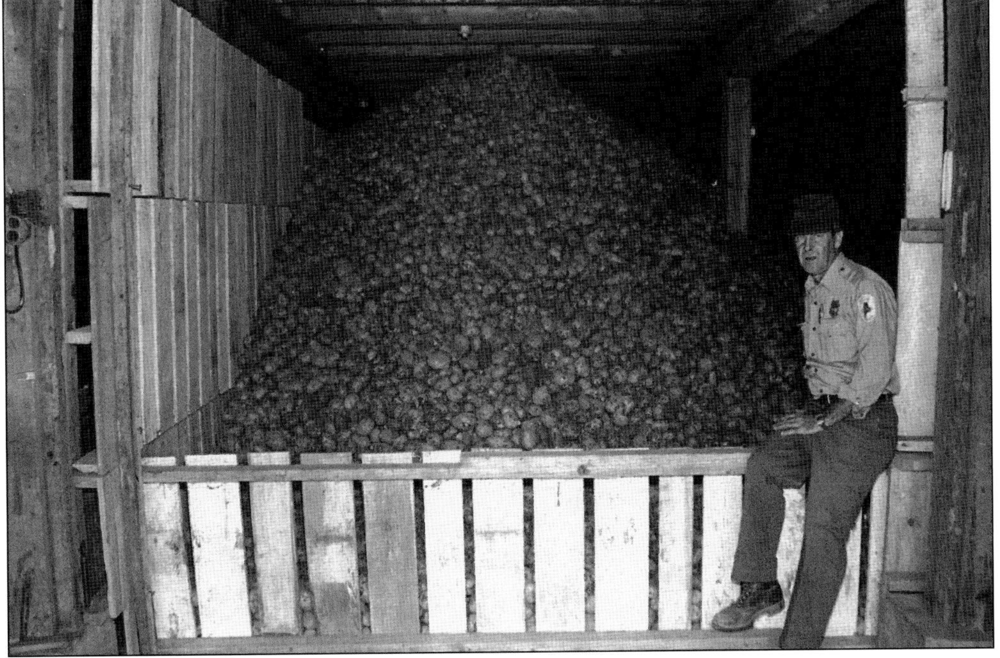

An annual fall potato crop harvest is shown in this photograph.

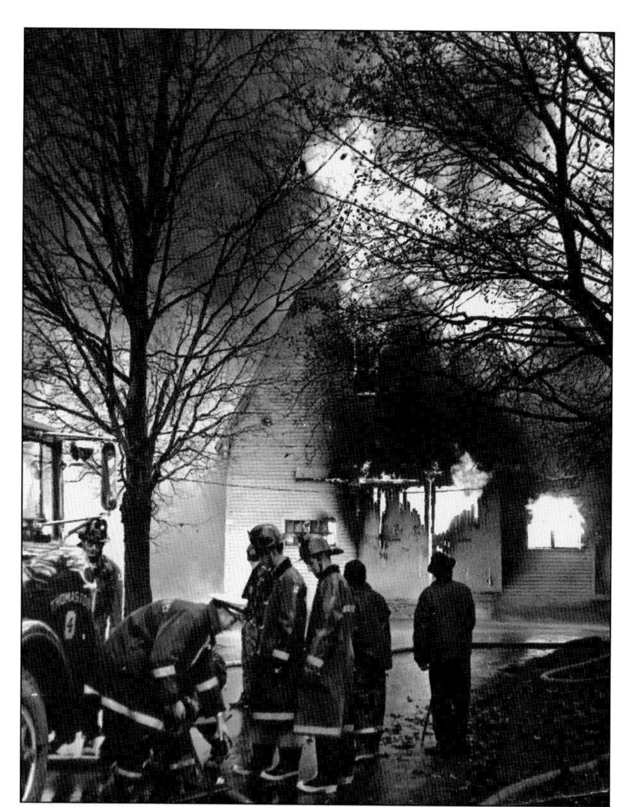

In 1971, fire destroyed the dairy barn and other buildings at the farm, although no livestock were lost. The Thomaston firefighters battled the blaze.

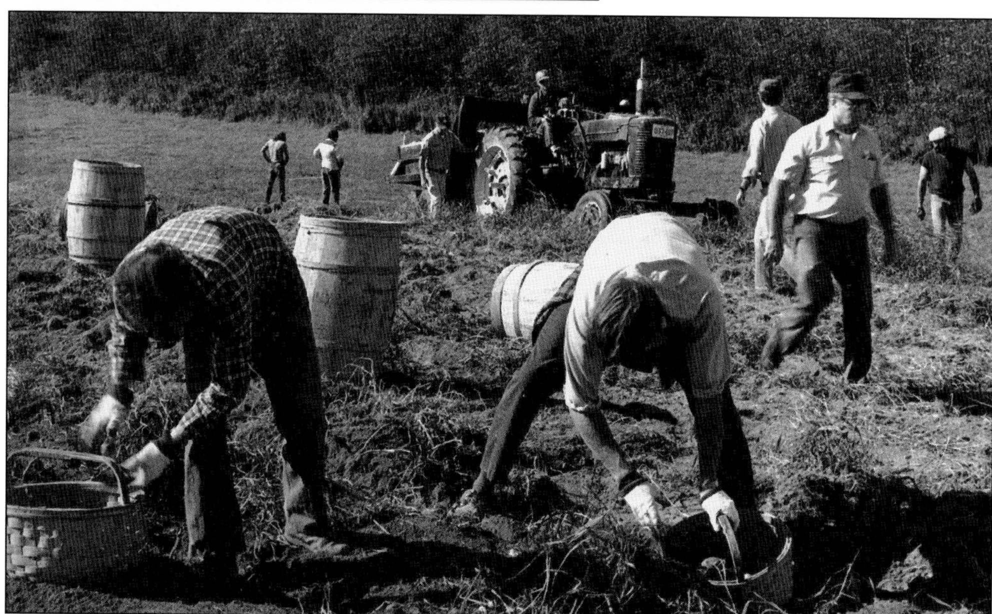

A general decline in farm profitability and the 1971 fire brought farm operations to an end. In the 1980s, farm manager Edward Barrett and Deputy Warden Joseph Smith brought the farm back into operation with just three acres under cultivation. Cultivation increased to 68 acres by 1991 under manager Harold Doughty. Pictured on the right, Deputy Warden Smith inspects the potato harvest.

Three

THE INDUSTRIAL EVOLUTION

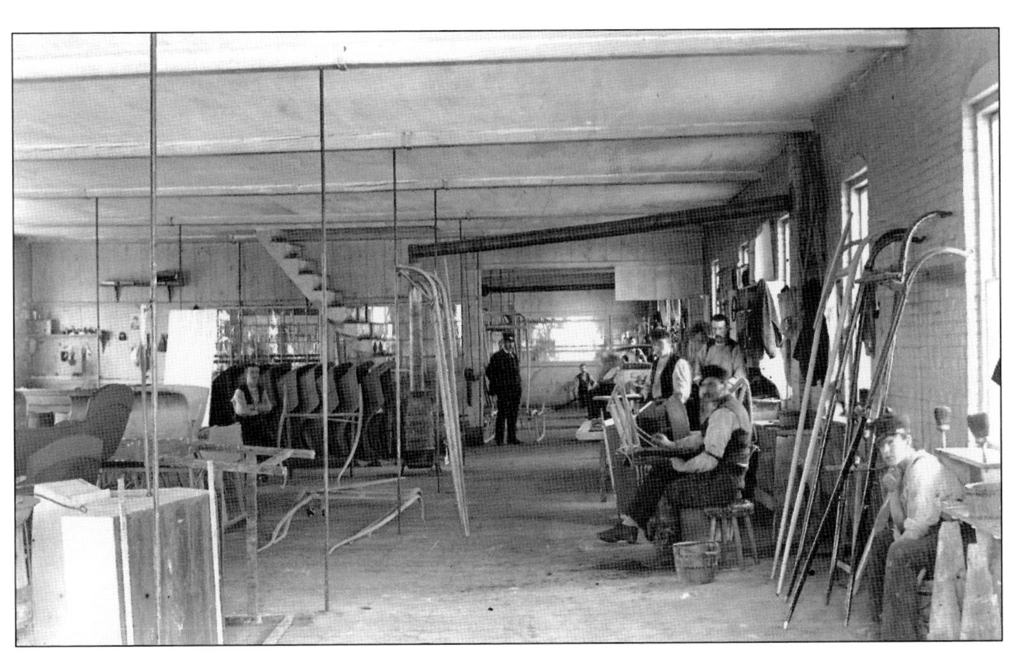

The Maine State Prison Industries Program dates all the way back to the prison opening in 1824. Over the Thomaston prison's 178-year history, the industries program has provided productive work for thousands of inmates in a wide variety of shop settings that included granite and limestone mining, harness making, carriage and sleigh building, blacksmithing, a cobbler, tailor, and woodshop, the craft room, a machine shop, license plate and metal sign making, and print and upholstery shops.

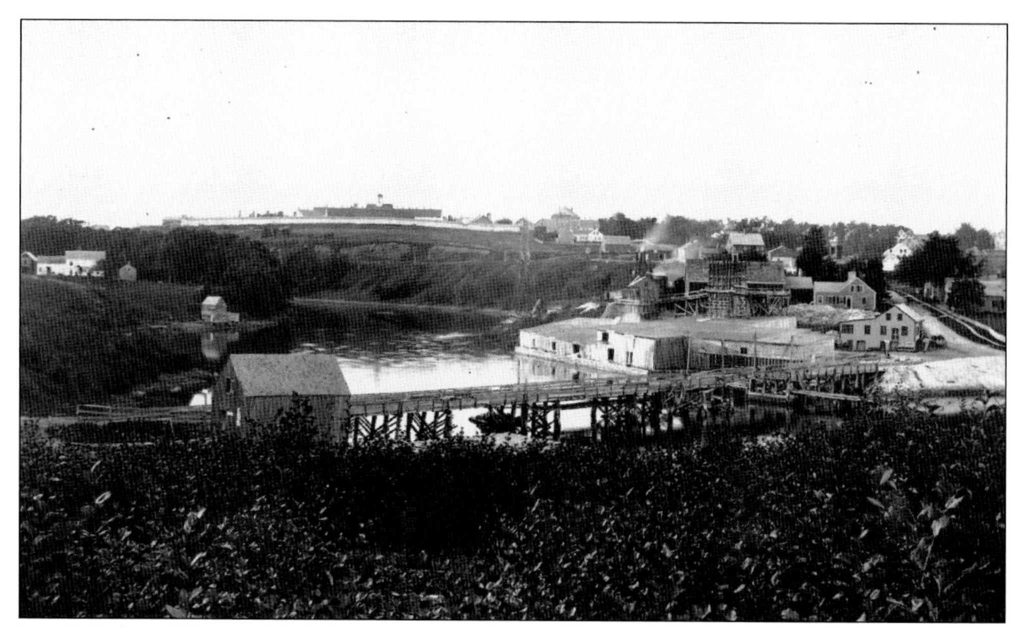

In 1826, the use of too many convict laborers overstocked the market with lime and therefore inspectors recommended hammering granite instead. In 1827, a granite quarry was purchased at Long Cove, St. George. A prison wharf was built with a crane for hoisting granite onto ships, a stonecutting shop was added, and in 1828, a gondola was built to transport granite up the St. George River. These changes improved commerce conditions.

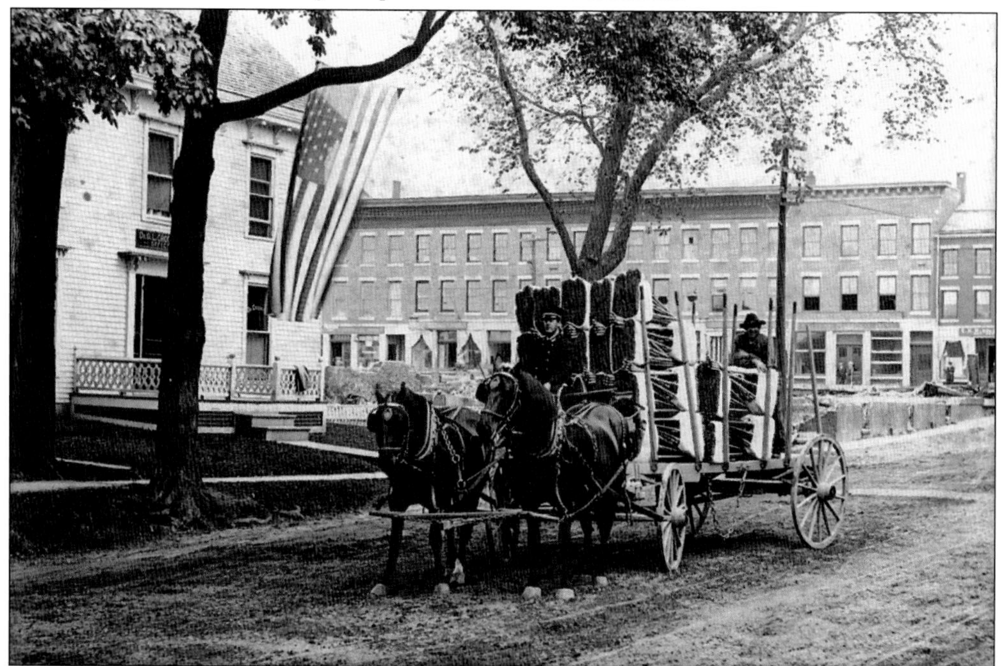

A wagon loaded with newly made brooms by convicts makes its way down Knox Street to the Thomaston railroad station for shipping. Behind the wagon is the rubble of Watts Hall, collapsed from the recent fire that took down the entire block on the south side of Main Street on June 6, 1915. A 1902 prison report stated the prison broom department made a gain of $3,002.24.

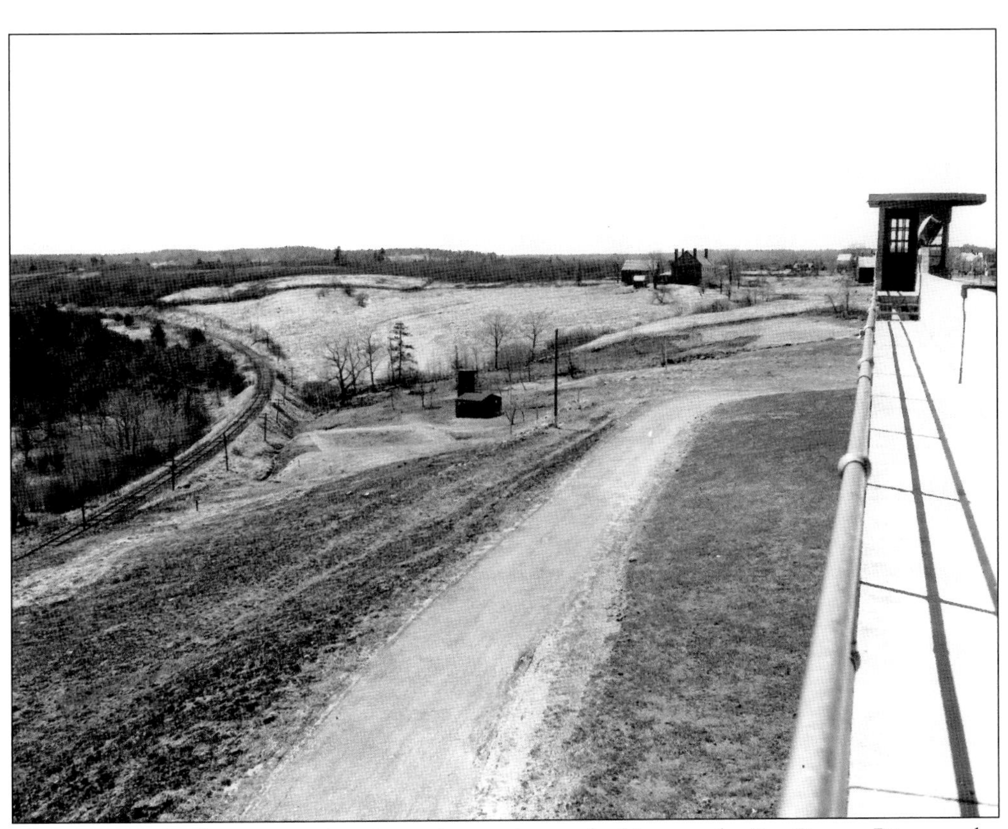

The photograph above was taken from the south post looking up the St. George River to the railway that in previous years had transported lime from the prison quarry. The photograph below shows a train pulling out of the Thomaston station on the east side of lower Knox Street. The brick building on the left, formerly the Knox farmhouse, was a structure built in 1796 to house the farm workers of Gen. Henry Knox. In 1870–1871, when the Knox and Lincoln Rail Road came through Thomaston, the original Knox mansion, Montpelier, was razed, but this building was spared to serve as a depot. It is the only building still remaining on the original site and currently serves as the headquarters for the Thomaston Historical Society. (Courtesy of the Thomaston Historical Society.)

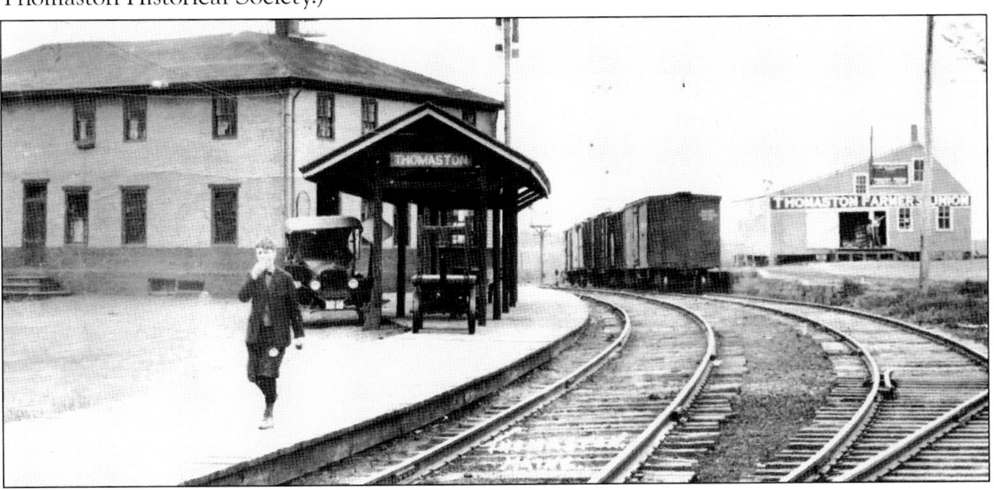

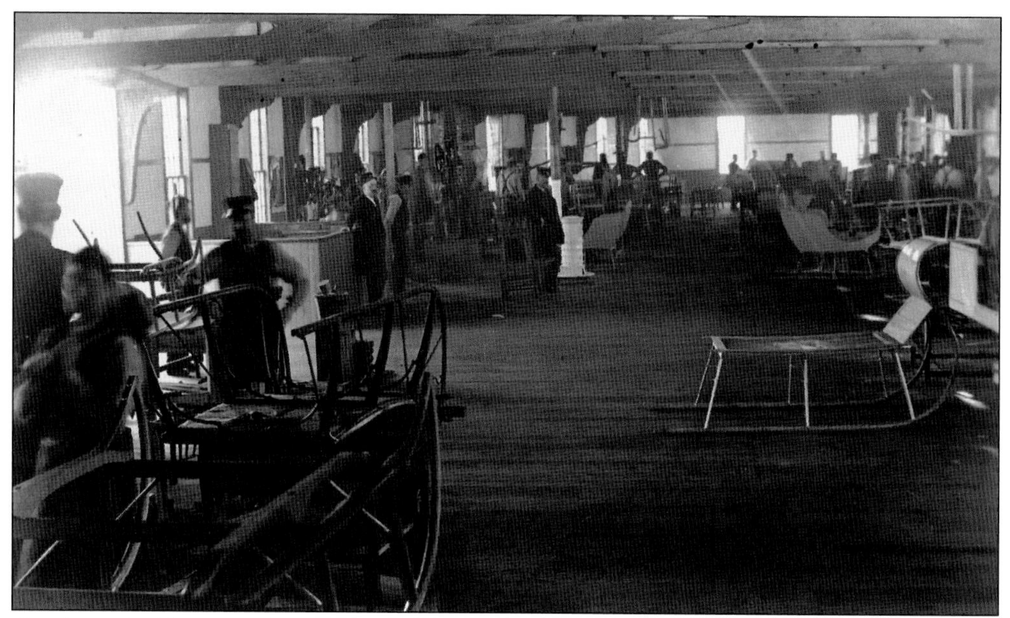

Sleighs crafted from wood were an important part of the convict work program in the 1800s and well into the 1900s. A variety of sleigh styles were custom built with detail and pride taken in the workmanship.

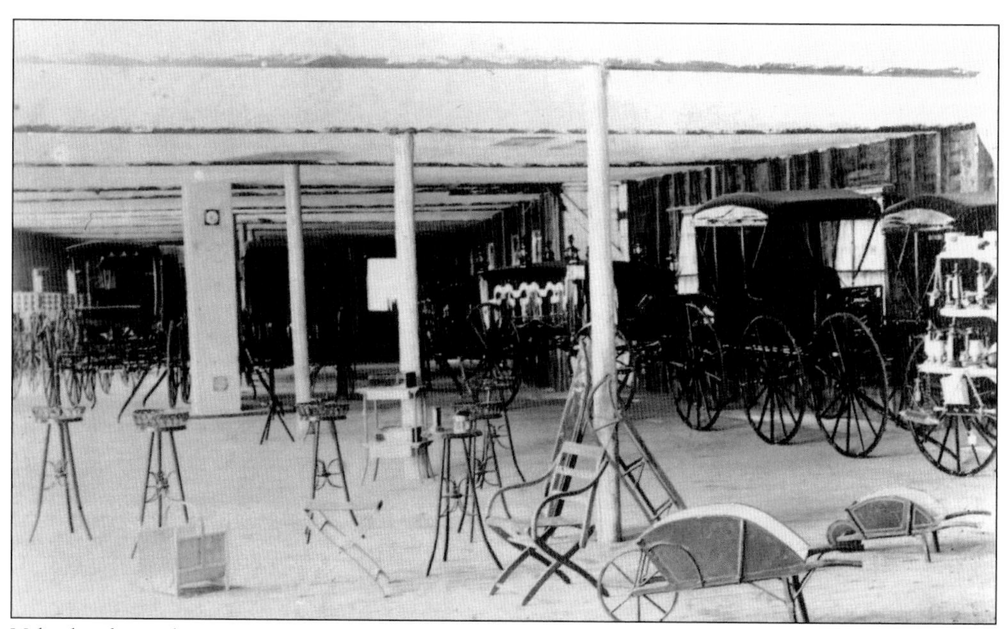

Vehicles from the carriage shop were in great demand when wagons were the only mode of transportation. Farmers and quarrymen required wagons for hauling while businessmen required not only wagons for merchandise but also carriages for their families. Physicians and itinerant tradesmen expanded their range of travel through the use of these well-built vehicles. The 1902 annual prison report states that the carriage shop made a gain of $3,129.20.

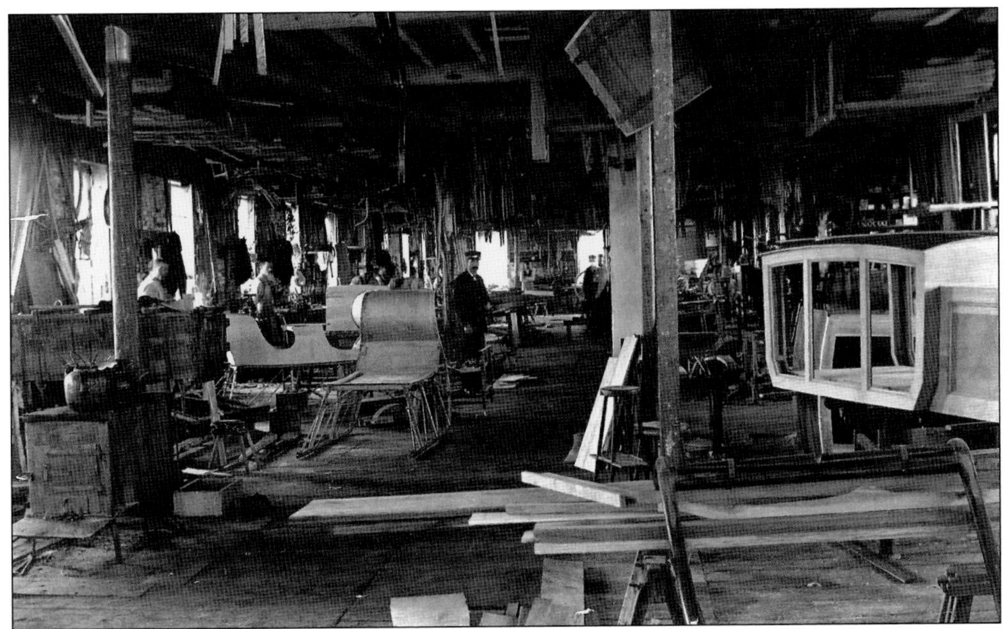

Pictured above are the sleigh and carriage shops, which produced high-quality horse-drawn modes of transportation from the mid-1800s through the 1920s. In addition to the sleighs pictured on the left, to the right is a wooden hearse. The prison produced many hearses for townships during the influenza years of the late 1800s and early 1900s.

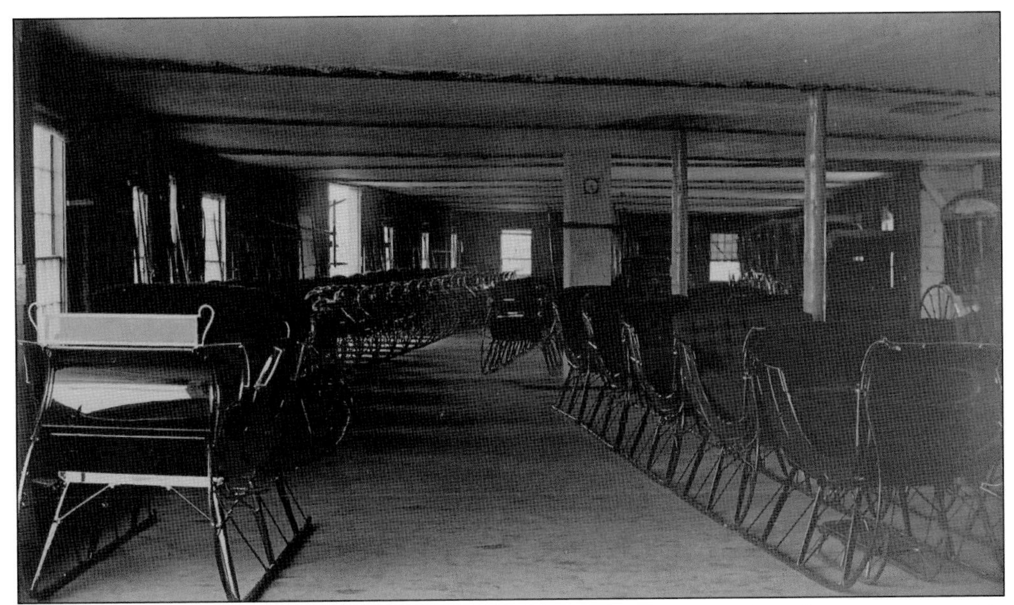

The manufacture of shoes, brooms, harnesses, and wagons was carried on for many years with some profit, or at least a smaller loss than stonework. The repository for sleighs and carriages in the late 1800s was believed to have been situated near the current location of the showroom.

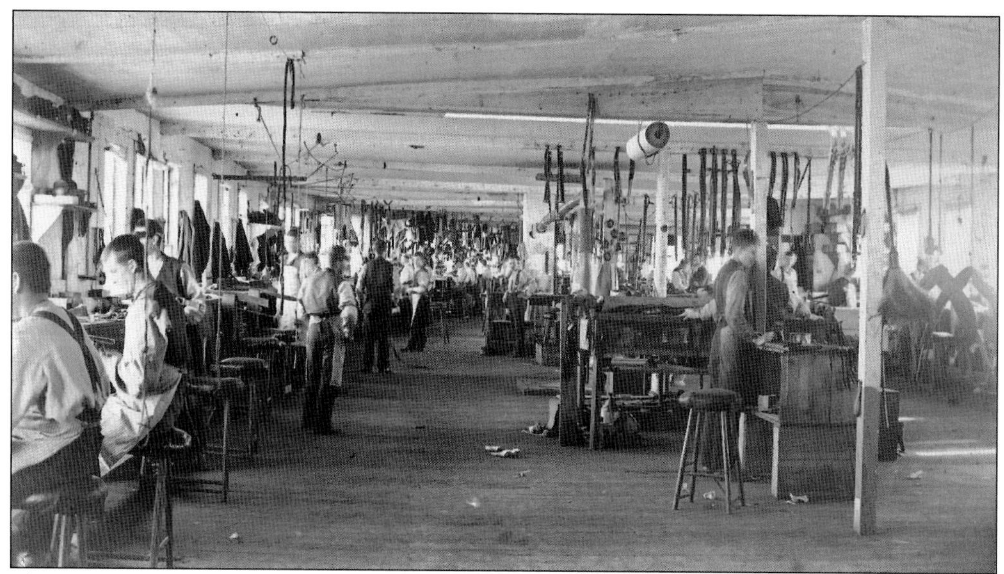

The prison harness shop has a long history dating back to mid-1800s and was once a primary industry employing the majority of the convict population. With the invention of the horseless carriage, demand for harnesses dropped dramatically.

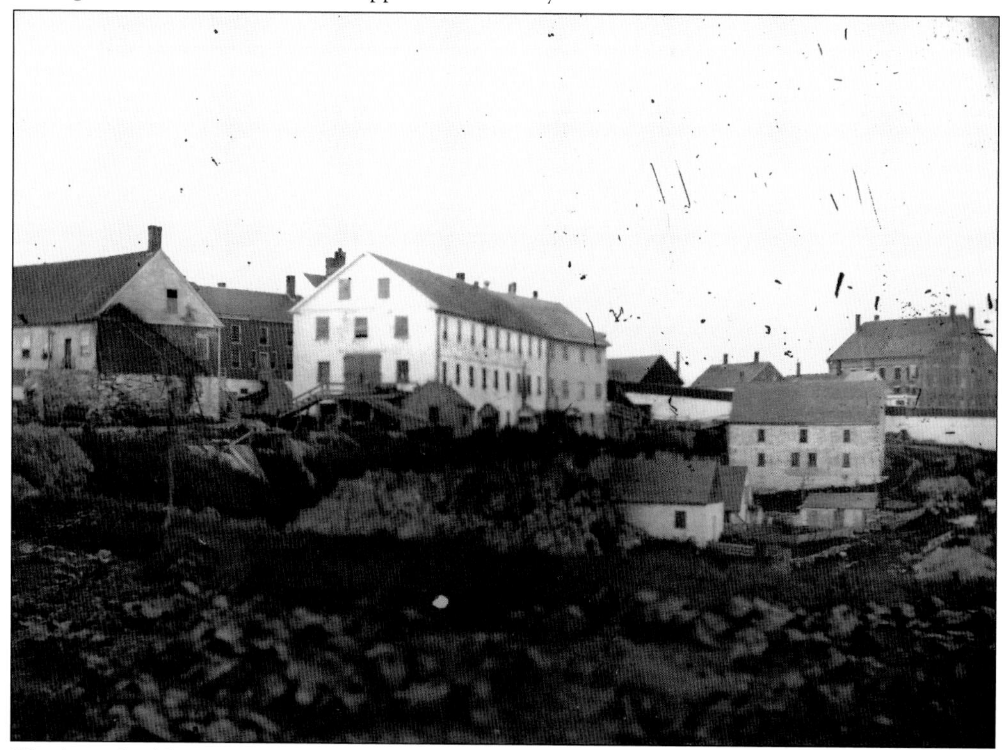

The large building pictured above housed the carriage and woodworking shops. Before these shops existed, convicts had to mine lime with profits earmarked for the state. In June 1824, Warden Daniel Rose contracted to sell lime rock for 15.5¢ per cask. Later extensive granite land in St. George was acquired and a stone shop was built at the prison. Granite work was abandoned as unprofitable in 1837.

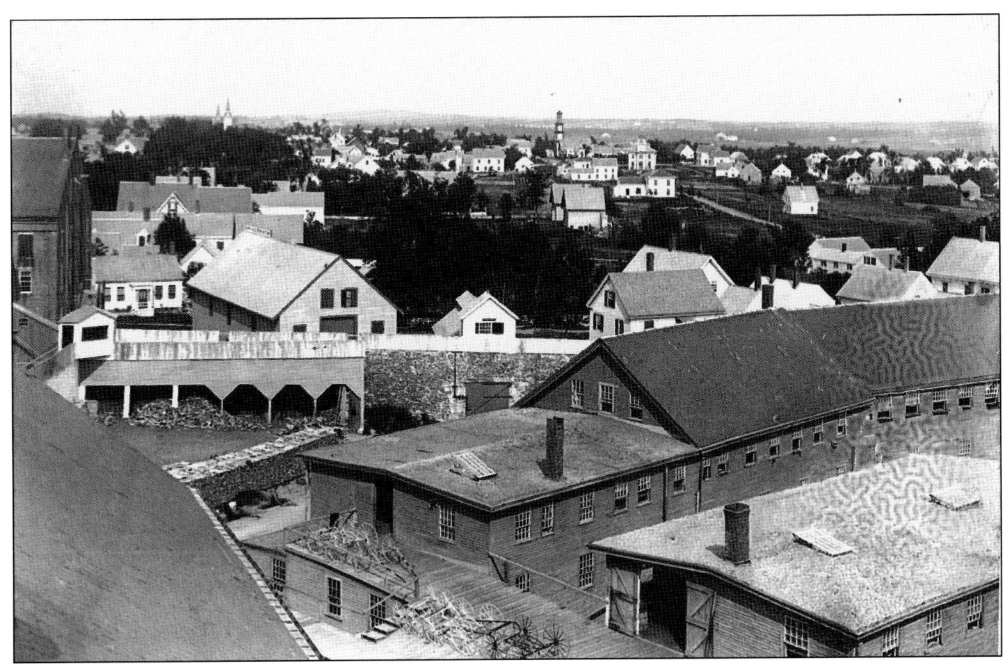

This bird's-eye view is of industrial buildings and shops located inside the prison walls. Cords of firewood are neatly stacked in the yard, and wagons can be seen on the rooftop of a shop.

MAY,
-1882-

PRICE LIST

-OF-

Goods Manufactured

AT

MAINE STATE PRISON

THOMASTON, ME.

G.S. BEAN, Warden

-LIST OF CARRIAGES-

Grocery, Portland, Concord, Bangor, Piano Box Cutdown Open Wagon......................	$100 to $125
Express Wagons, with Straight or Crank Axles.................	125 to 135
Regular and Standing Top Phaetons	175 to 200
Bangor, Corning, Box and Cutdown Top Buggies................	175 to 250
Side Bar and Cut Under Extension Tops..........................	250 to 300
Buck Boards...........................	50 to 80
Hearses, fitted to wheels and runners,	250 to 500
Toys, Boy's and Men's Wheelbarrows,........................	1.25; 2.50; 5.00
Hand Carts............................	5.00; 6.00; 7.00
Clipper and Framed Hand Sleds,......	1.00 to 3.00
Jumpers and Wood Pungs.............	25 to 35
Traverse Runner Pungs................	65 to 105
Single Sleighs..........................	50 to 75
Double do.............................	120 to 225

-LIST OF HARNESSES-

No.1	Rubber	$52.50
No.2	Regular or S.S.,R.,............	42.00
No.10.	do do R.,....	31.50
No.10.	do or do N.or D.R...	$26 to 28
No.8.	do N. or D.R.........	20 to 22
No.6.	do Br.N.and Jap....	23.25
No.0.	Bastard N.,................	13 to 15
Express.	4 to 4½ in.,N. or B..........	35 to 37
do	5 to 5½ in., do...........	42 to 45
do	6 to 6½ in., do...........	50 to 53
do	7 in., do...........	62 to 65
No.1.	Double Driving, R.,.........	$115
No.2.	do do R.,..........	95
No.10.	do do	55 to 65
No.8.	do do	45
	do Farm,..................	35 to 45
	do Team,..................	40 to 75
	do Stage,..................	35 to 50
	do Express,...............	45 to 65

This is a May 1882 price list of goods manufactured at Maine State Prison. G. S. Bean is listed as warden.

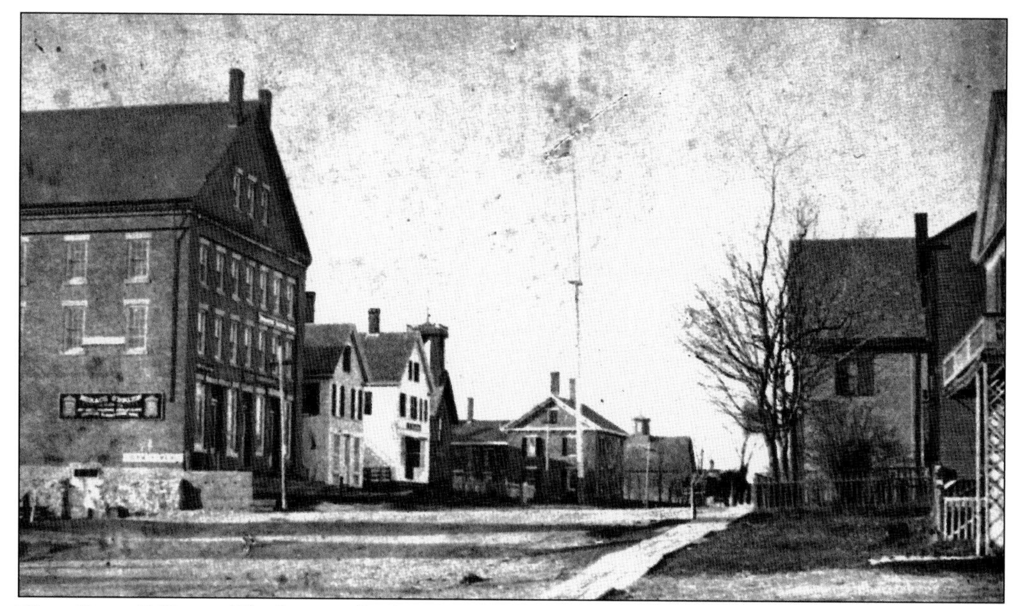

The Carr O'Brien Block was built in 1852 on the southwest corner of Country Road (Route 1) and Prison Lane (Wadsworth Street) for Benjamin Carr and Edward O'Brien, as seen in the above picture. Built of brick by E. Demuth, it was designed for Thomaston's shipbuilding millionaire Edward O'Brien's Georges' Bank, the Georges' Insurance Office, and other new stores at the upper or prison corner. After the closing of the J. B. Pearson Manufacturing Company, the prison purchased the building in 1957 for use as a store for products assembled by the inmates. It later became known as the prison showroom.

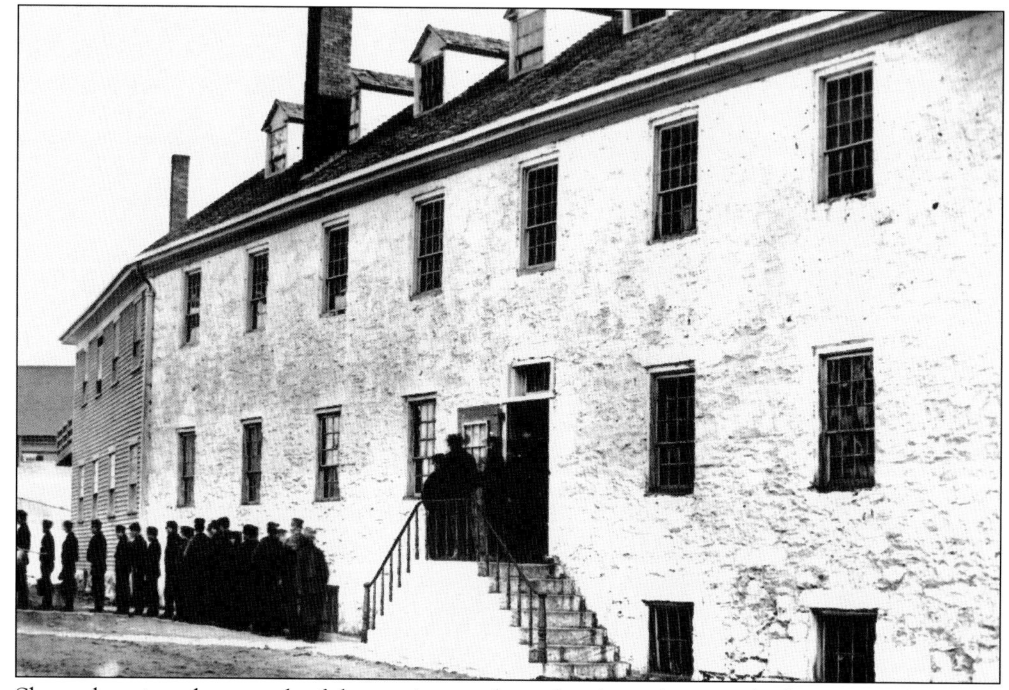

Shown here is a photograph of the carriage and woodworking shops in the late 1800s. (Courtesy of the Thomaston Historical Society.)

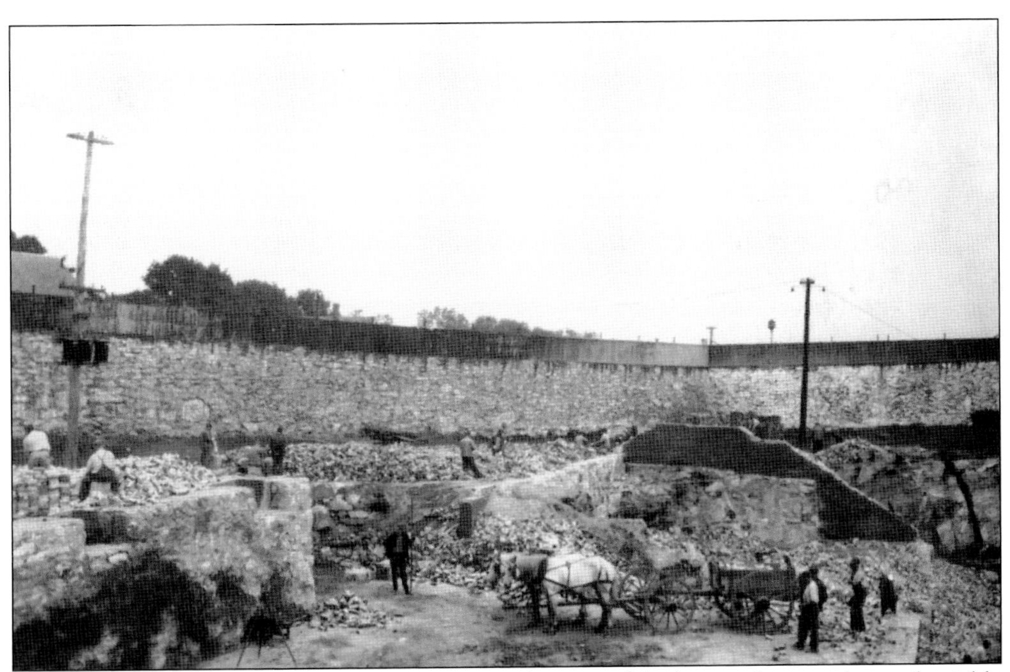

The blaze of Saturday, September 23, 1923, started in one of the broom shops and spread quickly to the other shops. The new brick blacksmith shop that was the pride of the prison was destroyed by flames that also destroyed the west wing. Cleanup started immediately after the fire, and plans for reconstruction began. (Courtesy of John Struk.)

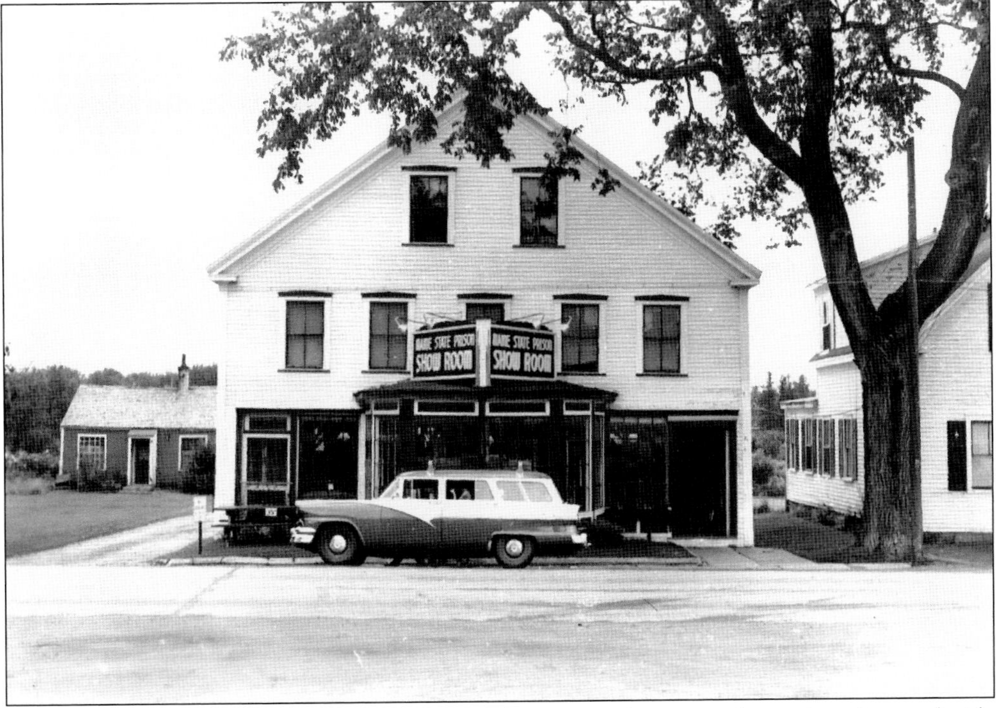

This is an early-1950s photograph of the prison showroom when it was located on the north side of Route 1.

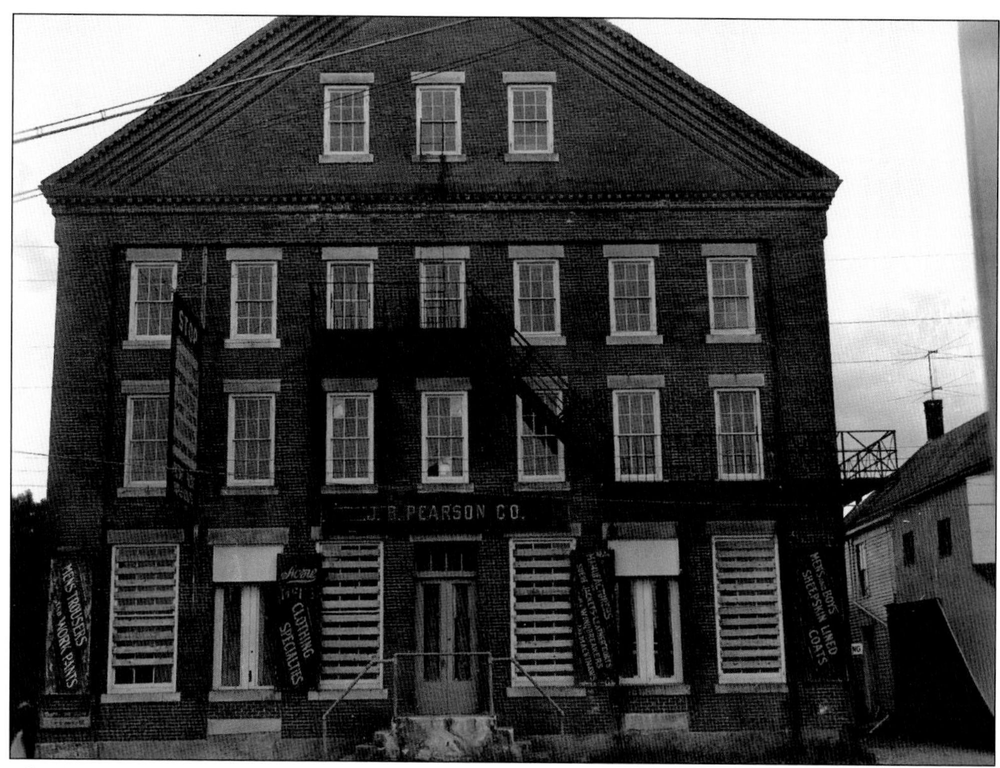

The former J. B. Pearson Company building was purchased by the state in 1957 and has been the site of the prison showroom for over 50 years.

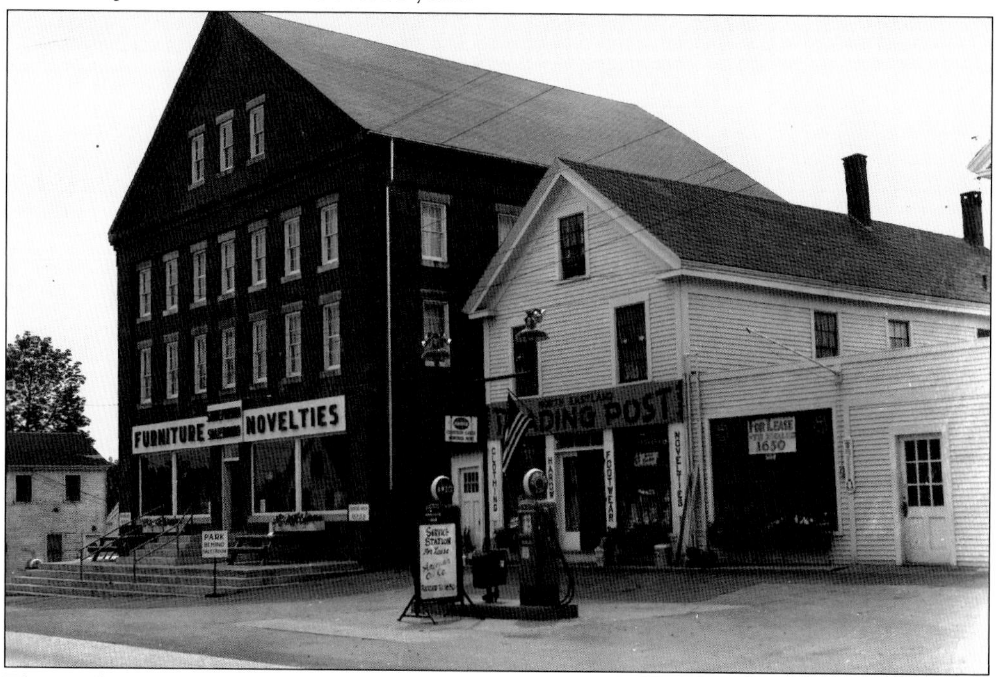

This early-1960s photograph shows the prison showroom advertisements of furniture and novelties alongside the North Eastland Trading Post that also sold gas.

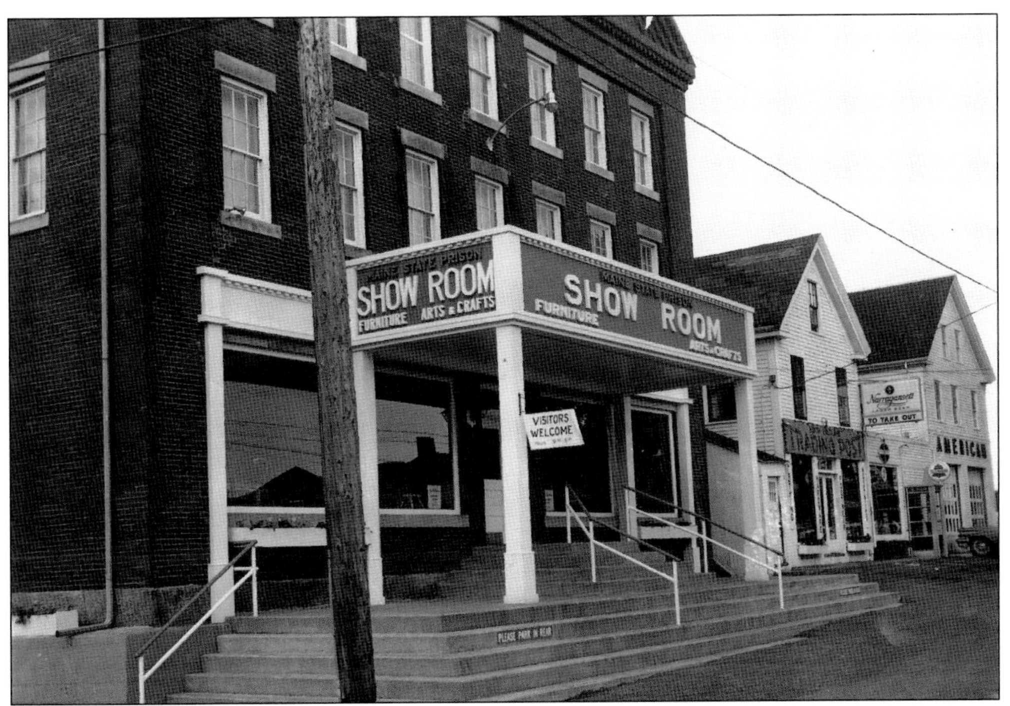

The prison showroom has had several different storefronts over the past 50 years. This mid-1970s look may have been the most decorative of them all.

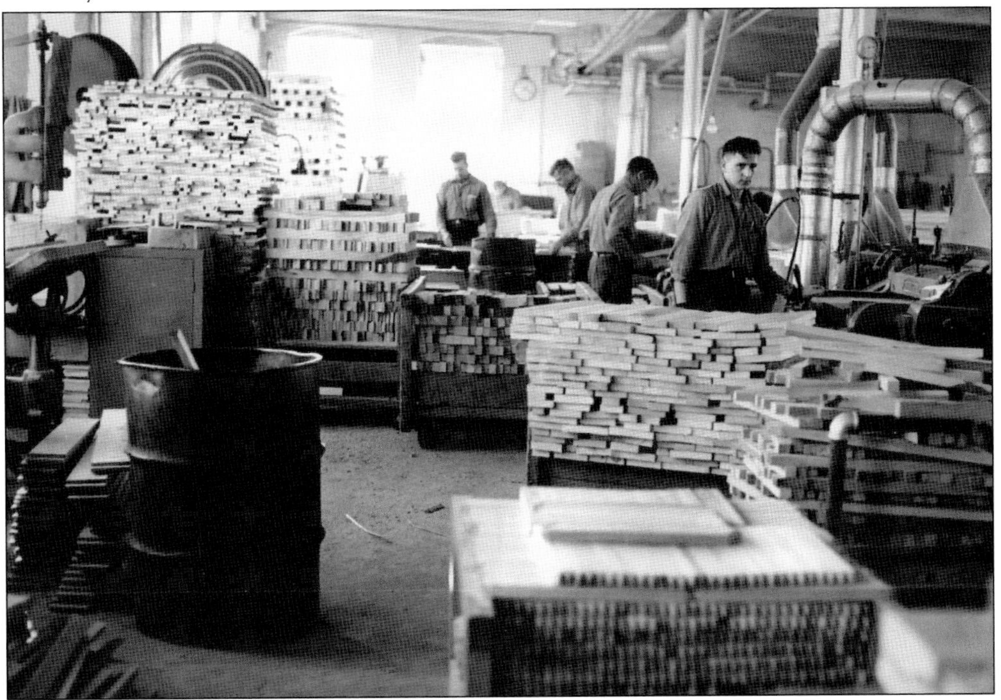

Over the years, inmates made a large quantity of office furniture and filing cabinets for state offices. They have also manufactured institutional uniforms, leather goods, Sam Brown belts and holsters, and even 500 garden wheelbarrows annually for a time.

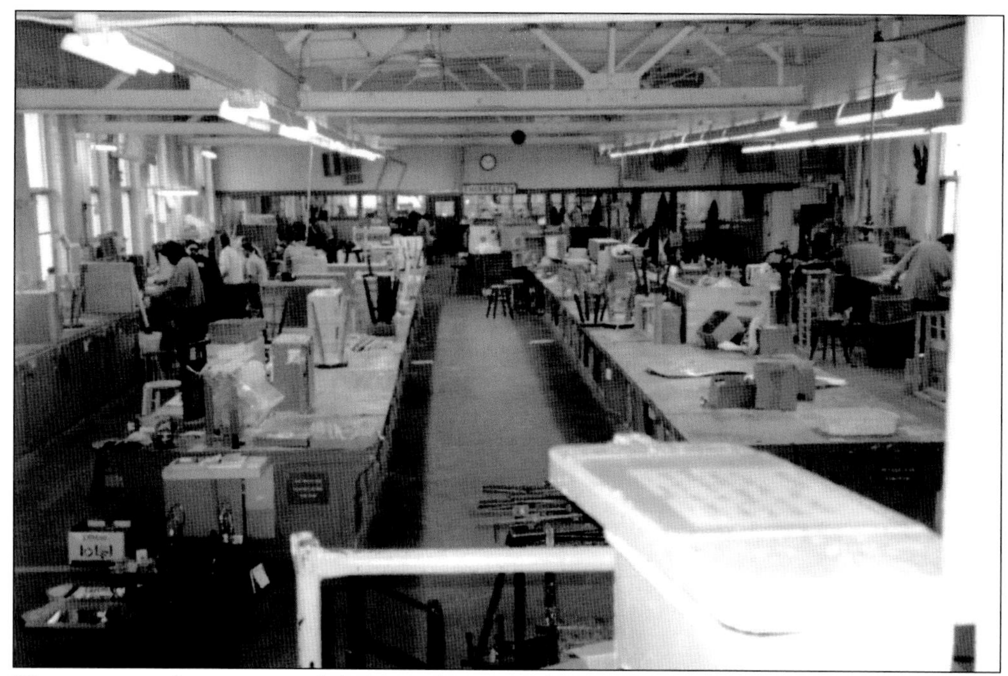

The prison craft room provided the work setting for inmates to build their novelty items for resale in the prison showroom. The craft room was opened in the 1930s. Each worker had an assigned workbench and locker. It was not uncommon for more than 100 workers to be active in this craft room at any given time.

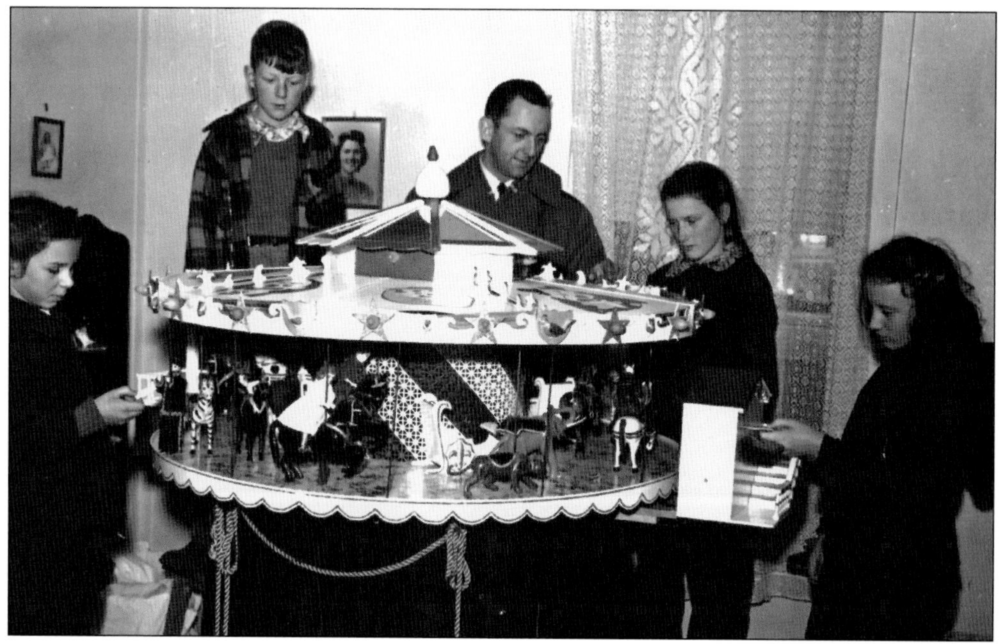

Deputy Warden Allan L. Robbins is shown in this 1949 photograph demonstrating to young visitors a merry-go-round constructed by inmates. The carousel was part of a Christmas display for the prison showroom. A coin placed in the switch brought the carved figures to life under flashing electric lights.

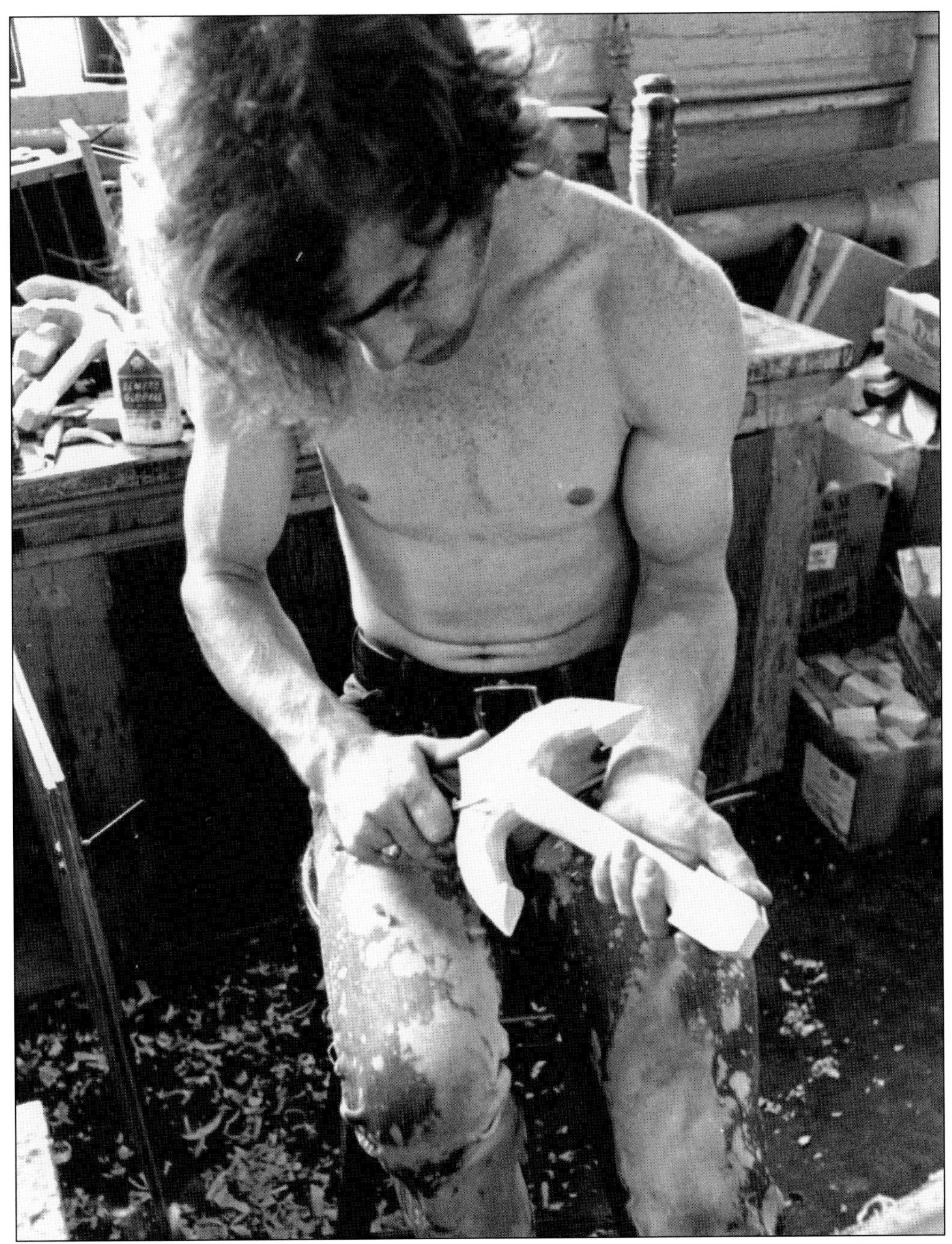

The seafaring coast of Maine has long influenced the look and type of crafts that dominate the shelves of the prison showroom. An inmate is shown carving a nautical anchor, one of the fine woodworking products that has established the outlet as a popular Thomaston tourist destination. A wide variety of crafts ranging from detailed model ships, to jewelry boxes, to toys were built by inmates in the craft room.

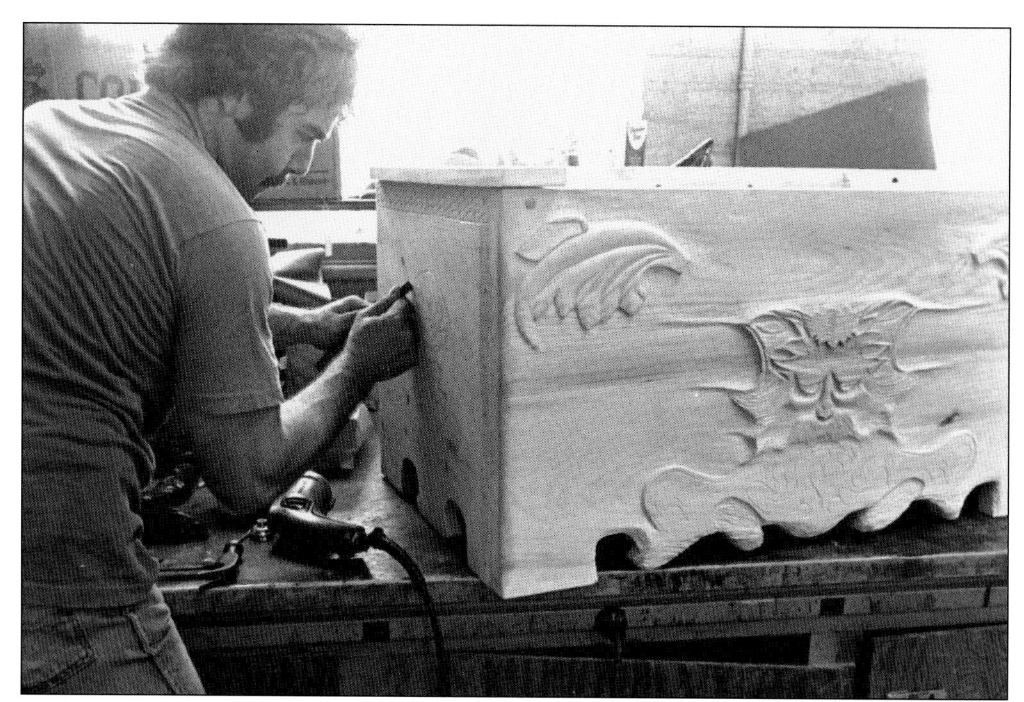

Hundreds of different handcrafted wood products have been and continue to be available for purchase at the prison showroom. The above photograph shows an inmate applying his creative carving skills to a wood chest. Many of the woodcrafters had no prior experience until they came to prison and learned their skills from the experienced inmate woodworkers.

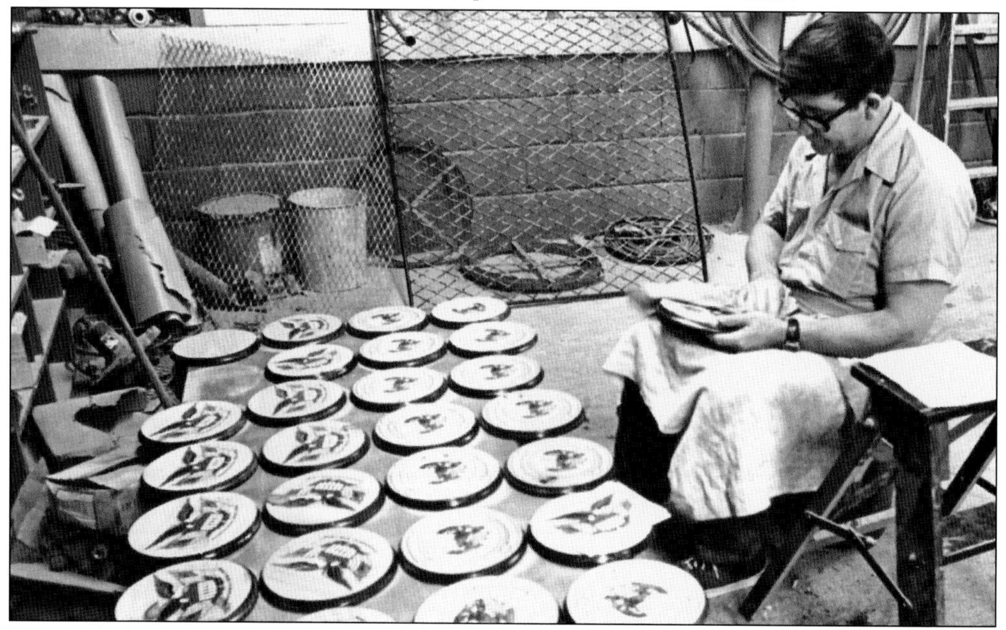

During the lockdown ordered in April 1980 by Gov. Joseph E. Brennan, inmates were not allowed to work in the craft room until it was reorganized and brought back under prison control. Retail sales of crafts and novelties at the prison showroom fell by 45 percent during the usually busy summer months.

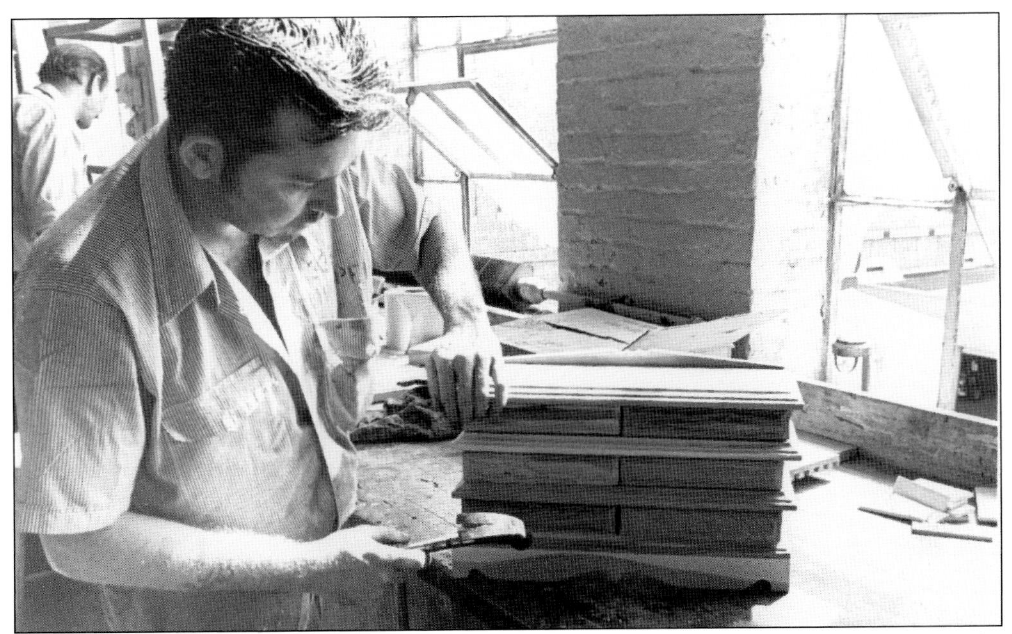

Novelties, such as jewelry boxes, have been a popular item for the public to purchase since the 1930s when small crafts and novelties were first introduced.

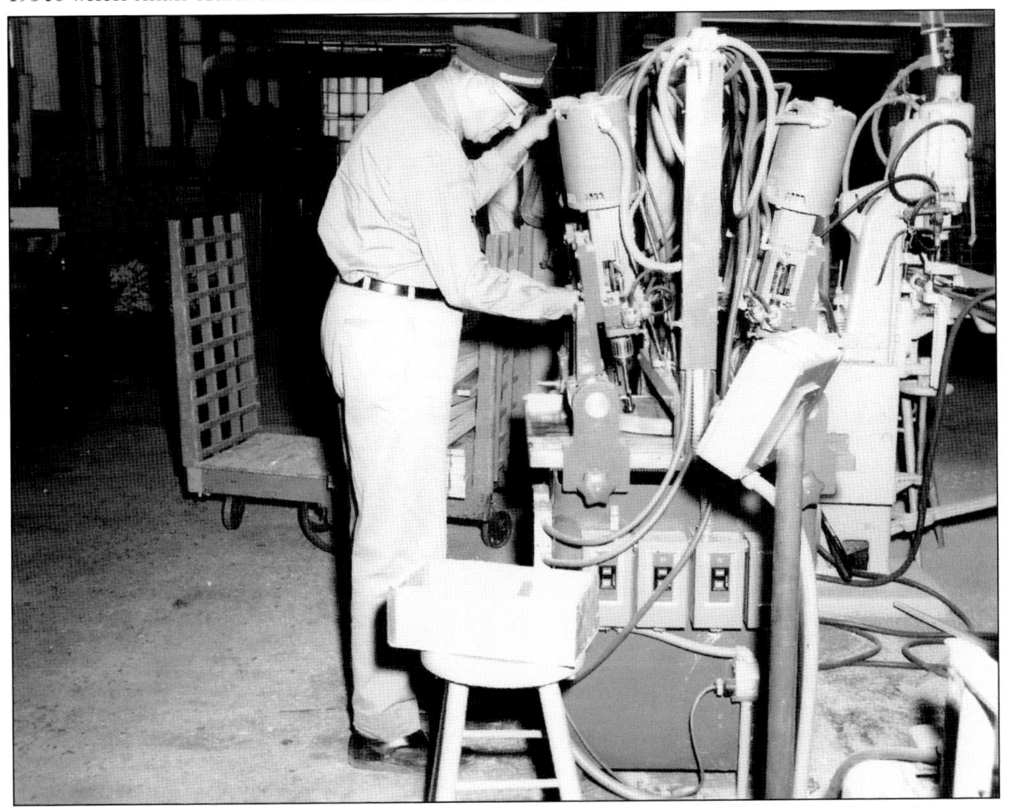

A 1960s photograph shows the quad press that was used in the manufacture of the well-known hardwood prison stools still in use today.

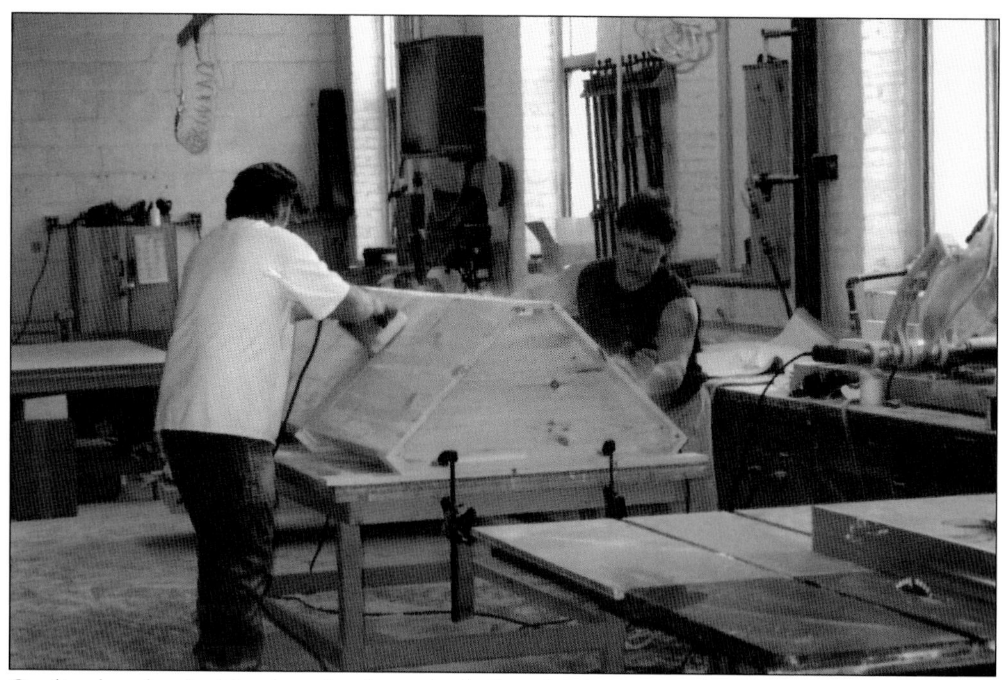

Quality, handcrafted furniture has been the hallmark of prison products for over 100 years. Here two inmate workers are seen hand sanding a corner hutch built from pine lumber.

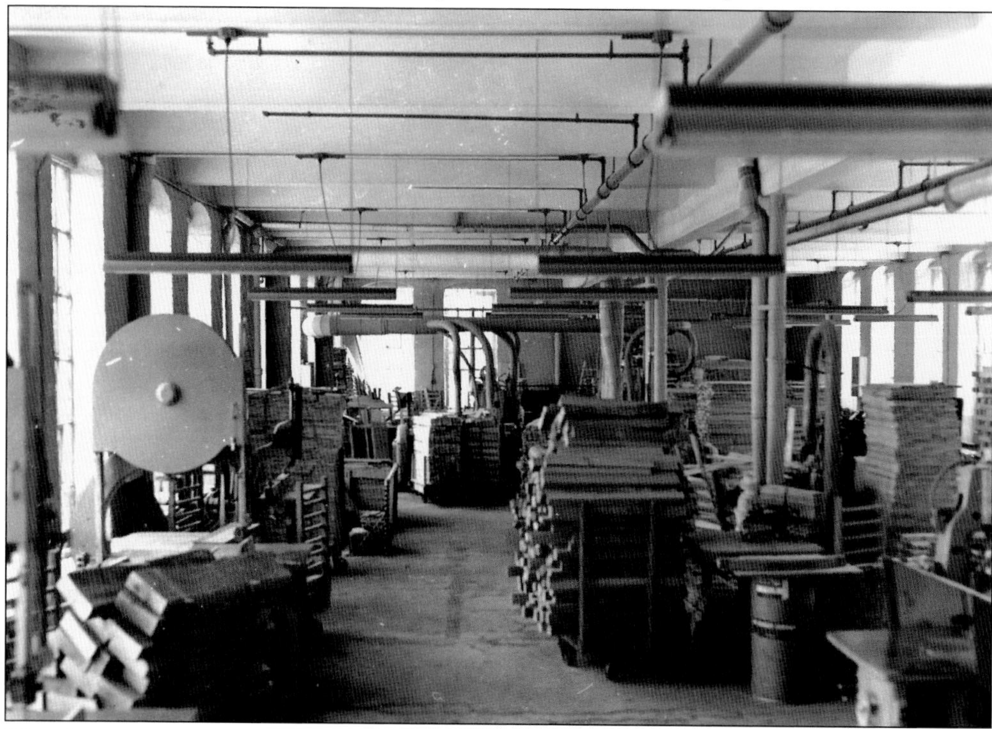

The above picture shows the woodshop layout as it appeared in the 1960s. Through careful machine maintenance, much of it done by the industries machine shop, most of this equipment is still in service today.

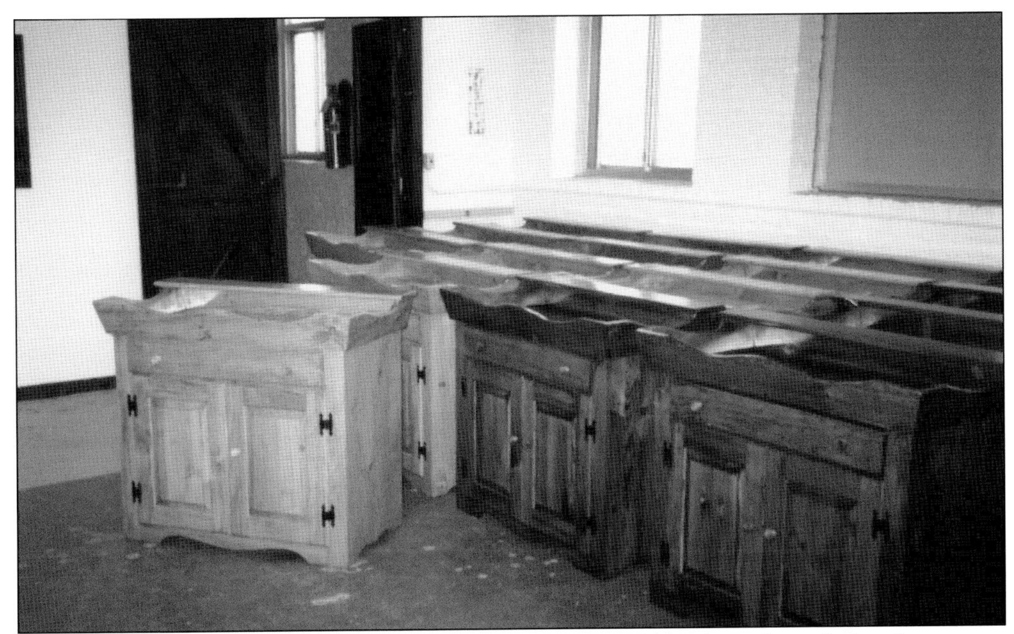

Cupboards and cabinets of many shapes and sizes are still built with pride by the inmate workforce. Inmates continue to believe that having an opportunity to work for pay in a prison industries shop is an earned privilege.

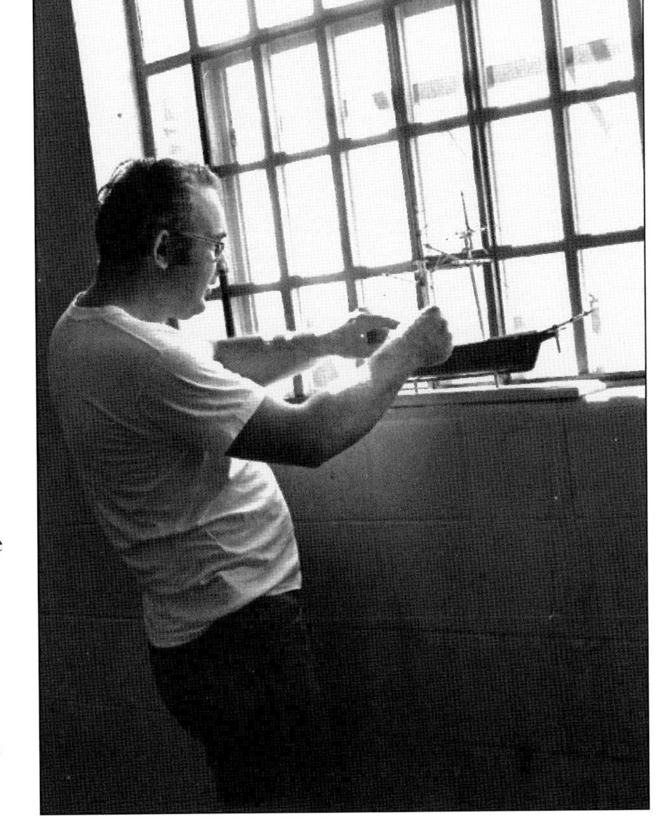

Elaborate model ships were built from lumber purchased through the woodshop program. These ships were accurate replicas of the ships that docked in Thomaston in the 1800s that carried local products to other ports. The models quickly became a tourist hit and one, a model of the USS *Constitution*, sold for $2,000. As many as 200 bus tours a year may stop and shop for quality items.

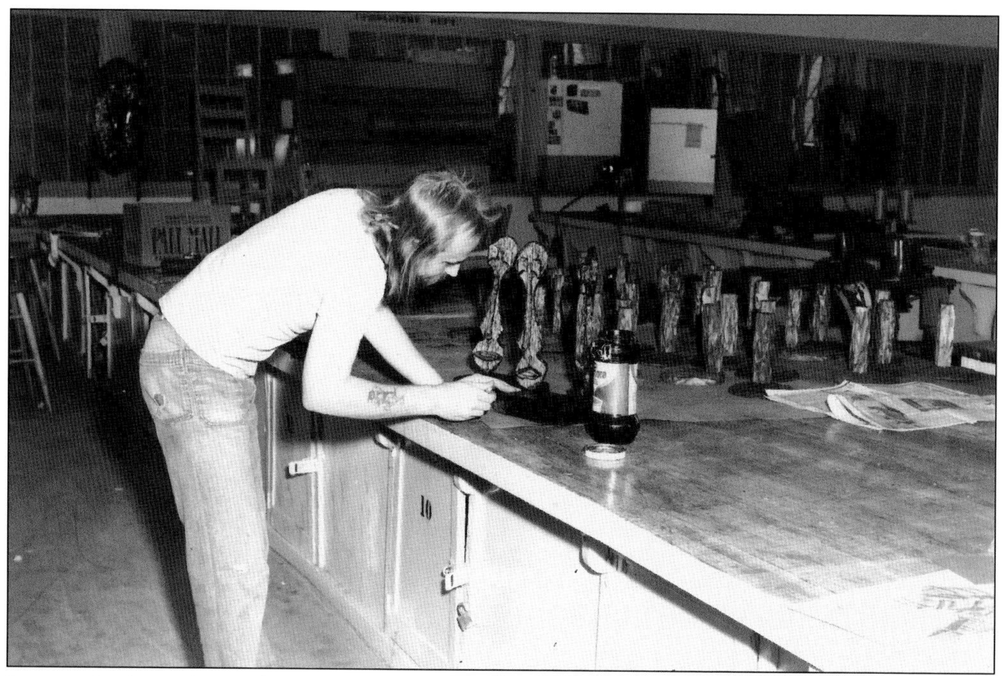

Inmates had to take a safety training course and meet other criteria before they were eligible to work in the craft room.

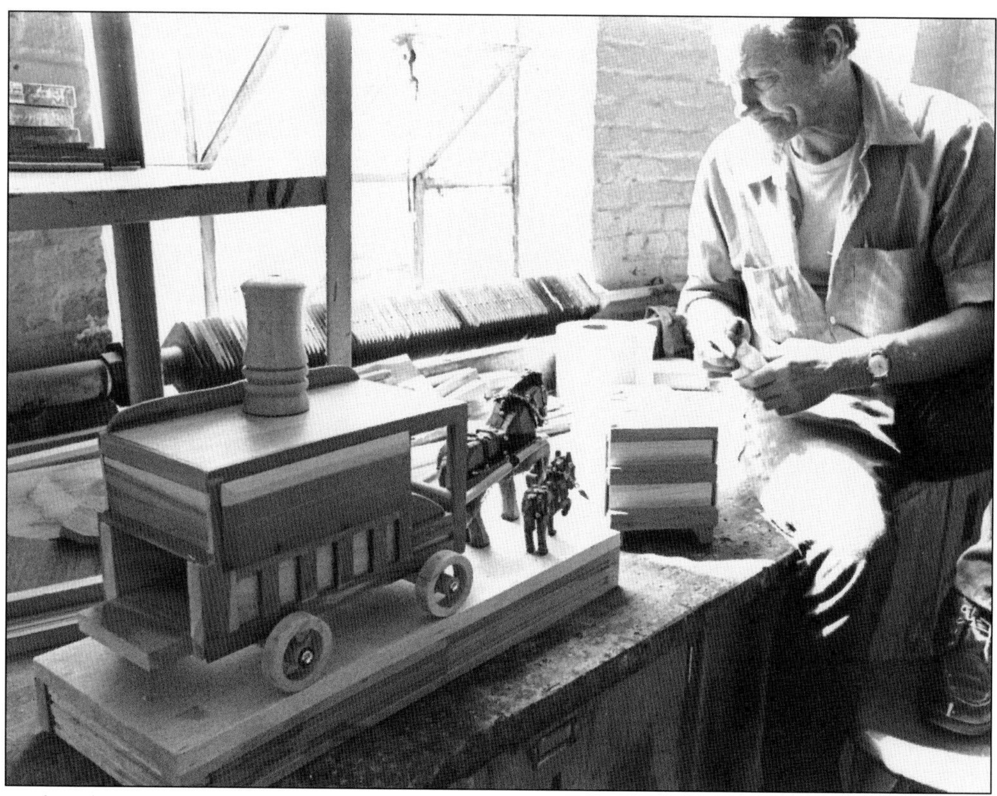

In this photograph, an inmate carves a toy horse-drawn wagon for sale in the prison showroom.

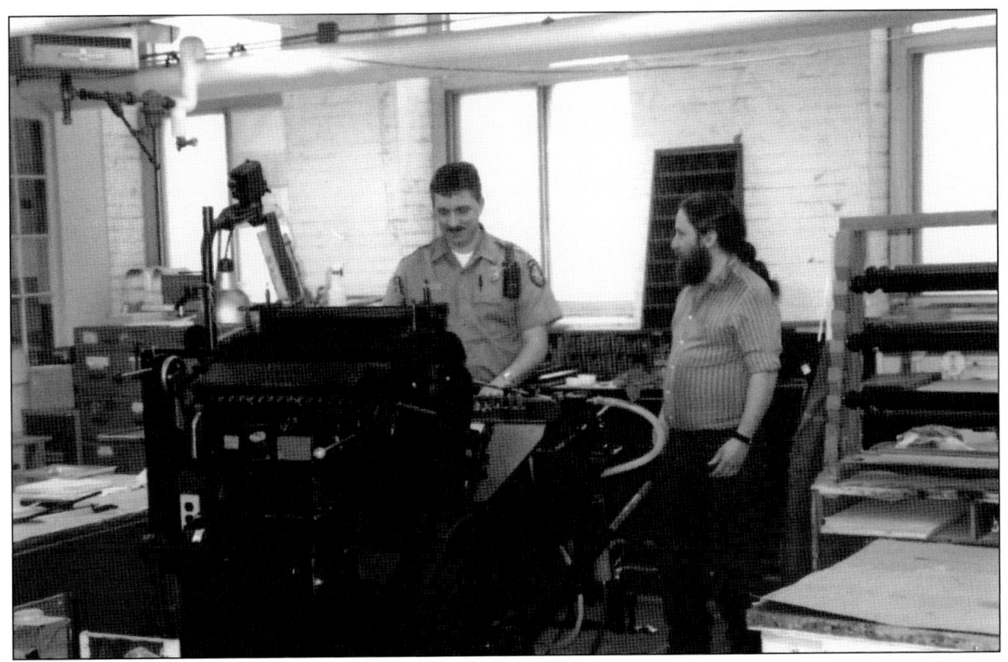

The print shop was always a busy area in industries right up until the time of the prison closing. Along with the routine printing needs of the prison, many local schools and municipalities had their printing done over the years as well. Shop supervisor Ken Lindsey (left) and an inmate worker can be seen setting up one of the presses.

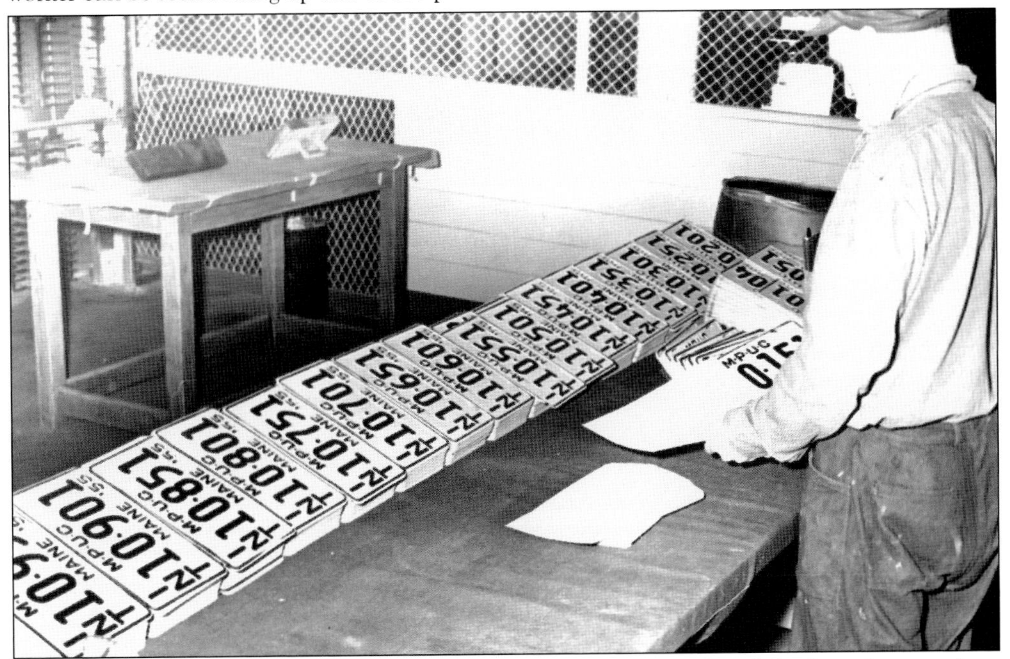

In 1905, Maine legislation required motor vehicles to be registered and display a license plate. The first plates were made from porcelain. Here an inmate works on a 1955 run of plates at the prison. In the majority of states today, license plates are made in correctional facilities. Many popular stereotypical prison movies show inmates making license plates.

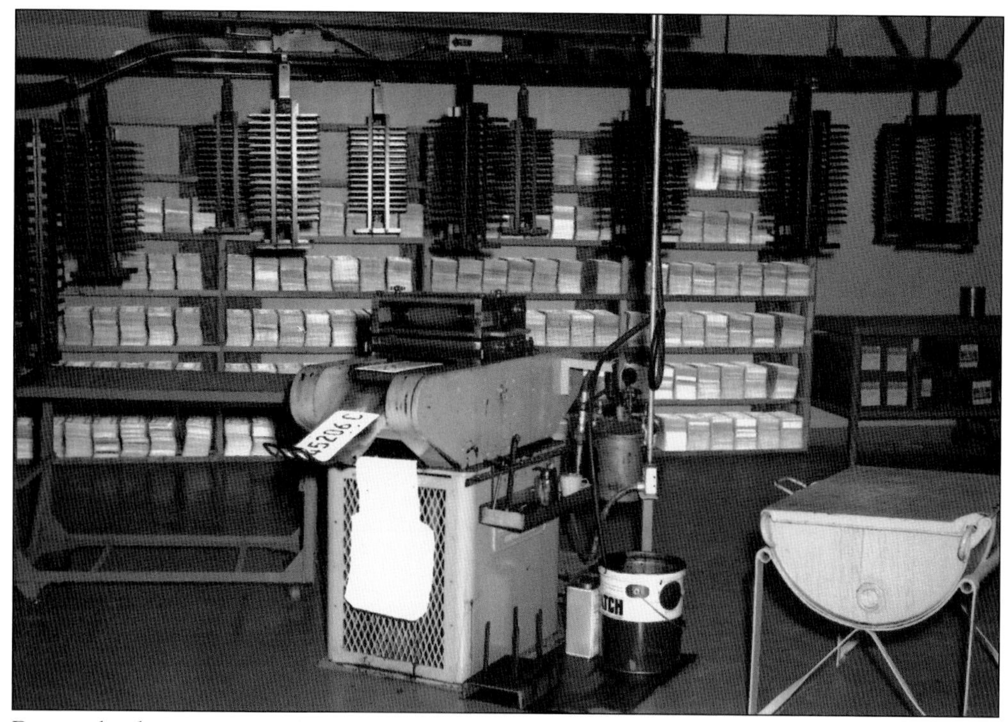

During the three-year period that license plates were not made at the prison, they were purchased from Massachusetts and New Hampshire. The quality of the plates during this time was reported to be poor. Above, freshly painted plates are hung in racks to dry, and shown on the shelves in the background are stacks of blank plates waiting to be processed. In 1977, the prison stopped its long-standing license plate manufacturing for three years as a result of inmates sabotaging the equipment.

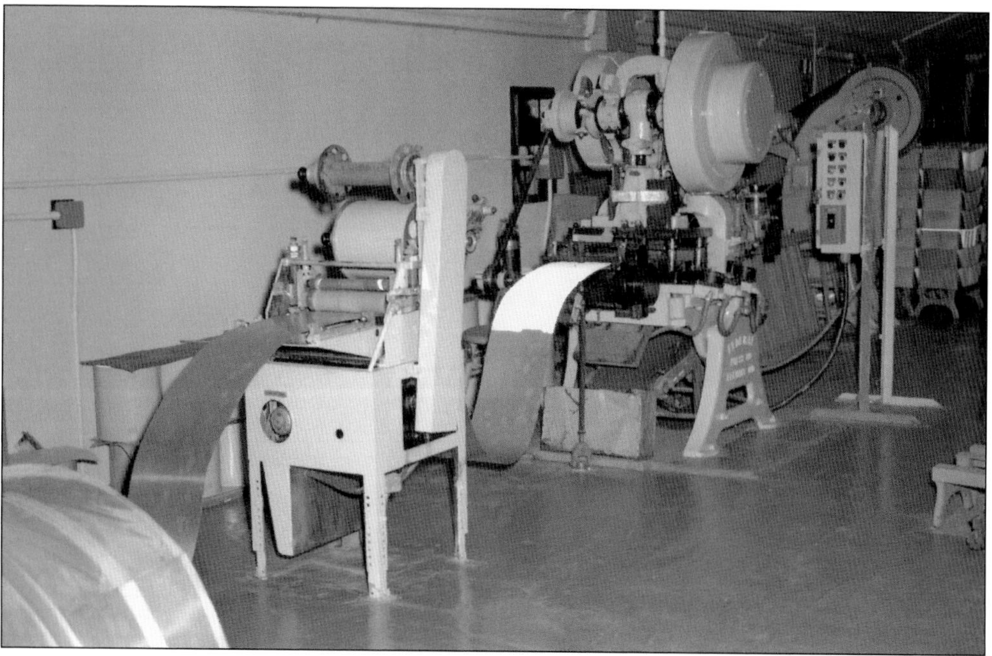

Four

The Human and the Hardware

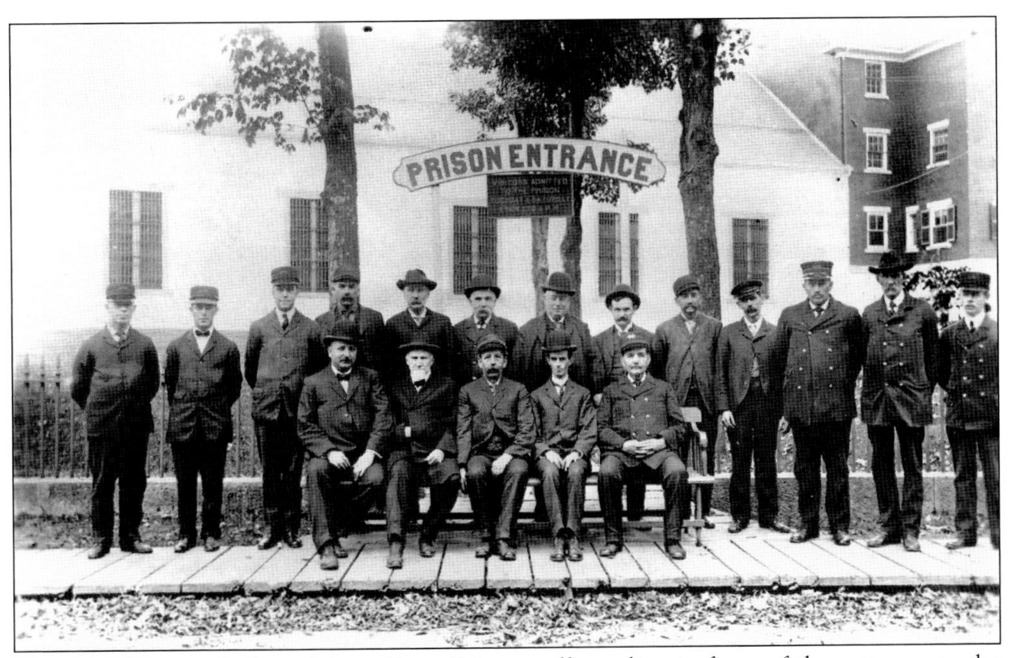

An early photograph shows Maine State Prison staff standing in front of the entrance to the prison. The sign hanging just below the entrance reads, "Visitors Admitted to the Prison Tuesday and Saturday from 1 to 4 P.M."

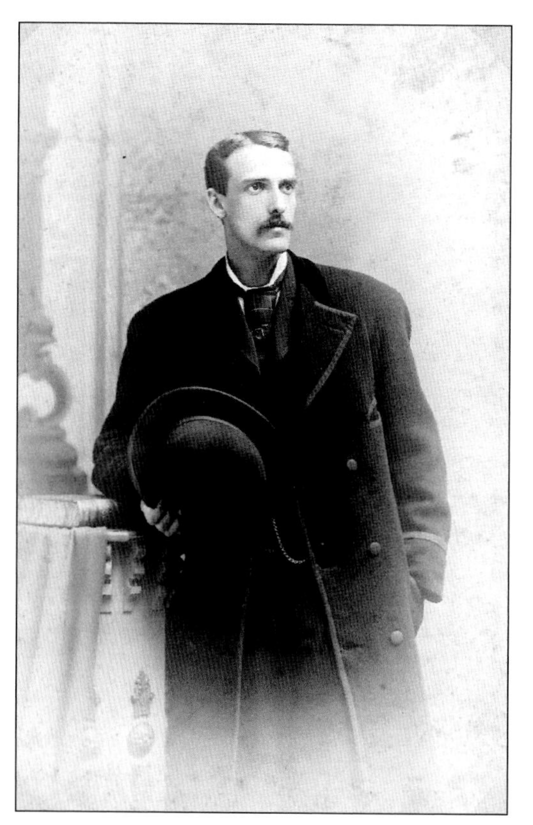

Wendell Phillips Rice, pictured here, was the son of Warren W. Rice, who was warden in the 1860s. Wendell was appointed deputy warden of the prison at a young age and became well respected. His success brought him an offer to manage the Vermont State Prison. He later followed the 1880s westward expansion and settled in Kansas, where he became a successful entrepreneur. (Courtesy of Katy Tripp.)

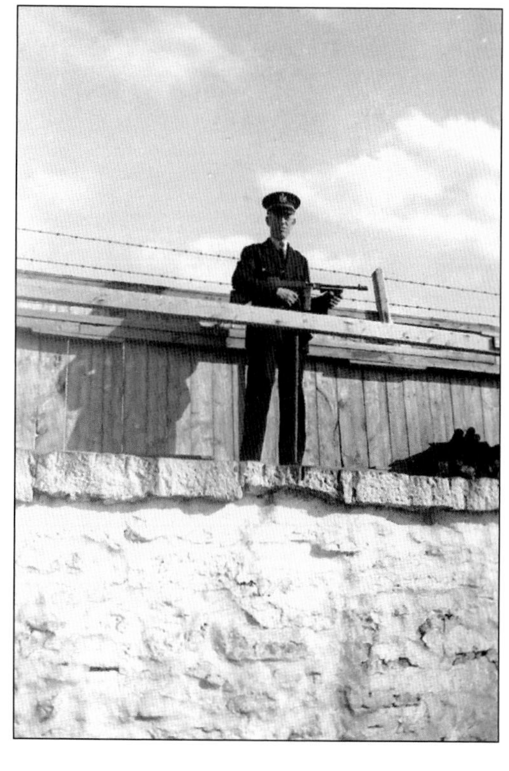

Walter Anderson fondly remembers his father Albert "Doc" Anderson, photographed here standing on the wall of the south post with a machine gun, lowering a bucket to the ground in which he would be raised up to sit with his father and watch inmates play baseball in the yard. (Courtesy of Walter Anderson.)

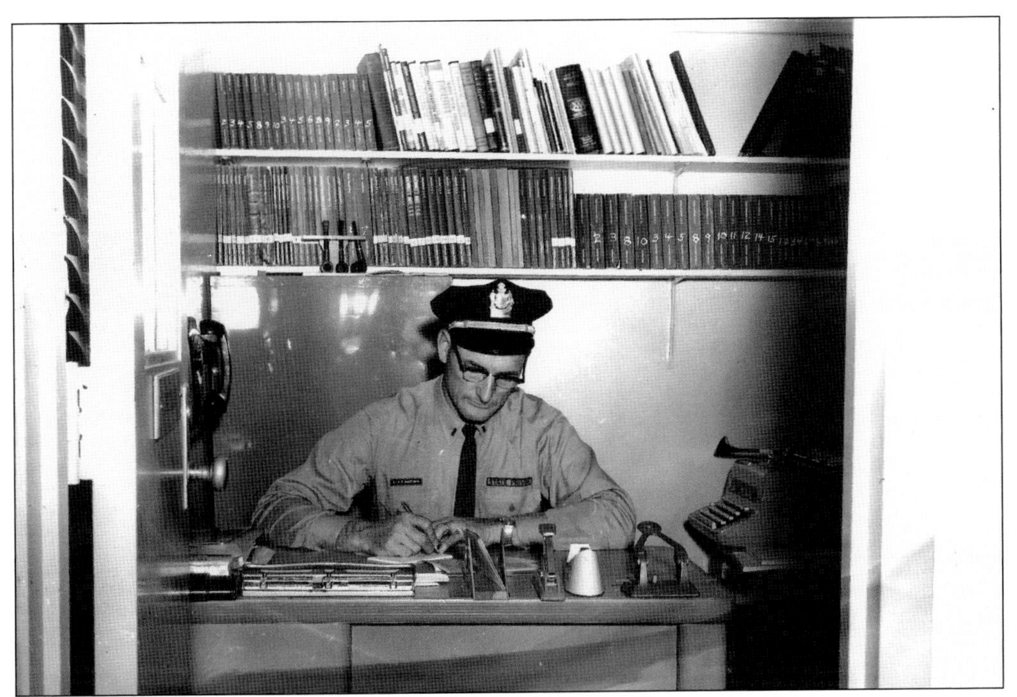

This 1960s photograph shows classification officer Richard Sukeforth in his office working on inmate files.

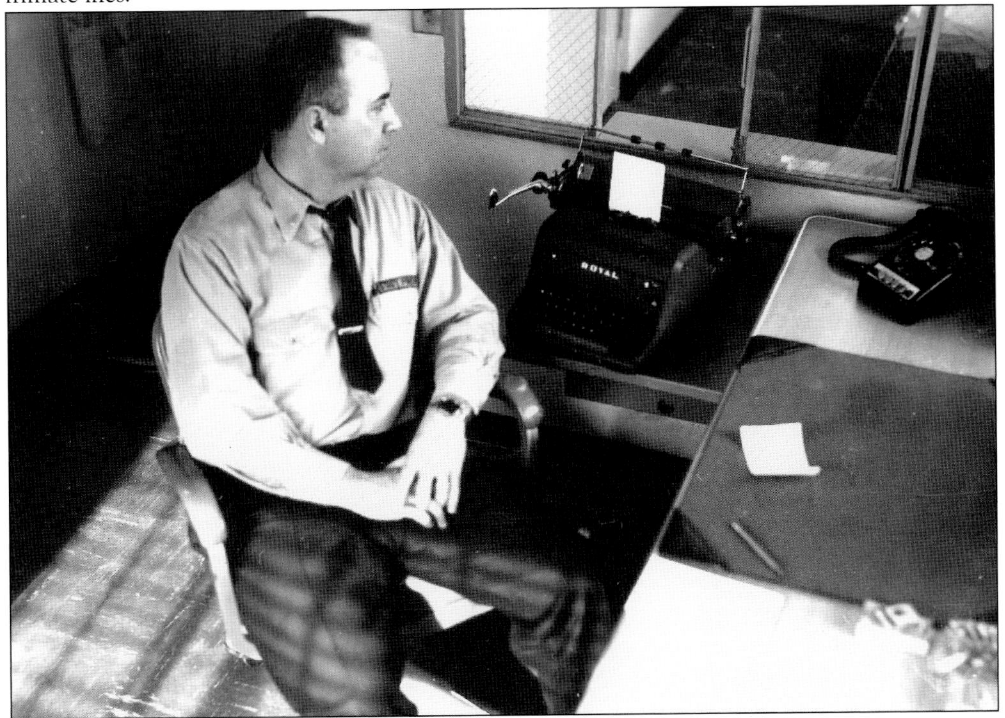

Maj. Ronald Bolduc contemplates the future of the prison sitting in his sunny office. Major Bolduc would be instrumental in shaping the development of the Bolduc Correctional Facility after the fire at the farm.

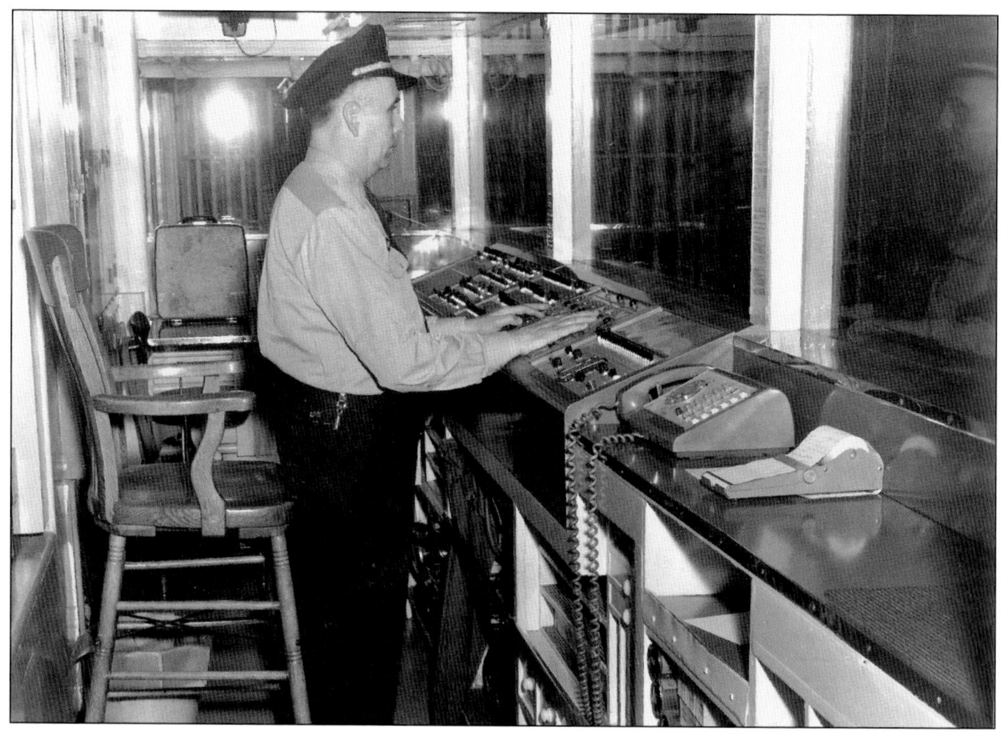

Third shift officer Robert Polky is seen at the console of central control in the late 1970s.

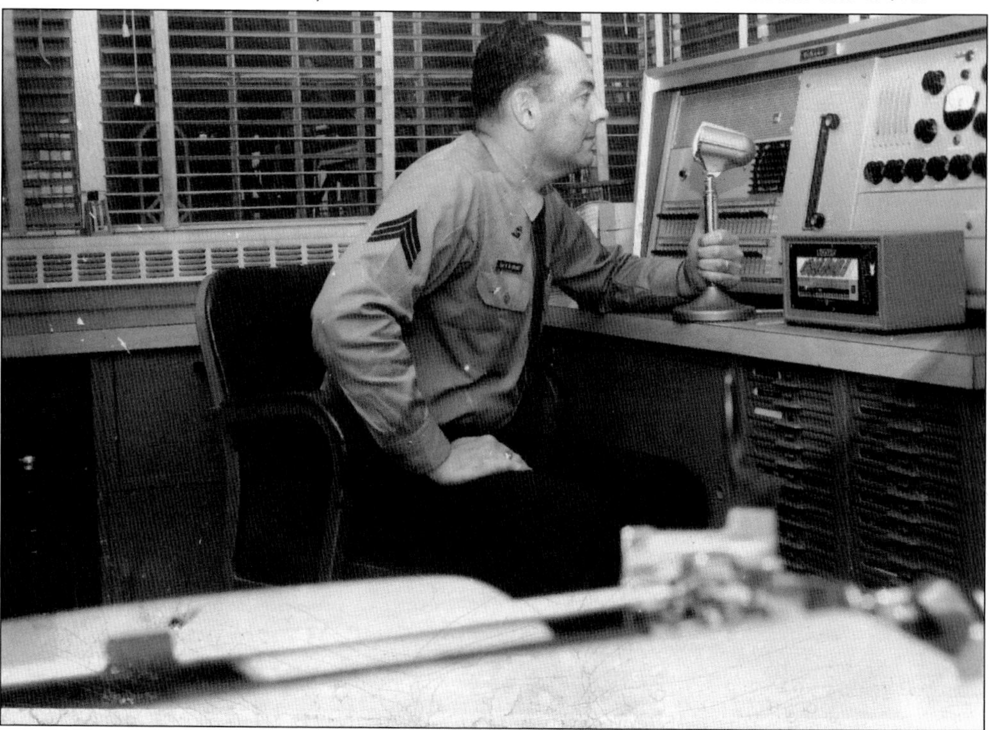

Sgt. Frank Grant sits in the old deputy warden's office where announcements and assignments were made and count taken. This room was the central communication area.

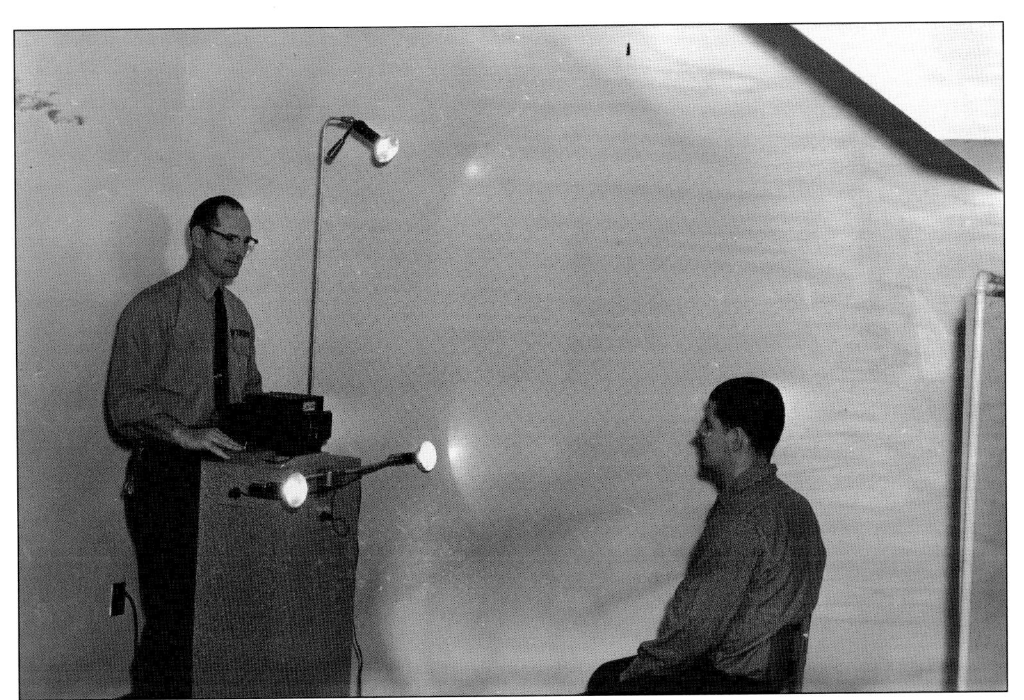

Officer Richard Sayward begins the process of documentation by photographing this prisoner. The prison had its own darkroom during the 1960s, and many of the photographs found in this book were developed there.

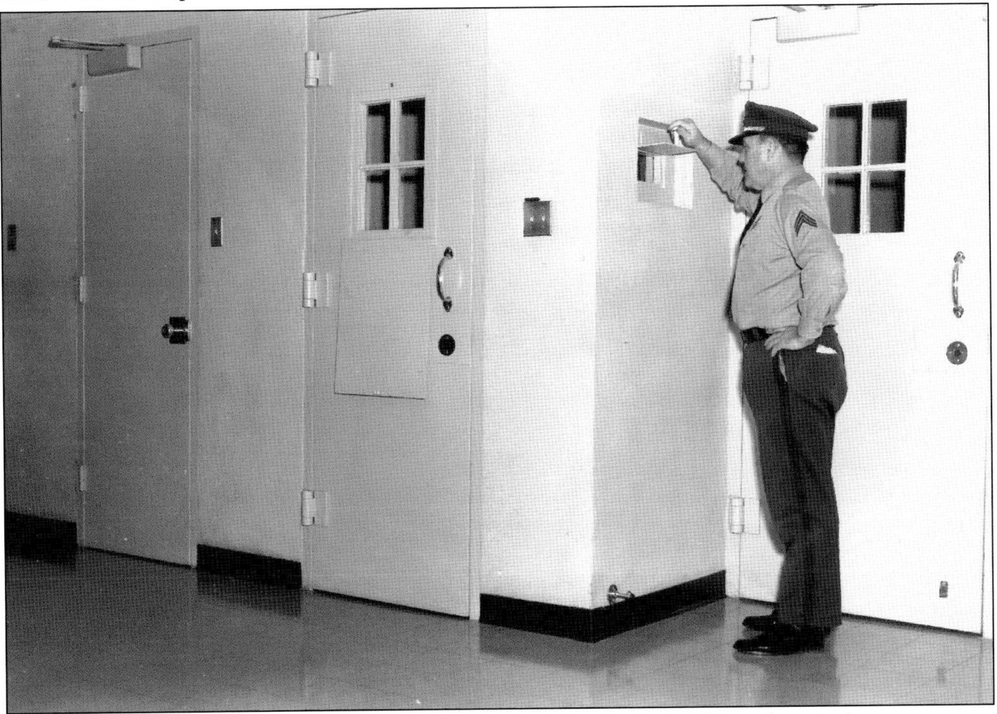

Sgt. Henry Worster observes an inmate through an observation cell window in the segregation unit in the 1960s.

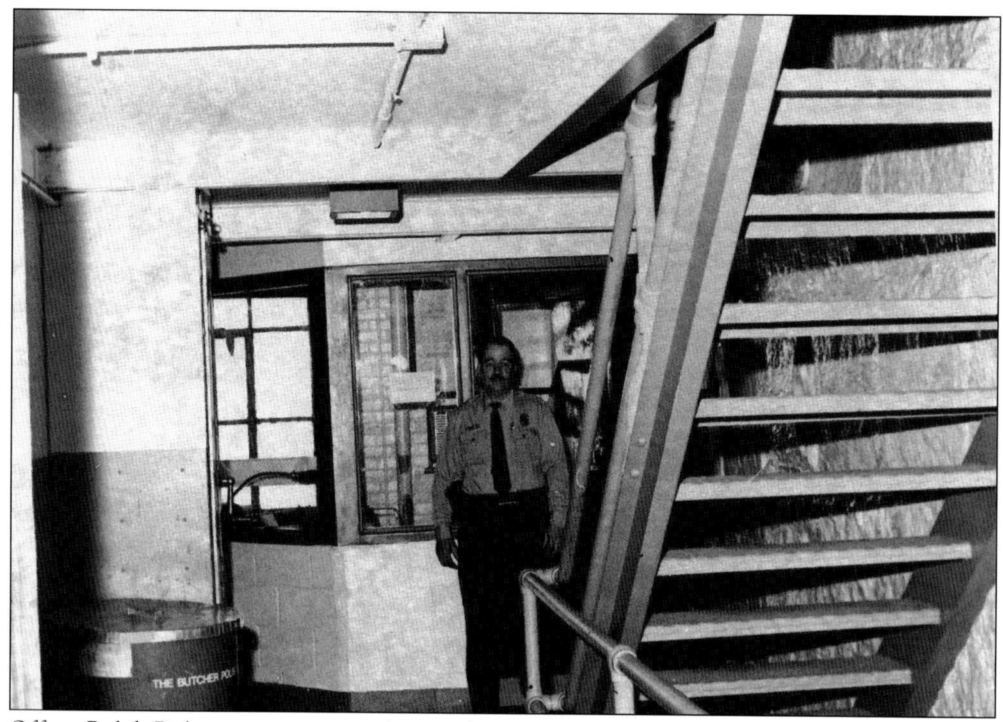

Officer Ralph Robinson is seen standing at the foot of the stairs in the west block.

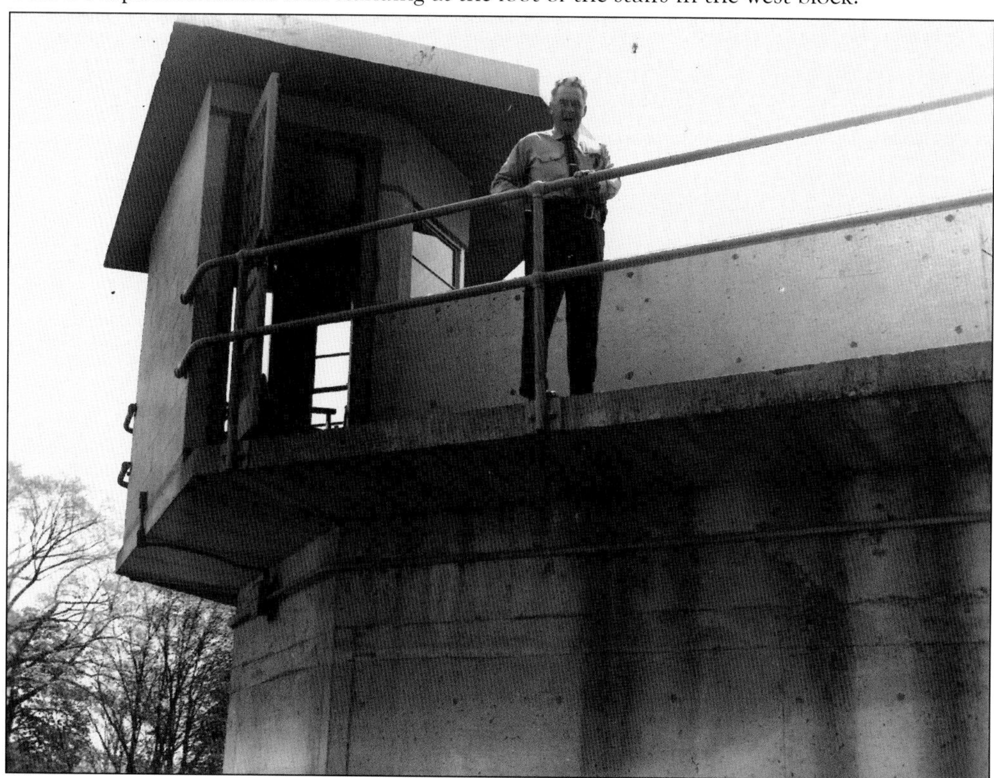
Officer Linwood Williams is photographed here standing outside the north wall post in the 1960s.

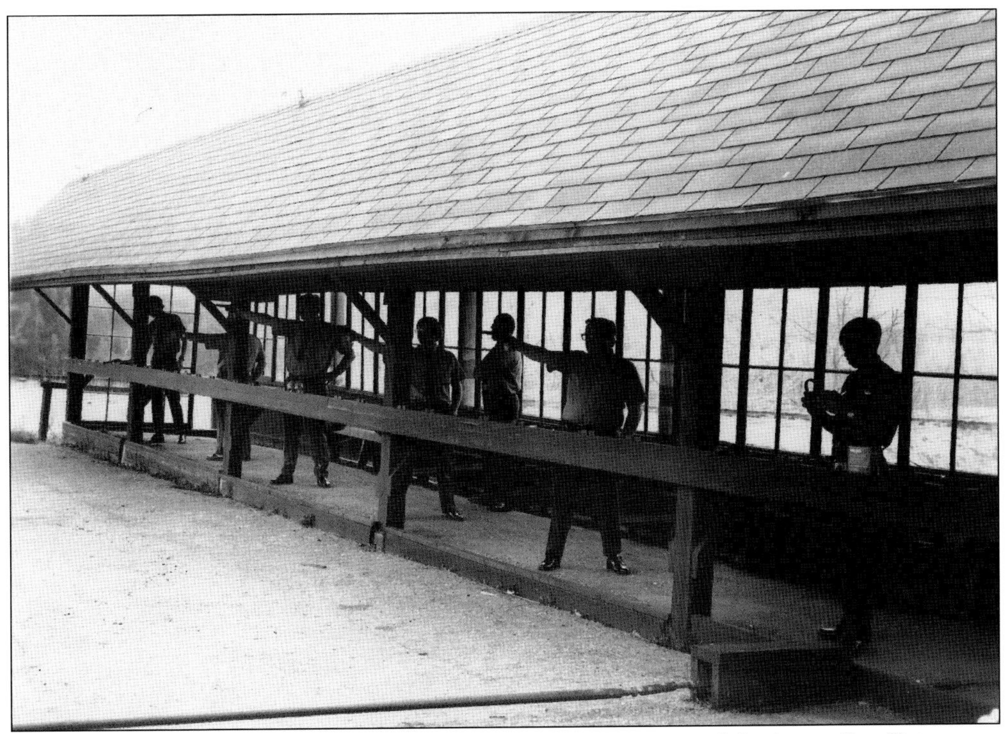

Officers practice at the pistol range in the 1960s preparing to requalify. Annually officers were required to demonstrate their shooting skills.

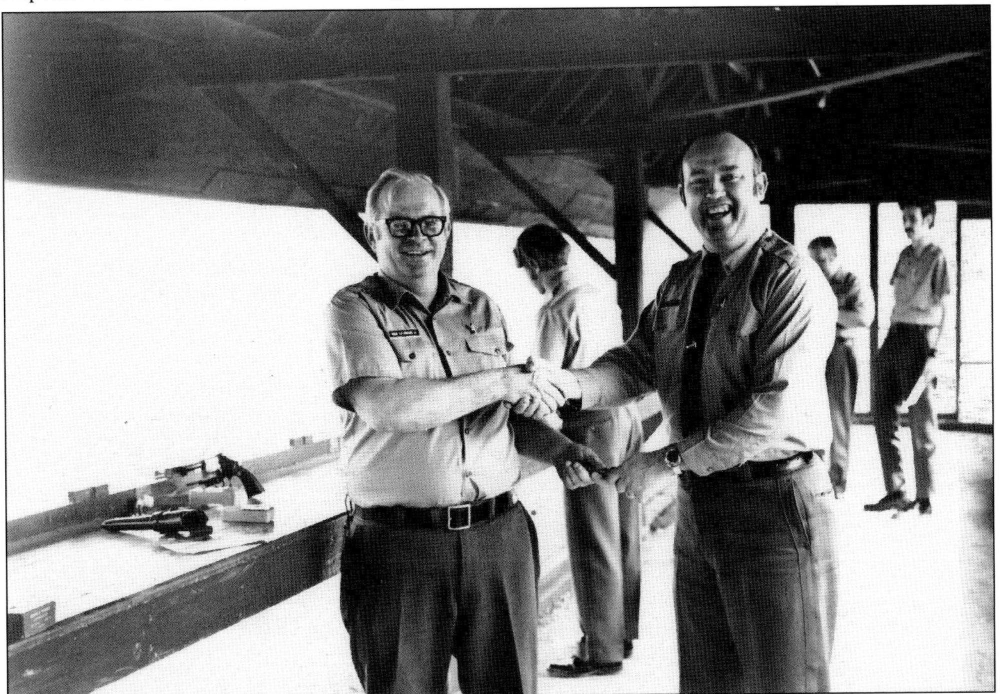

Lt. Richard Belanger congratulates an unidentified officer after qualifying on the pistol range. Lieutenant Belanger was the training officer during the late 1960s and early 1970s.

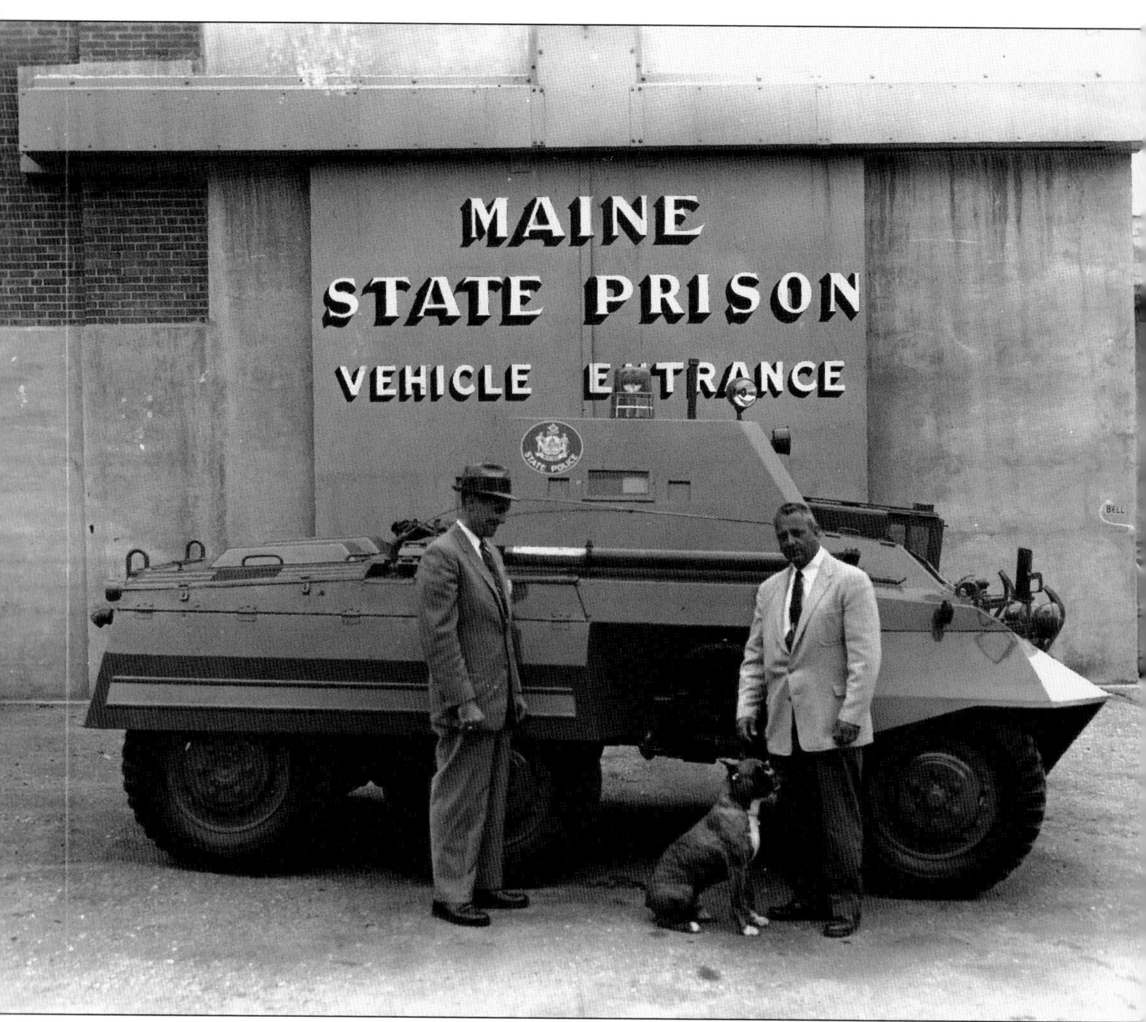

This armored car was built under the direction of Lionel Cooper, foreman of the prison's industrial shops, along with Lt. Robert McKinney of State Police Troop D and Warden Allan L. Robbins. It was constructed by inmates from an M-20 Cavalry reconnaissance car obtained through Civil Defense by Warden Robbins. A deflector plate of seven-eighths of an inch on the front and a half-inch armor plate protected the driver and covered the roof of the vehicle. In tests conducted at the prison farm, the turret withstood fire from 30-06 and 30-30 rifles with hardly a dent. The vehicle was powered by a 110 horsepower Hercules engine, and speeds of 60 miles per hour on the highway were possible. The eight-ton vehicle could maneuver over most terrain. Warden Allan L. Robbins (right), his dog, and an unidentified person are standing in front of the armored car.

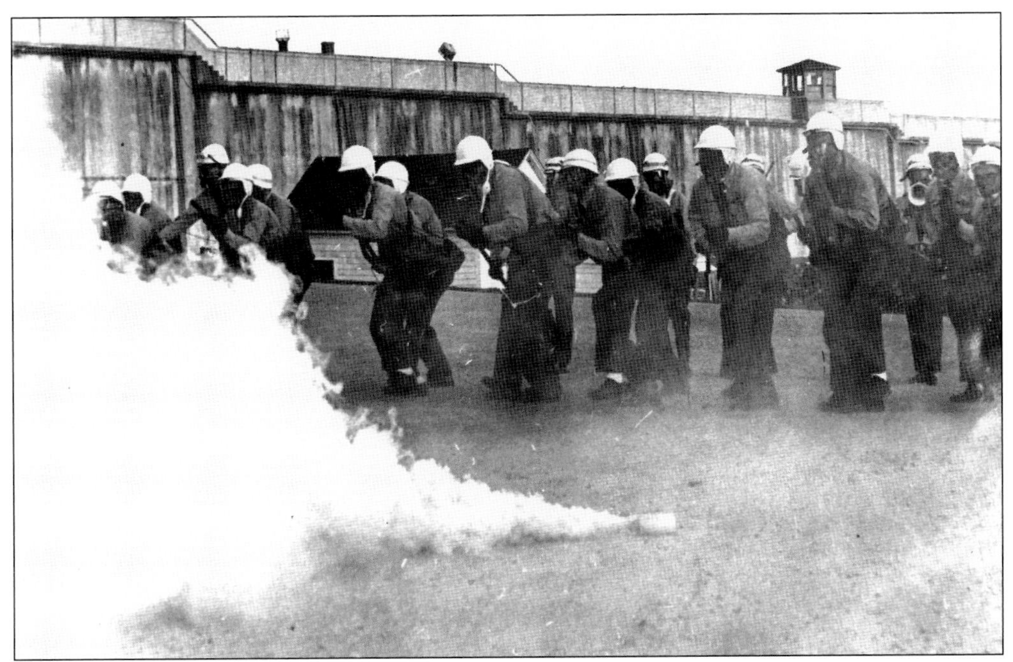

Maine State Prison Riot Squad, formed in the 1960s, is shown practicing with full gear and chemical agents.

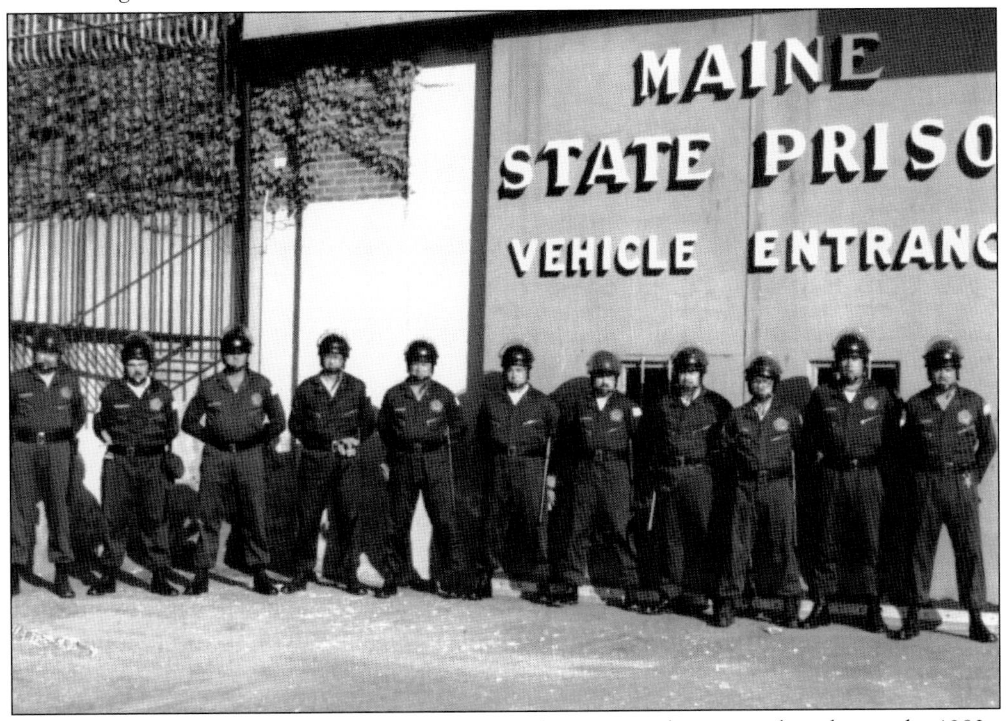

This photograph of the Maine State Prison Tactical Team members was taken during the 1980s. Standing from left to right are Richard Wellington, Hildane Polky, Gary Grant, Lee Kragh, Richard Ames, James O'Farrell, Wayne Page, Richard Schoonamaker, Steven Mahoney, Jay Carlson, and Scott Jones.

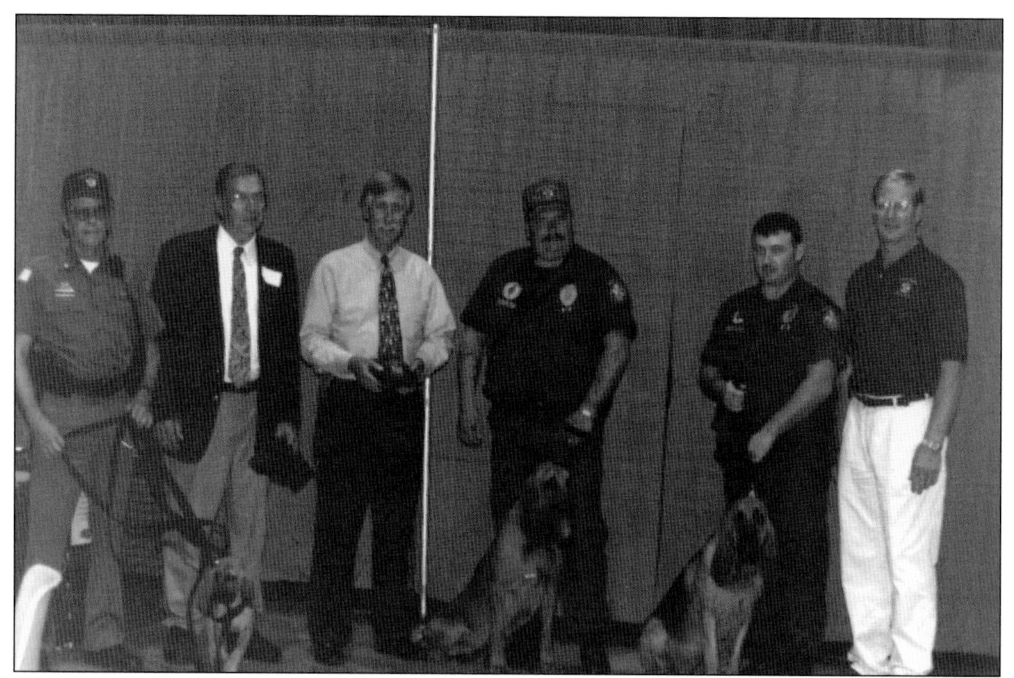

The Maine State Prison K-9 Unit was invited to the Augusta Civic Center to put on a demonstration. From left to right are John Struk, commander; Commissioner Martin Magnusson; Gov. Angus King; Doug Robinson, handler; Gerald Hartley, handler; and Warden Jeffrey Merrill.

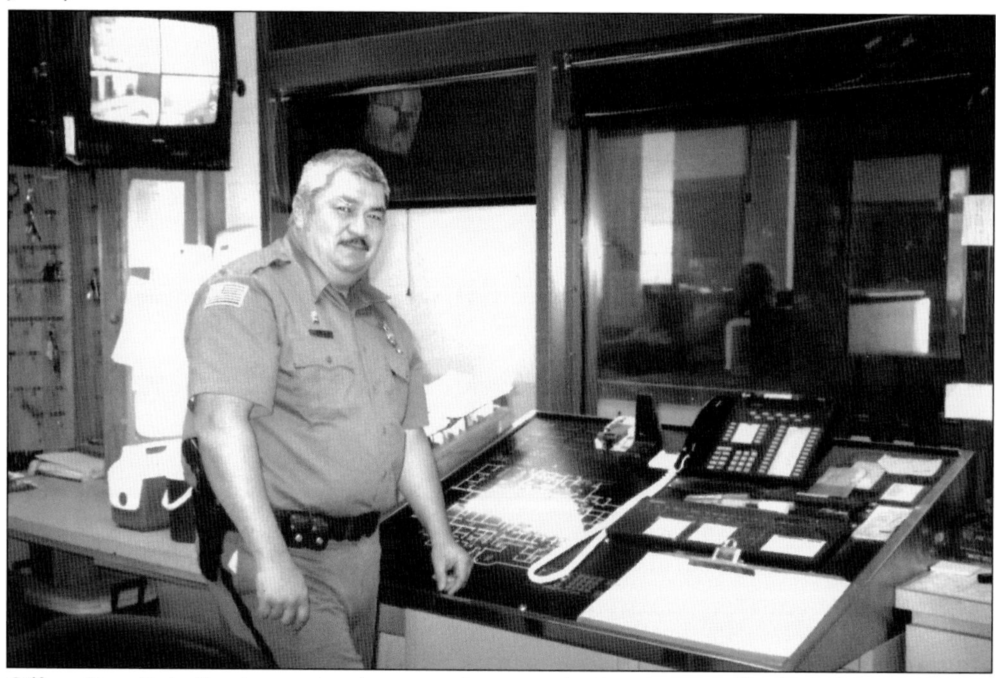

Officer Dan Swindler is seen in the control room, which was virtually the hub of the entire institution. From this point, entrance into or out of the institution was controlled by this armed post. The control room was part of an infrastructure update that occurred in the mid-1990s.

Photographs were used by senior officers to perform uniform inspections. In this picture, Gary Hyvarinen, a respected role model, is shown posing in the summer security uniform. Hyvarinen was hired as a guard in 1961, promoted to sergeant and then lieutenant, and retired in 1991 as the assistant classification officer.

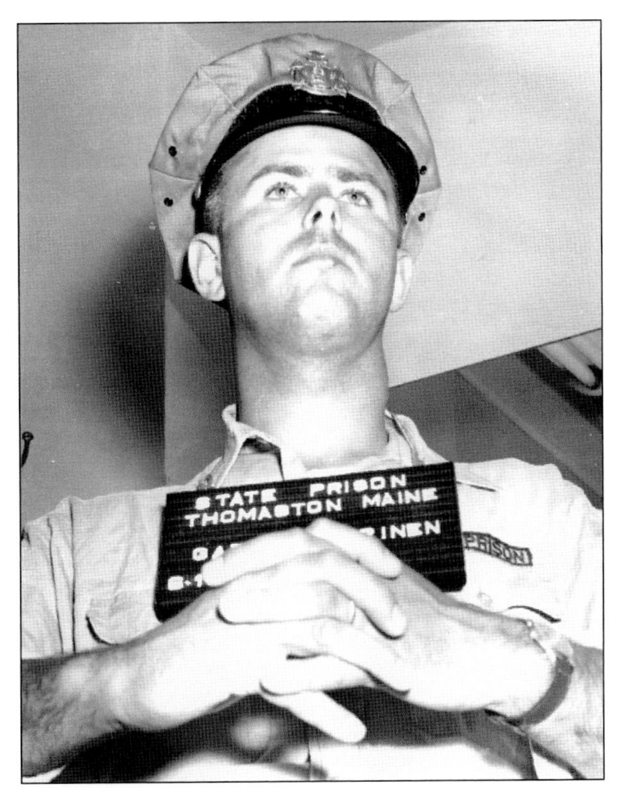

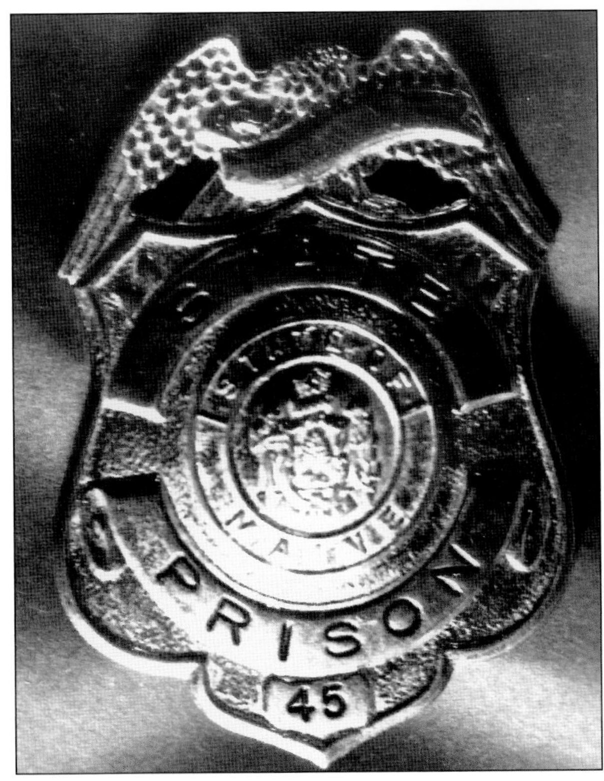

A symbol of respect and security is represented in this picture of a Maine State Prison officer's badge.

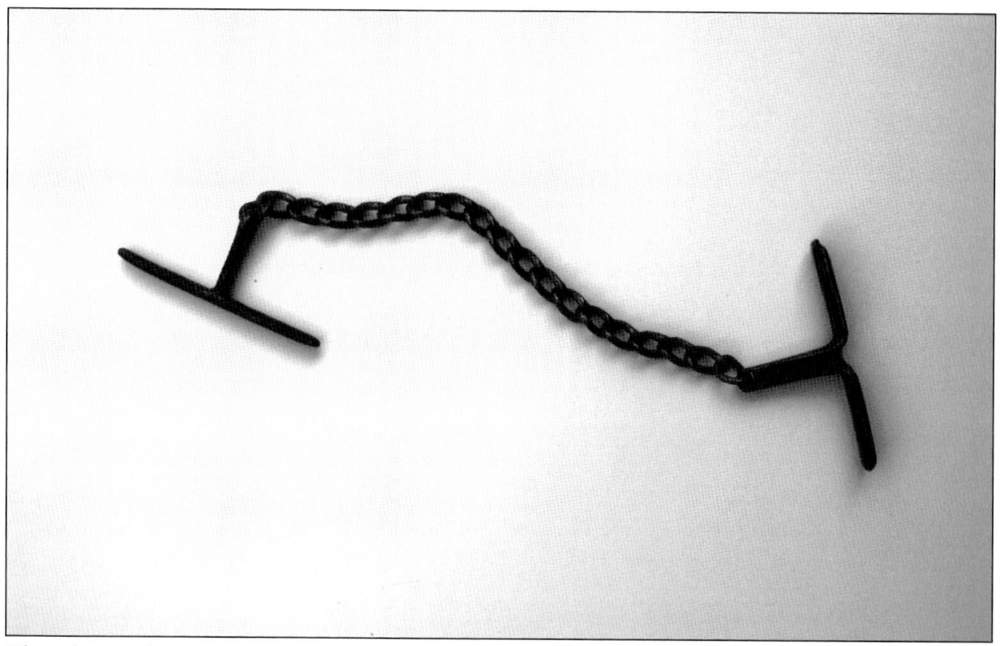

The above photograph shows an early wrist restraint that had been used at the prison. A guard would wrap this device around an inmate's wrist, applying painful pressure to force compliance.

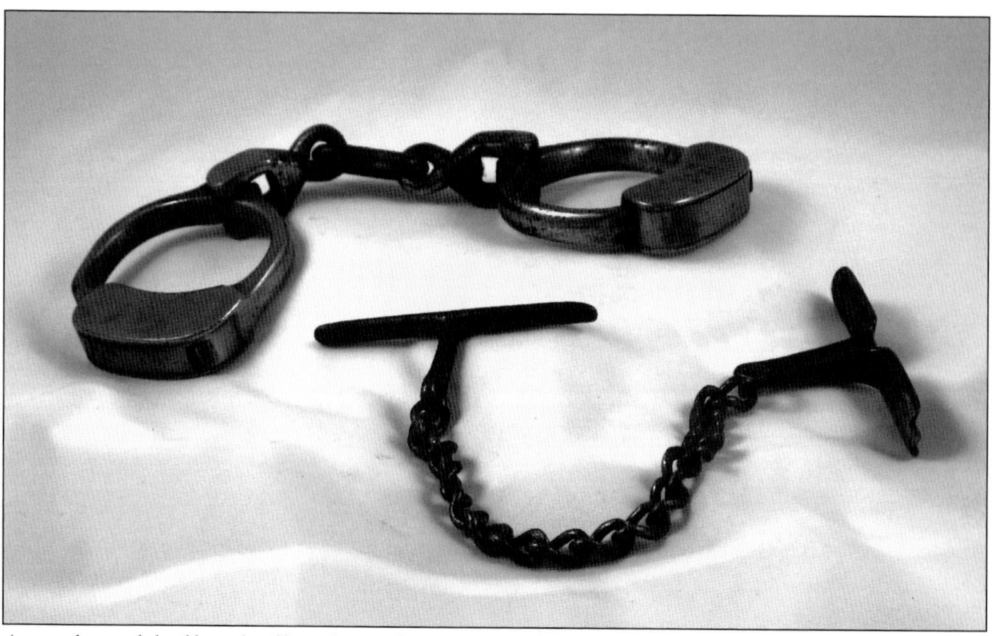

An early model of handcuffs is shown here next to the wrist restraint..

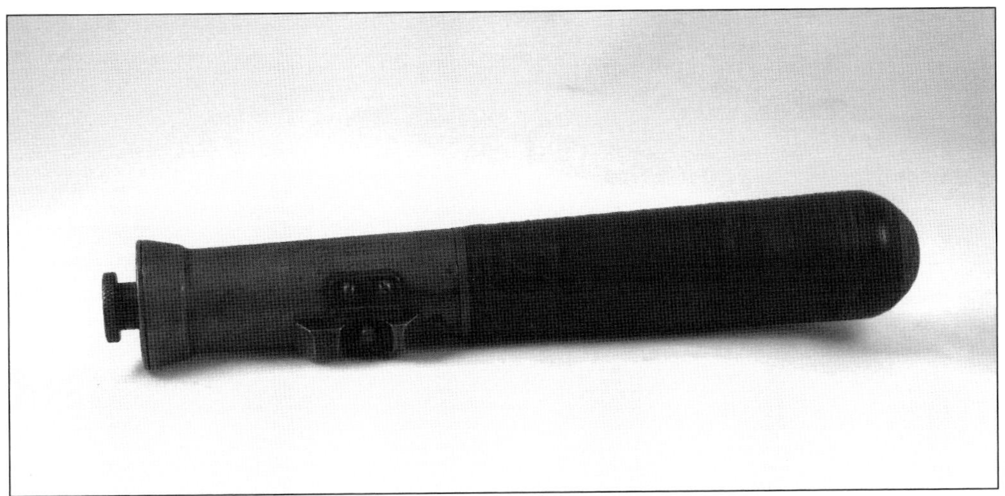

A captain's gas billy club from 1925 is shown here. It contained a canister of tear gas that could be discharged at unruly inmates if needed. Only captains or higher rank staff were issued this security item, and there is no documented use of this device at the prison.

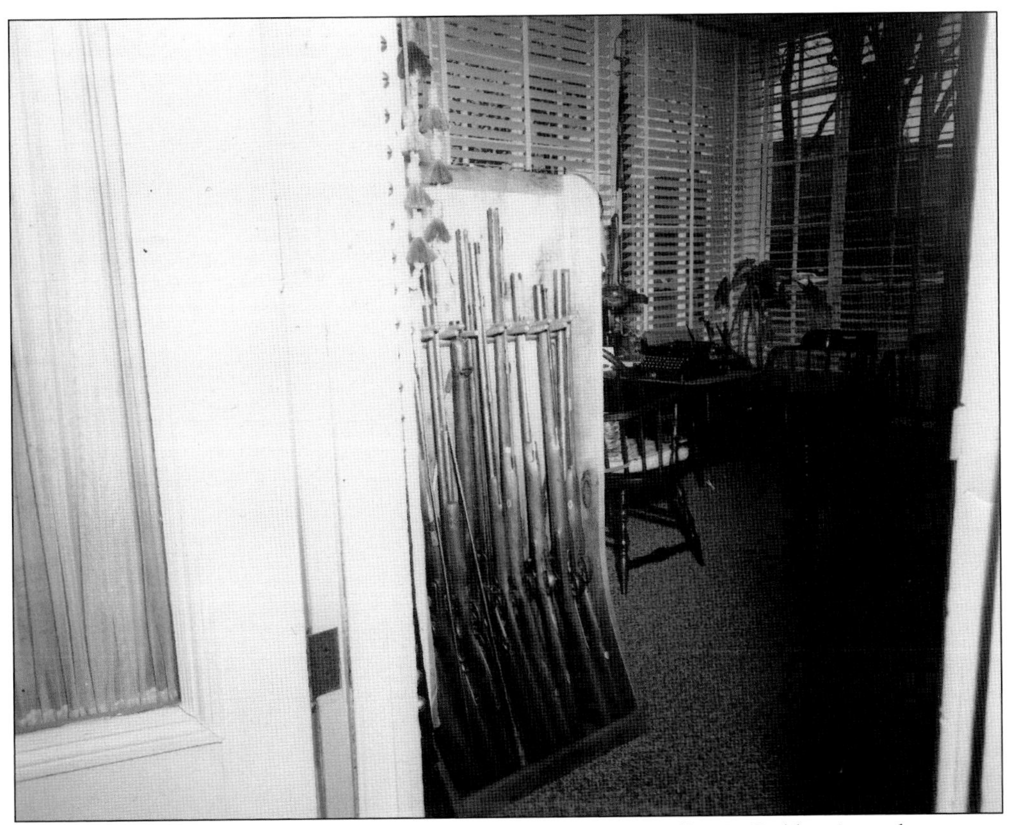

This is a 1960s photograph of rifles that were kept in Warden Allan L. Robbins's residence.

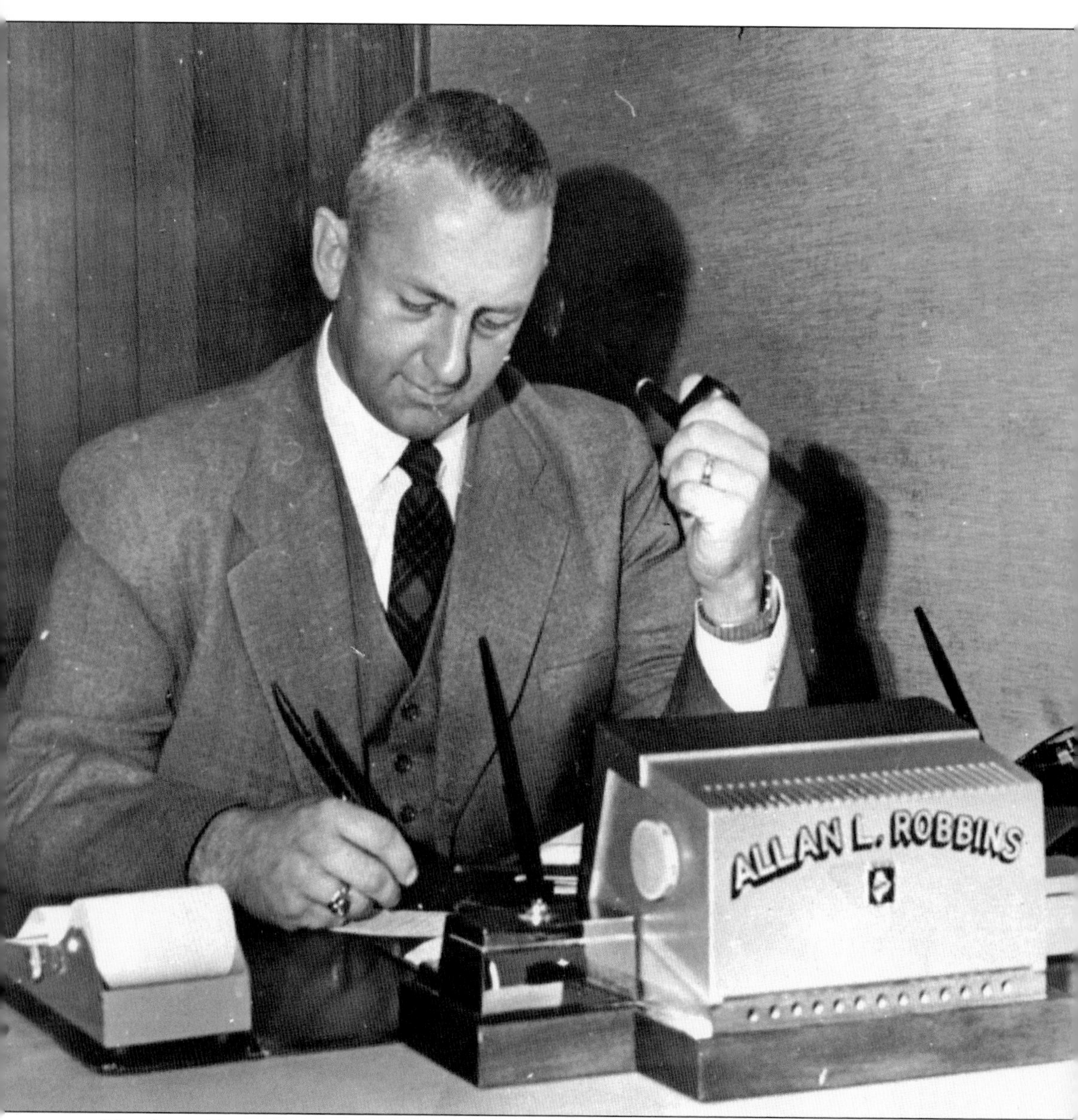

Warden Allan L. Robbins is shown in his office following the renovation of the prison in the early 1960s. Warden Robbins served as deputy warden for two years before being appointed warden in 1951 at age 30, the youngest warden in the country. He served as warden for 20 years and received national recognition for legendary accomplishments. He was a progressive reformer who brought about many positive changes in the prison operations. He was responsible for updating the prison, including the medical department by adding an operating suite, infirmary, dental unit, and x-ray facilities. The 1853 outer wall was rebuilt, and the kitchen and mess hall were redesigned, along with the chapel. The rock pile work program was done away with and relevant inmate programs developed. He also spearheaded many community projects using inmate labor. (Courtesy of the Robbins family.)

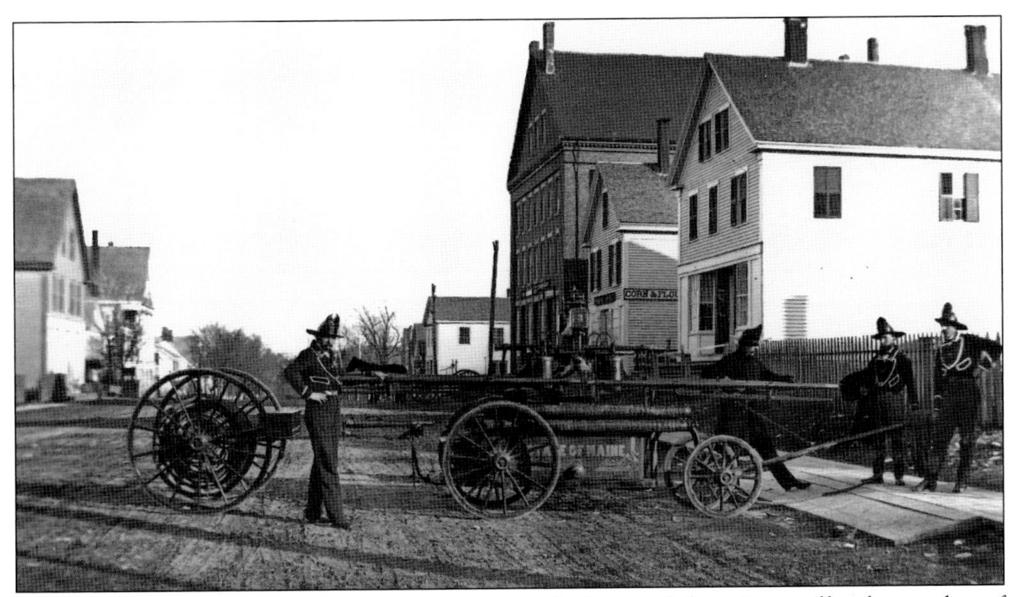

Fire is always a major concern for any correctional facility, and the prison suffered a number of them over its history. The fire company was composed of local citizens and prison staff.

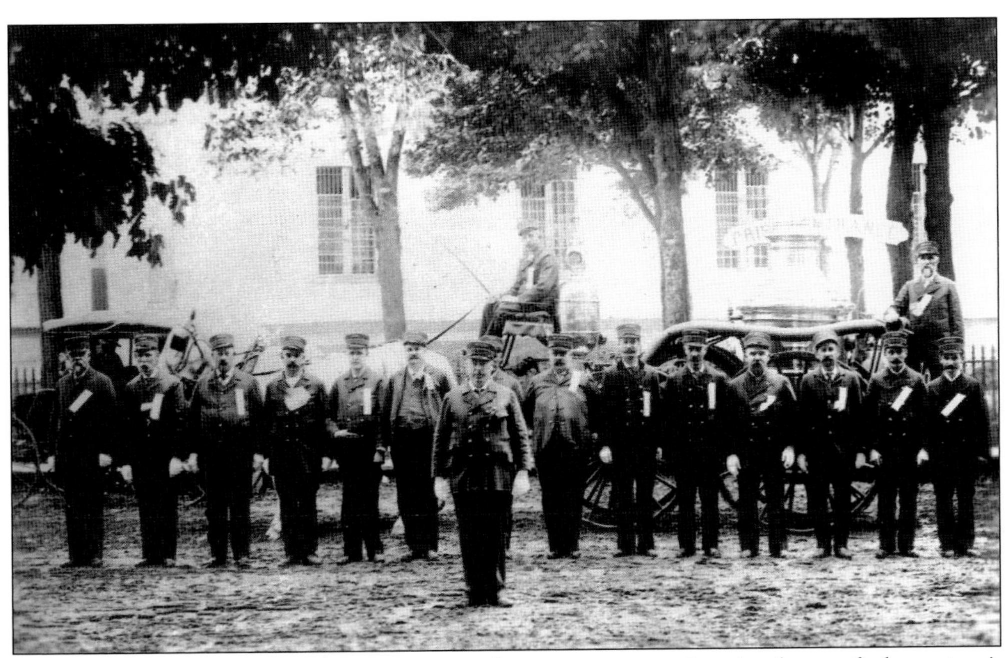

In this early photograph, the prison guards pose at attention in front of the prison's horse-drawn pumper.

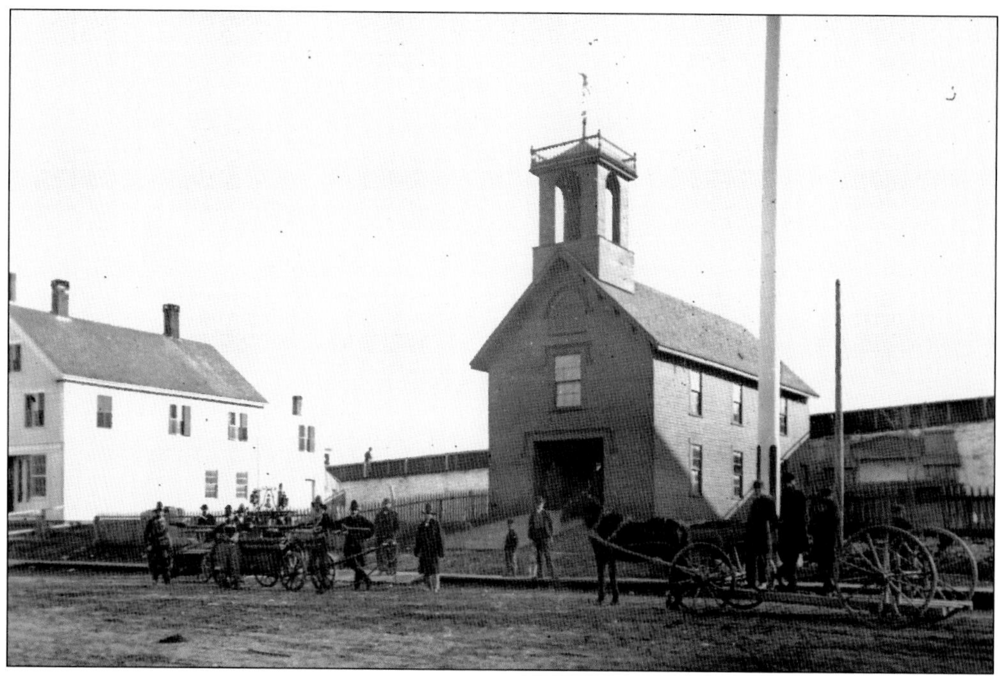

During a summer drought, the cabbage patch of Frank W. Morse on New County Road was parched and in dire need of water. He appealed to Warden Bernes O. Norton (1904–1911) to use the pumper to water the patch. Warden Norton agreed, and the cabbages were saved. Streetcars slowed down for this occasion, and passengers cheered. (Courtesy of Thomaston Scrapbook.)

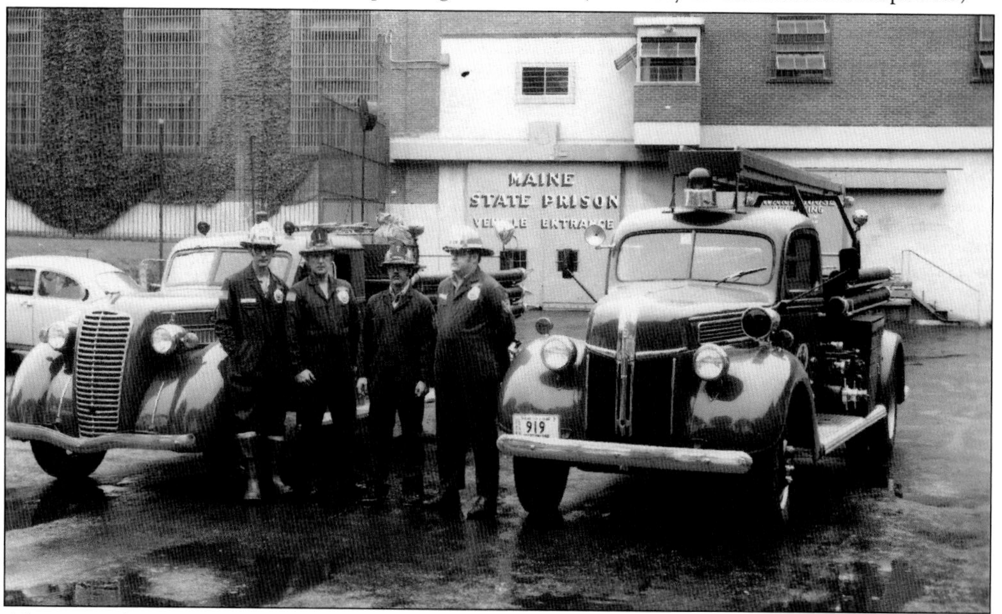

Always ready to respond, this pair of fire trucks shines on a wintry day. On the left is the 1937 Diamond T Pumper obtained from the town of Winthrop. On the right is a 1941 American La France, purchased in the early 1970s. Keeping with tradition, a name was sought after for the new truck. Katy Trip, granddaughter of Warden W. W. Rice, suggested *Clara* after her grandmother. The brigade settled on *Clara-Bell*.

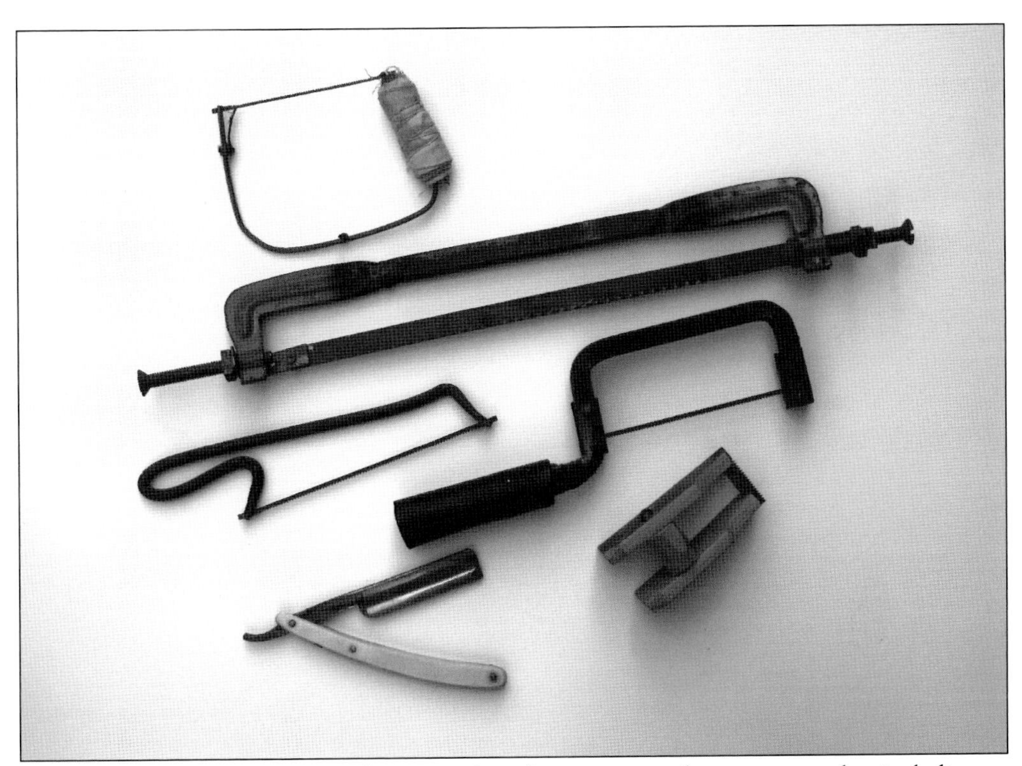

This photograph shows a collection of early inmate-made escape tools, including a handcrafted saw.

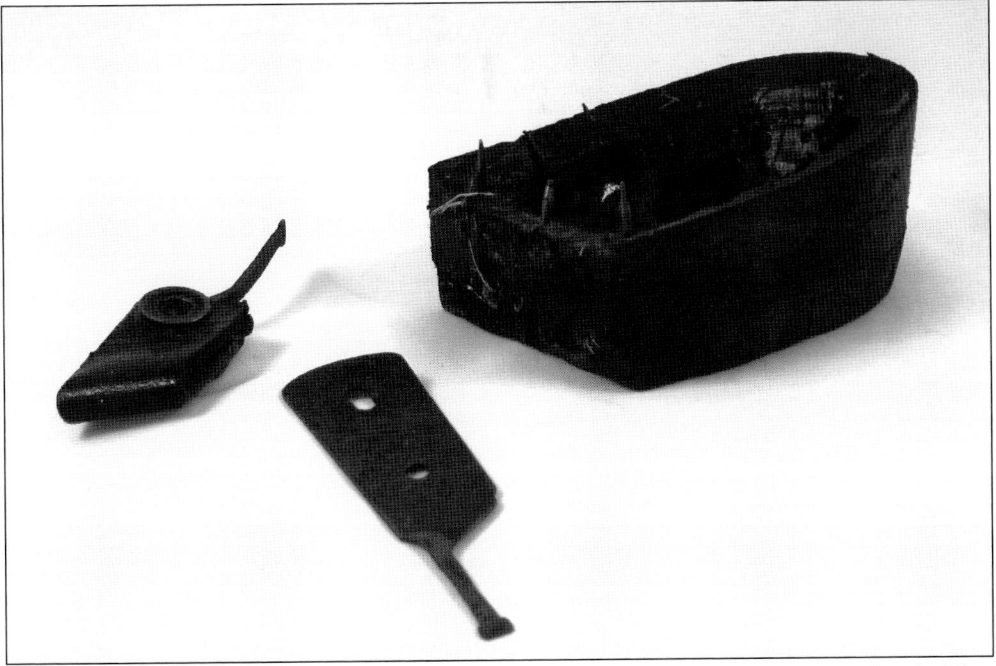

Hollowed-out boot and shoe heels are still common places to hide contraband. This hollowed-out boot heel held keys handmade from leather and metal.

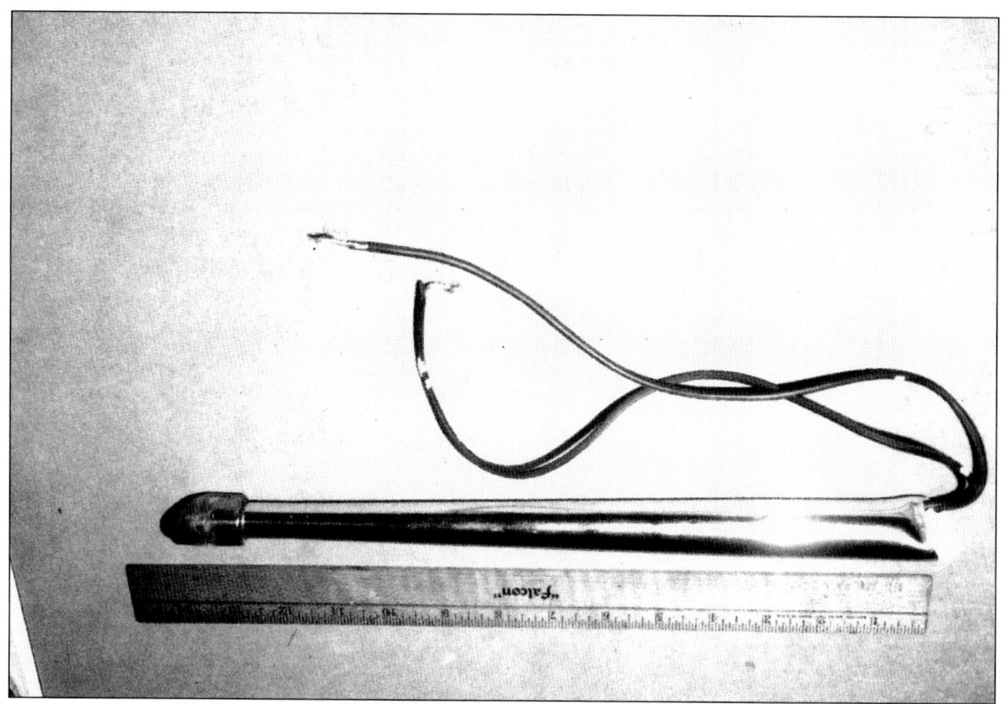

This is a photograph of a homemade pipe bomb found in an inmate's cell in August 1976.

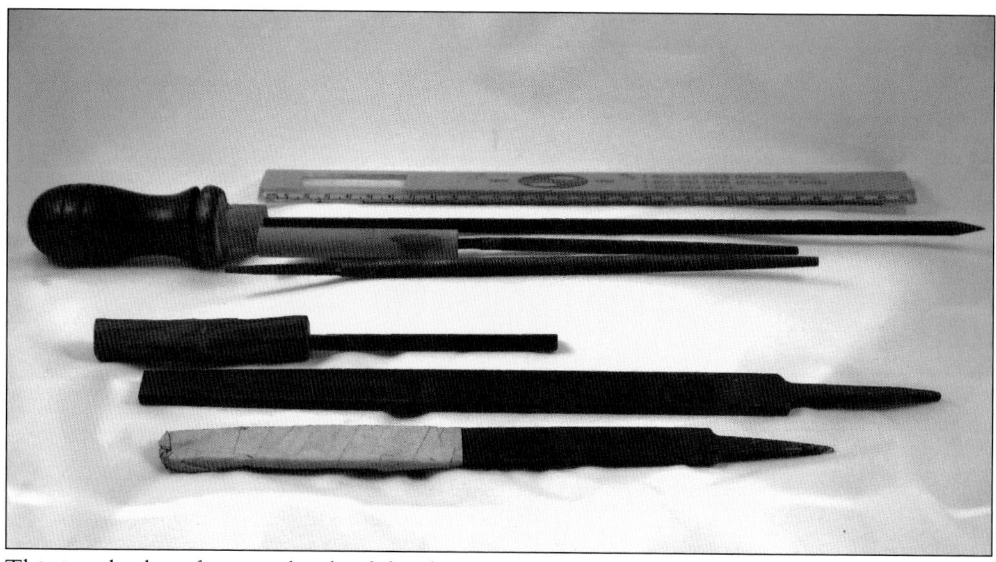

This is a display of various kinds of shanks confiscated from inmates. These were crafted from files and other metal objects and could be used to harm others or for an inmate's own protection. Inmates today still occasionally fashion shanks out of metal and plastic.

Pictured on the right is Martin A. Magnusson, who was appointed warden of the Maine State Prison in December 1982 by Commissioner Donald Allen and confirmed by Gov. Joseph Brennan. Warden Magnusson was appointed associate commissioner to the Maine Department of Corrections in May 1997 by Gov. Angus King. Below is warden Jeffrey D. Merrill, who was appointed by Commissioner Joseph Lehman and confirmed by Gov. Angus King. Warden Merrill was the last warden to serve at the Maine State prison in Thomaston when it closed in 2002, and he remains warden at the Maine State Prison in Warren, which opened in 2002.

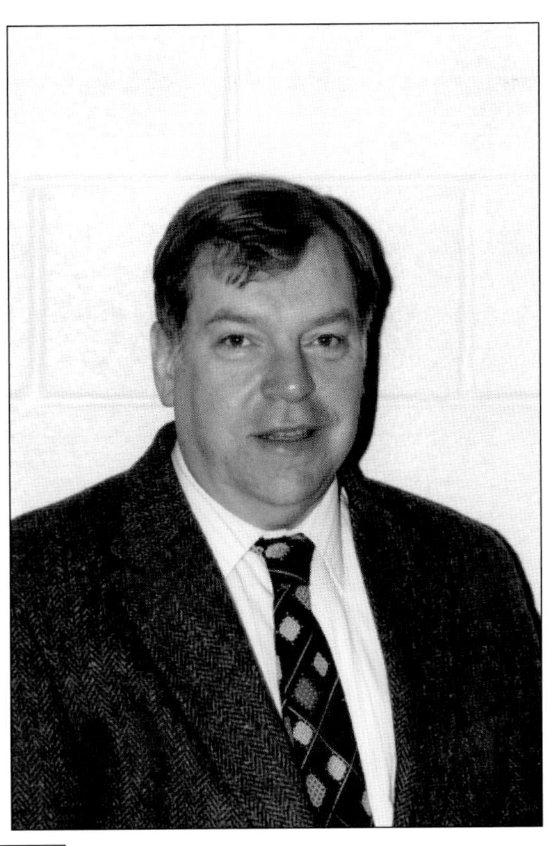

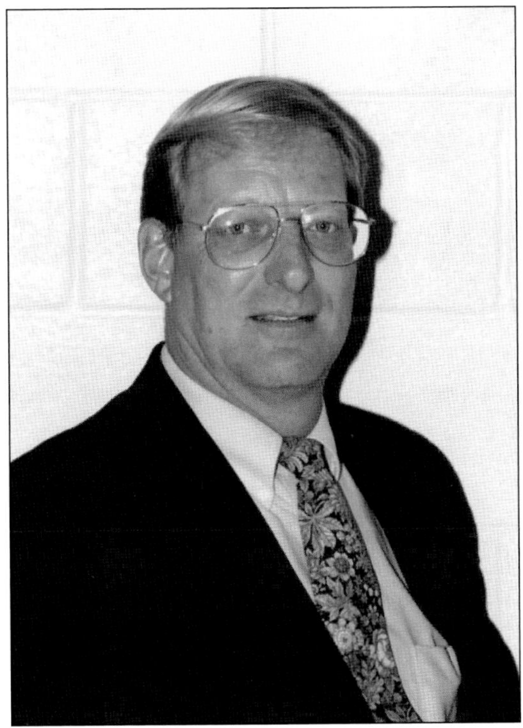

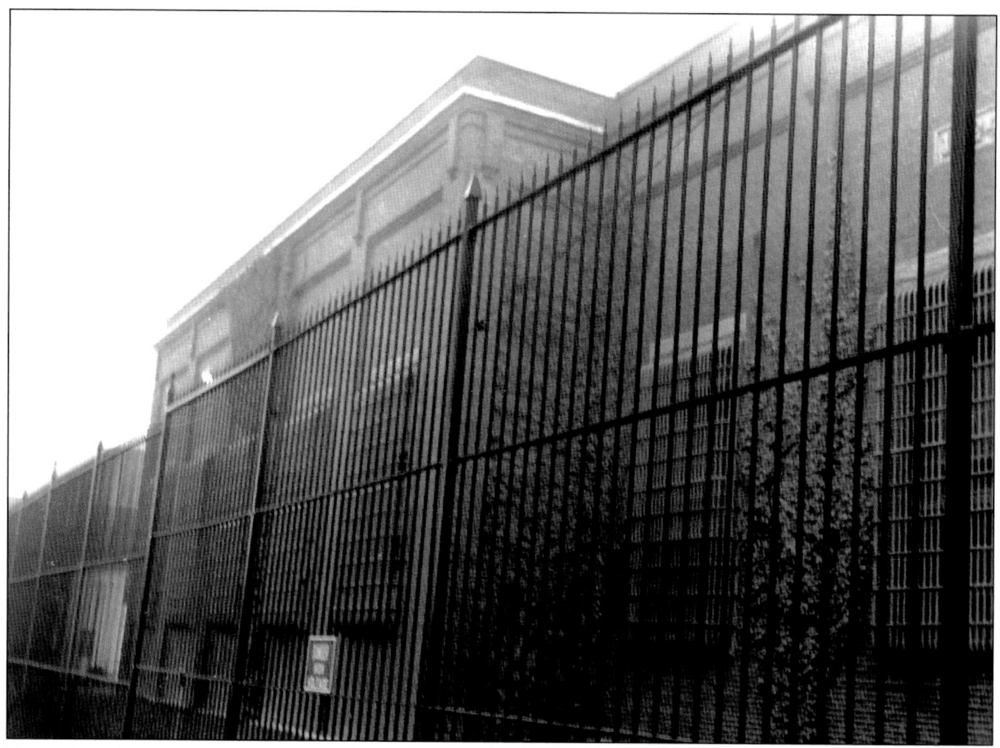

This is a lasting image of metal bars and brick that served so many years to provide the community, staff, and inmates with safety and security.

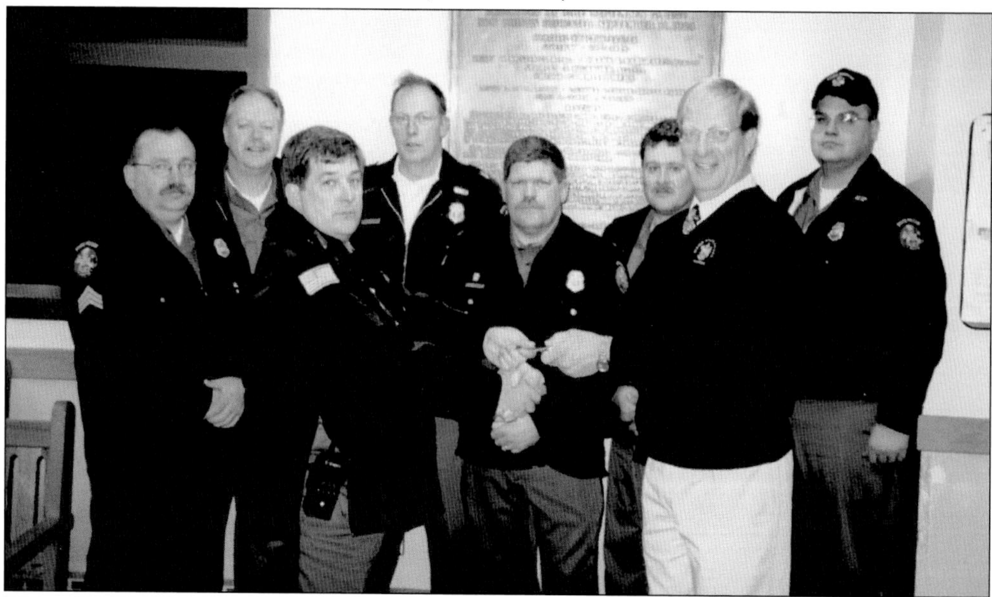

Maine State Prison staff and the warden gather in the prison lobby. Director of security James O'Farrell hands the front door key to Warden Jeffrey Merrill after the last inmate was transferred to the new facility. Also pictured from left to right in the second row are Sgt. Larry Worster, officer James Sturks, Capt. Dale Gardner, Sgt. Harold Abbott, officer David Shepard, and officer Jonathan Cunningham.

Five

MURDER, EXECUTIONS, AND ESCAPES

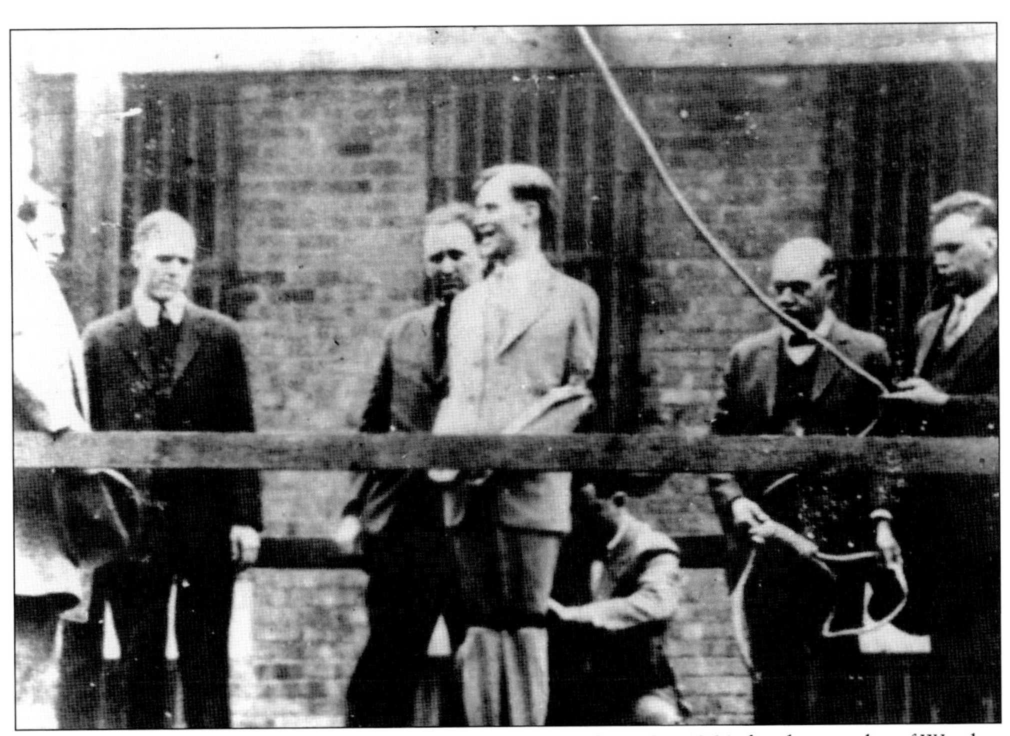

Convict Francis C. Spencer was executed by hanging on June 24, 1864, for the murder of Warden Richard Tinker. Spencer, serving a five-year sentence for assault, approached Warden Tinker from behind and stabbed him in the neck, severing his carotid artery. The "Gibbet," or gallows, was erected and Spencer put to death on the very spot where Tinker died. Warden Tinker was appointed in 1861 and had previously been a sheriff and senator in Hancock County.

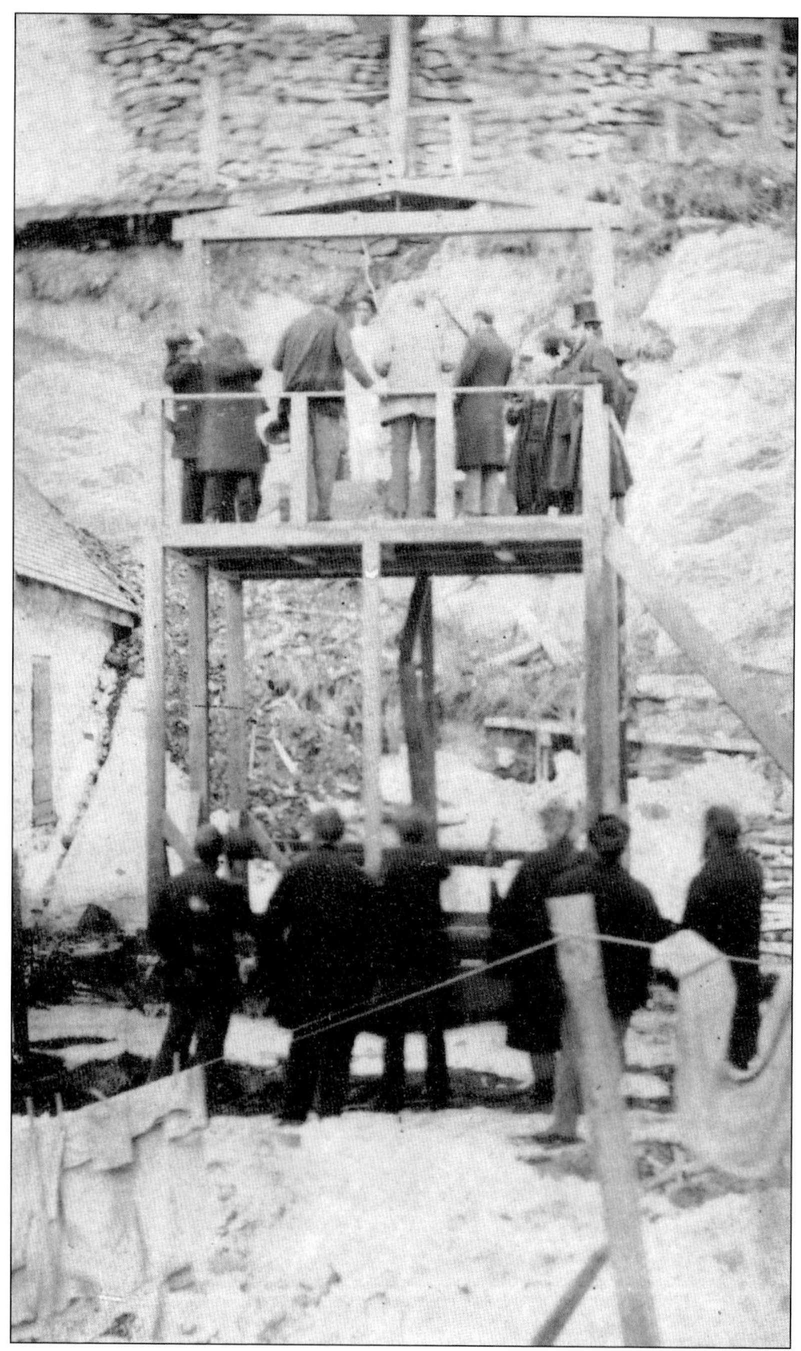

The above picture is believed to be the execution of Clifton Harris. Harris was executed by hanging on March 12, 1869, a year after being convicted of killing Susannah Kinsley and Polly Caswell of West Auburn. This crime was known as "the West Auburn Tragedy." Harris, a 19-year-old black man from Fortress Monroe, Virginia, had moved to Maine after serving in the Civil War. The law at the time required the death warrant to be signed before an execution could take place. Harris's death warrant was signed by Gov. Joshua Chamberlain, a Civil War hero and strong believer in the death penalty. (Courtesy of Muriel Heath.)

Louis Wagner was convicted of murdering two Norwegian immigrants, Anethe Christensen and Karen Christensen, on Smutty Nose Island March 5, 1873, which would come to be known as the Smutty Nose murders. Wagner was executed by hanging along with another convict, John Gordon, at the prison on June 25, 1875. A book, *The Weight of Water*, written by Anita Shreve, depicts the Smutty Nose murders. (Drawing courtesy of Ohlin Williams.)

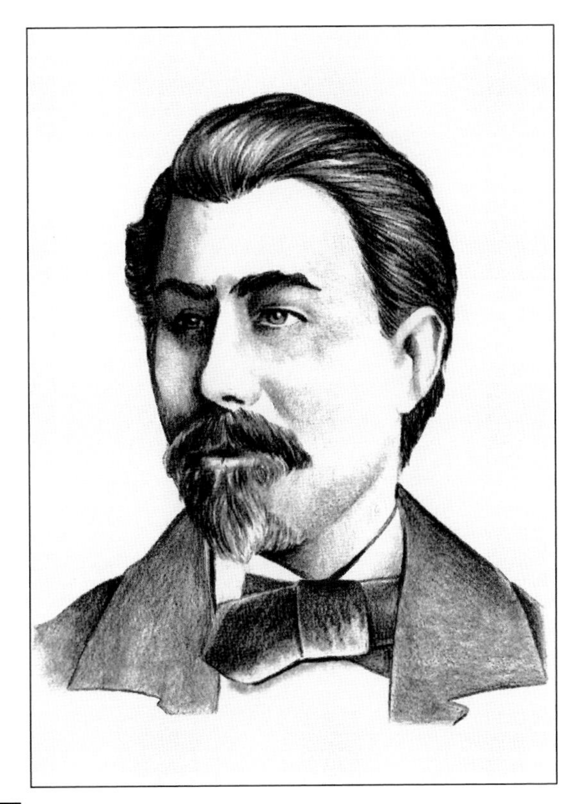

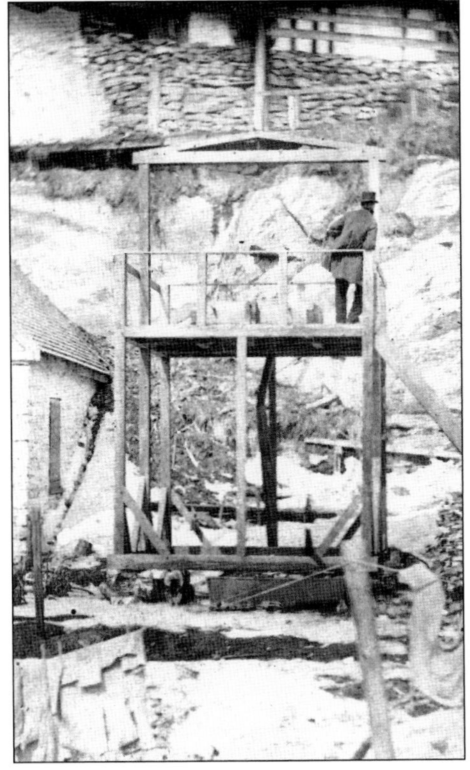

There were seven hangings at the Maine State Prison: Francis Spencer (June 24, 1864), Clifton Harris (March 12, 1869), Louis Wagner and John Gordon (June 25, 1875), Raffaele Capone and Carmine Santore (April 17, 1885), and Daniel Wilkinson (November 20, 1885). All were convicted for the crime of murder and were hung from the same gallows. (Courtesy of Muriel Heath.)

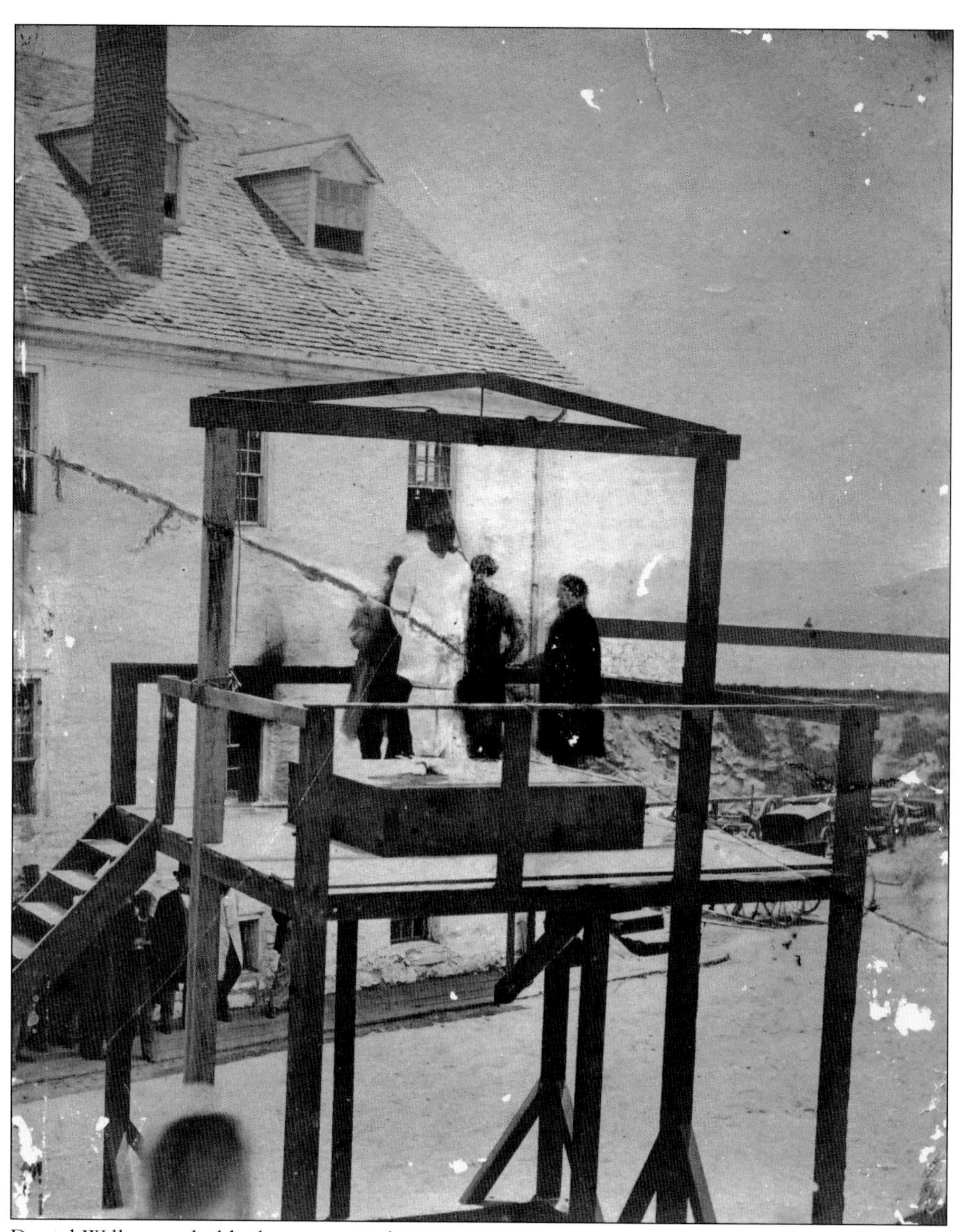

Daniel Wilkinson holds the ominous distinction of being the last convict executed in the state of Maine prior to the death penalty abolishment on March 17, 1887. Wilkinson was convicted of murdering Bath police officer William Lawrence. On September 4, 1883, officer Kingsley came upon an attempted break-in at the D. C. Gould Ship Chandlery and Provision Store. During the ensuing foot chase, Wilkinson ran into officer William Lawrence and in an attempt to escape from him, Wilkinson shot Lawrence at point bank range with a .32-caliber revolver. The bullet killed officer Lawrence instantly. Sheriff Irish carried out the execution on November 20, 1885, at the Maine State Prison.

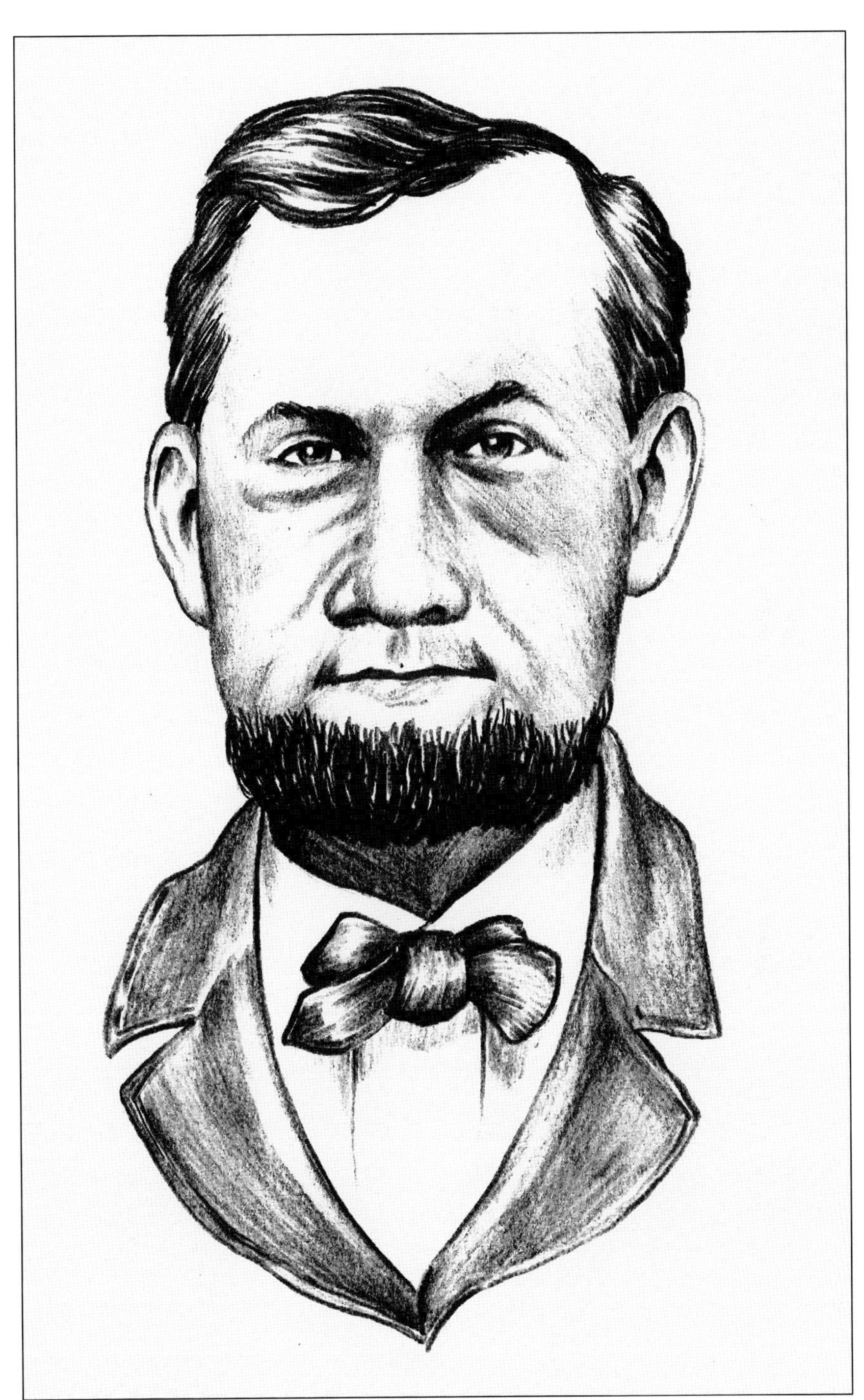

Written in 1882, the book *Innocent Man in a Felon's Cell*, loaned by Flora N. Chapman, was based on the murder of Sarah H. Meservey, found dead in her home in Tenants Harbor. She was strangled to death by a long woolen scarf wrapped around her head and neck. Questions still remain as to the guilt or innocence of Nathan F. Hart, who died in prison proclaiming his innocence to the end. (Drawing courtesy of Olin Williams.)

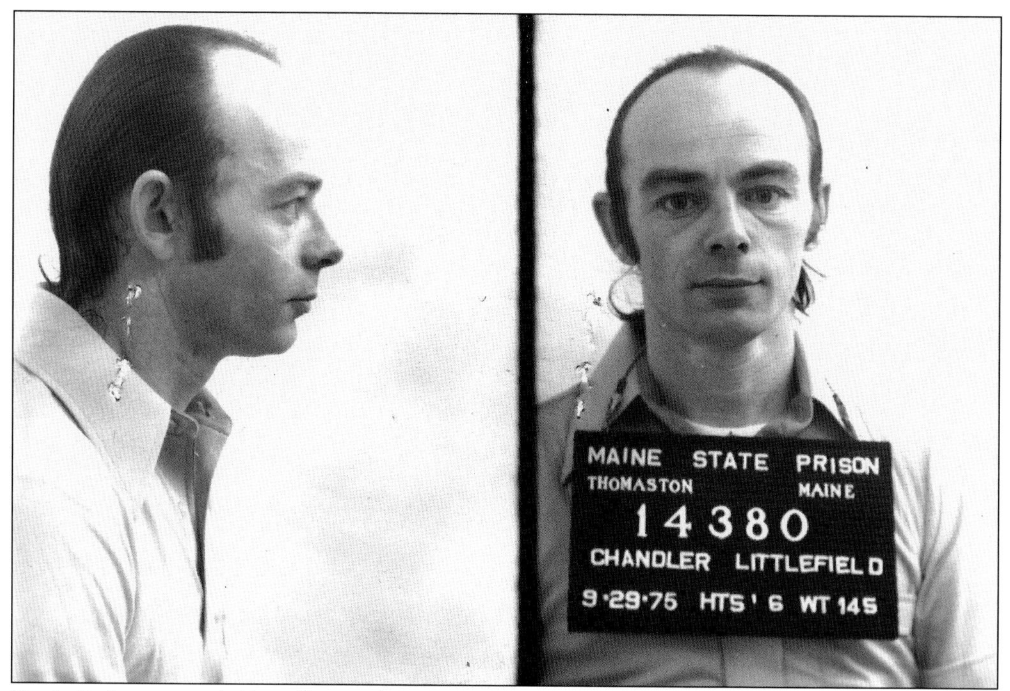

Keith Parkinson and Chandler Littlefield escaped from the Maine State Prison on January 25, 1977, by gaining access to the center block roof air vent. The inmates found the firearms left for them by accomplices outside the prison. They then kidnapped a local resident, forcing him to drive them to northern Maine. The inmates were captured in Millinocket by local authorities after they took a neighbor of inmate Parkinson's family hostage.

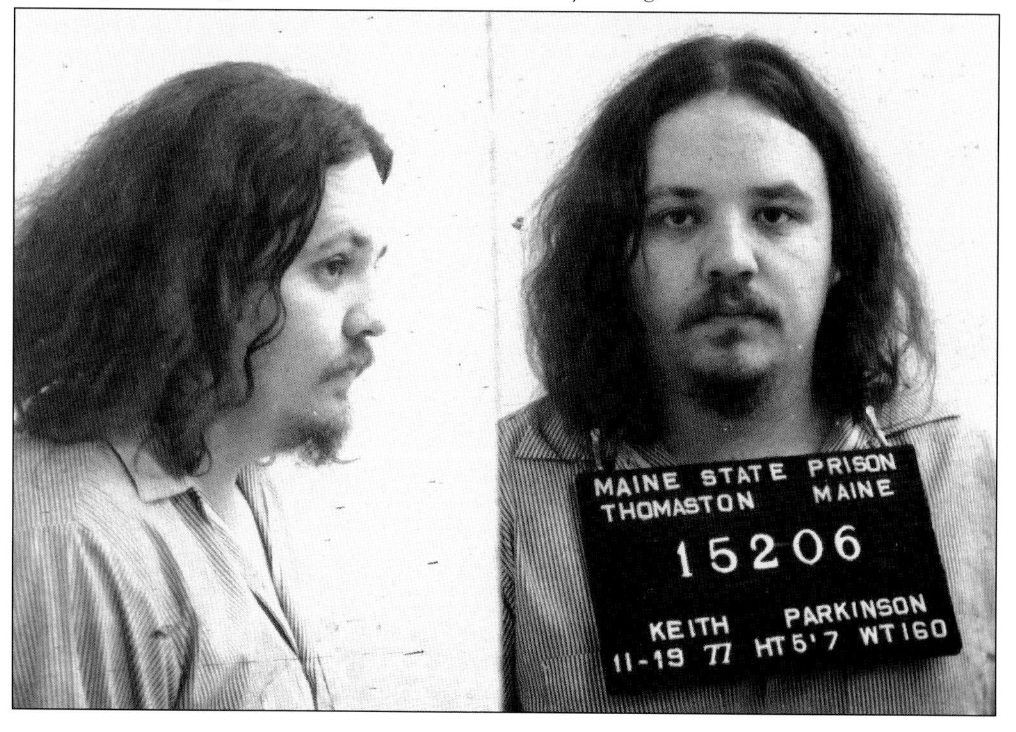

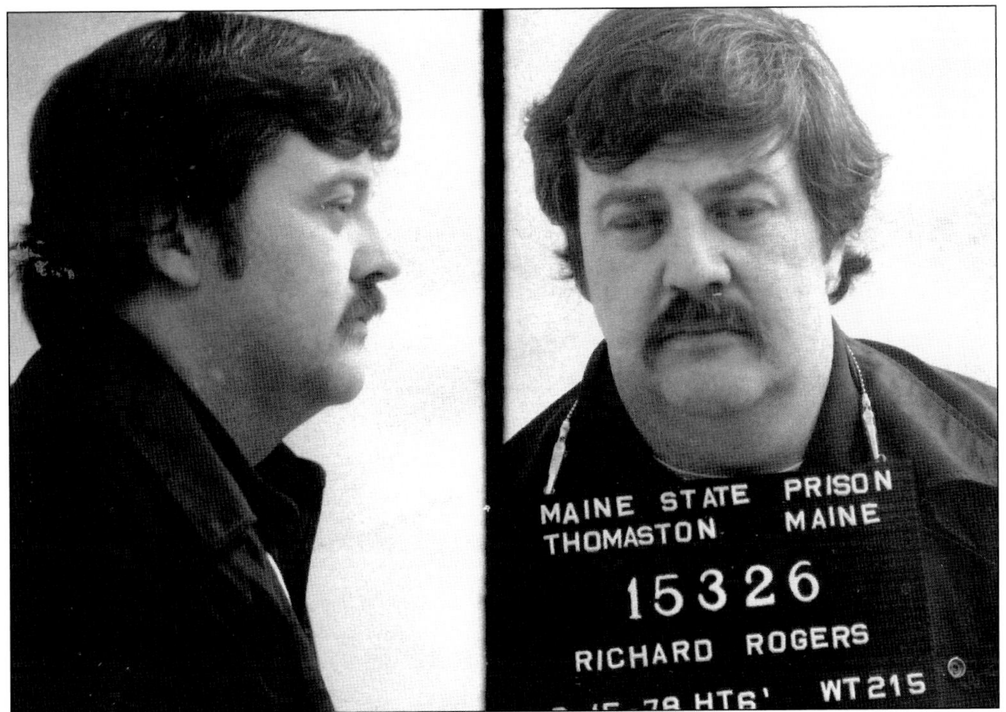

Inmate Richard Rogers escaped on November 14, 1977, during a medical trip to Penobscot Bay Medical Center. Rogers obtained a .38-caliber revolver left for him in a hospital bathroom and took officer Robert C. Thibodeau hostage. Rogers forced officer Thibodeau to drive the prison vehicle to a remote location and restrained him inside the vehicle. Rogers fled on foot and was captured days later. Officer Thibodeau was not injured.

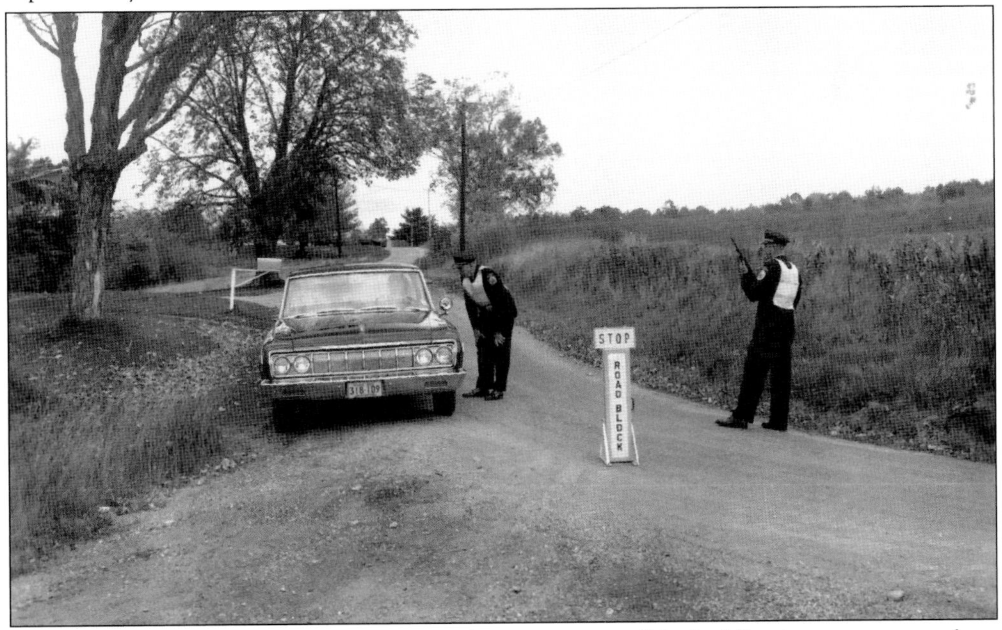

Officers of the Maine State Prison are shown at a roadblock following an escape from the prison.

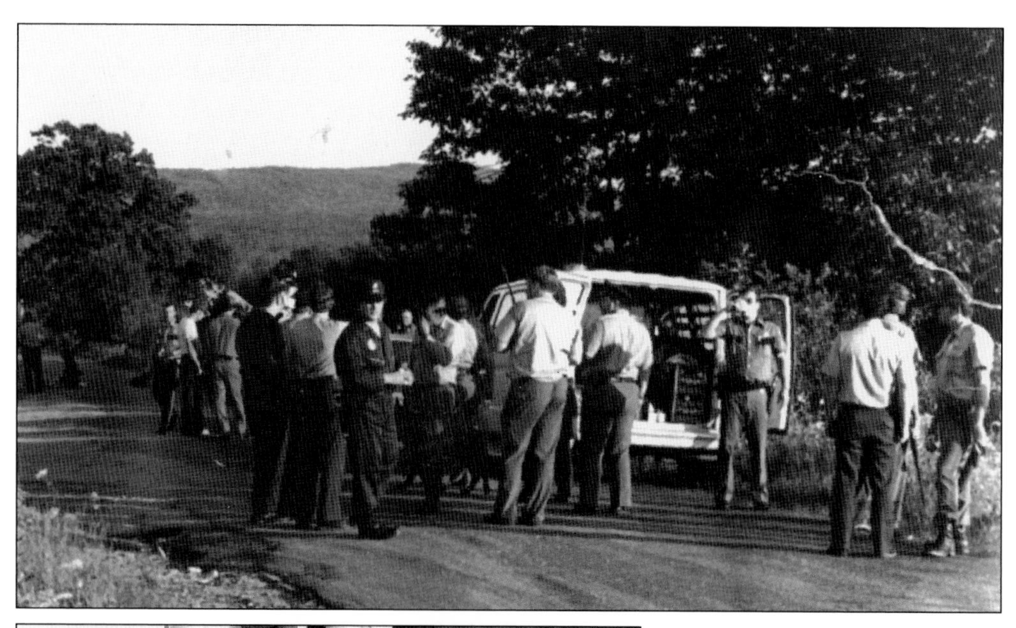

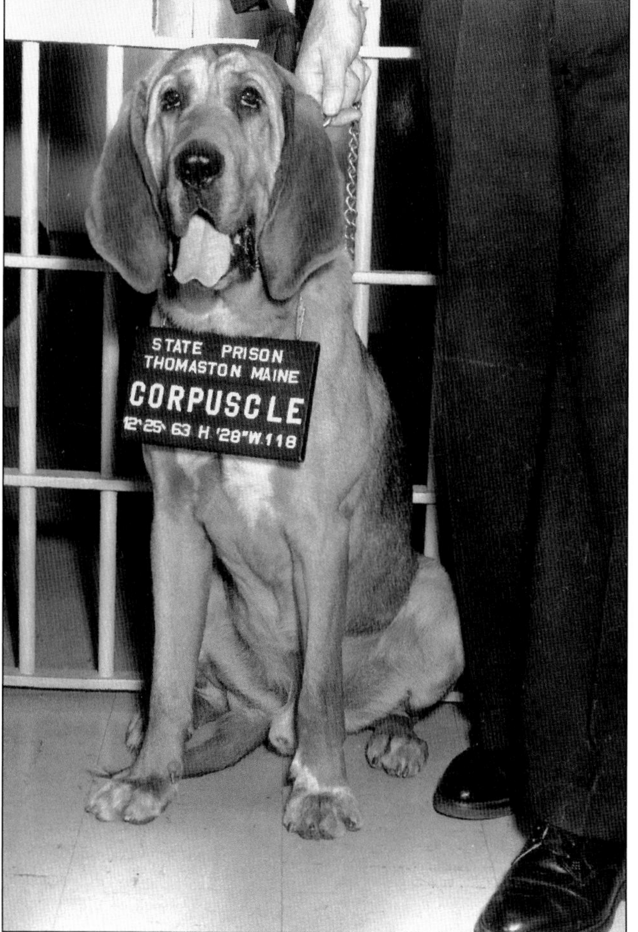

Inmates Arnold Nash and Milton Wallace escaped on July 15, 1981, while outside on a work detail. The search became known as the "Moody Mountain Manhunt" and was the largest of its kind in Maine history. The inmates were captured on August 5, 1981, after state police K-9 Skipper led searchers to their location. Identified Maine State Prison staff appearing in the photograph above, from right to left, are Scott Jones, Robert Costigan, Clifton Blakesley, Len Olsen, John Struk, Sgt. James O'Farrell, and Sgt. Richard Schoonamaker. At the prison, bloodhounds were first introduced in the 1960s under Warden Allan L. Robbins. Pictured here is bloodhound Corpuscle, photographed on December 25, 1963. Following Warden Robbins's retirement, the bloodhounds were also retired, but in the early 1980s under Warden Paul Vestal, bloodhounds were brought back into use.

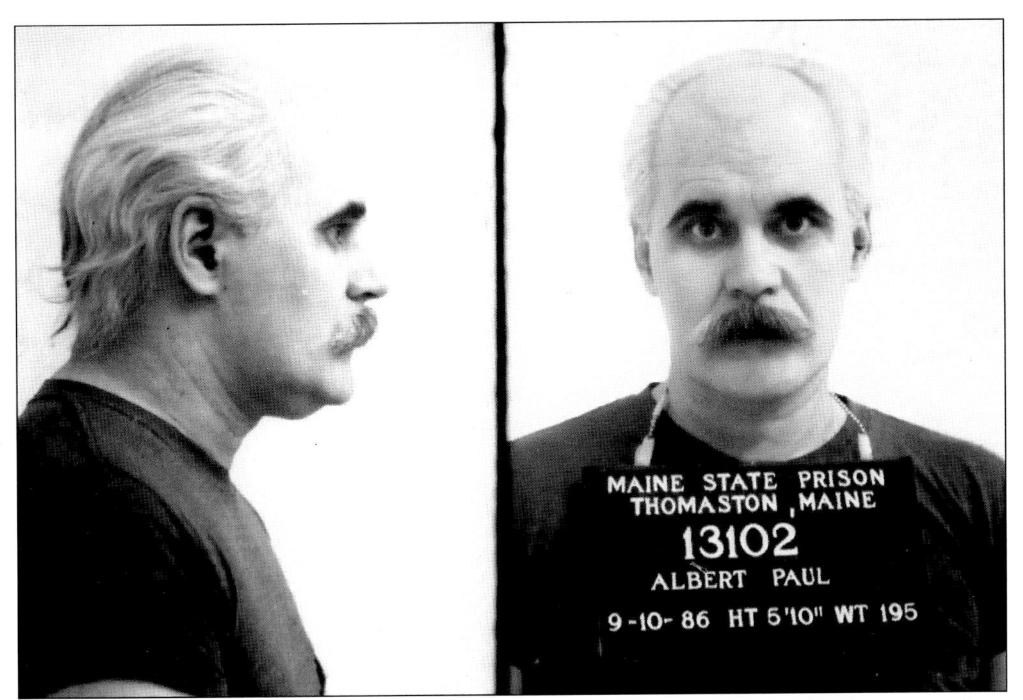

Inmate Albert Paul was noted for his ability and desire to escape from custody. He escaped from the Maine State Prison, the state hospital in Augusta, and the federal penitentiary in Lewisburg, Pennsylvania. Aside from these actual escapes, he also had several he attempted from the Maine State Prison and other facilities in Florida and Connecticut. In his most notable escape attempt, he dug a tunnel from his cell in the east wing 42 feet until hitting the granite foundation of the prison. He could not get through and had to give himself up.

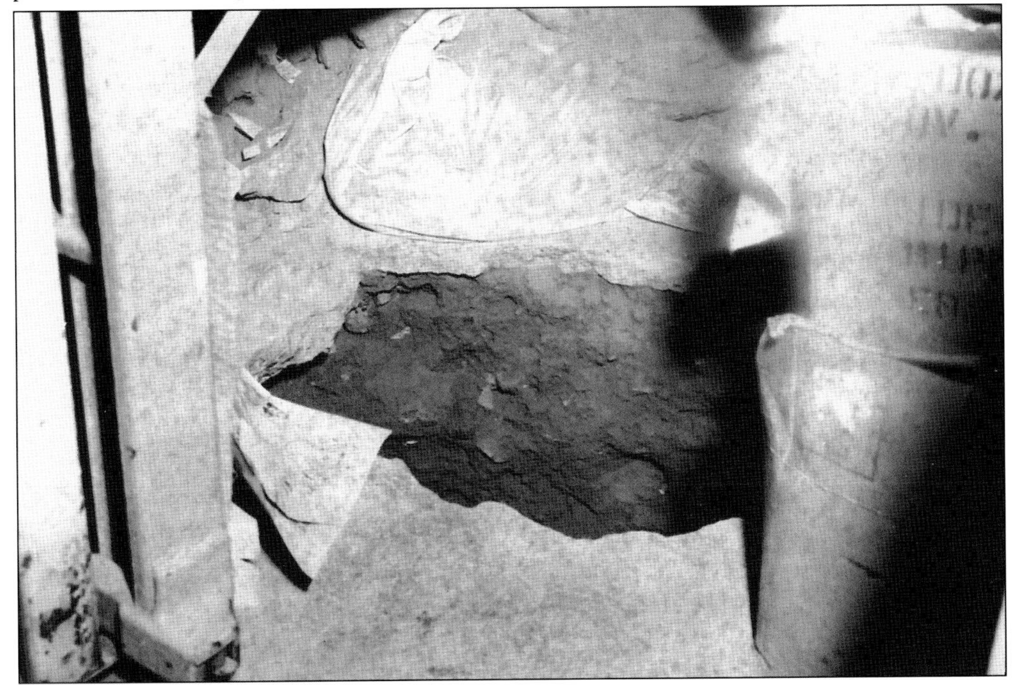

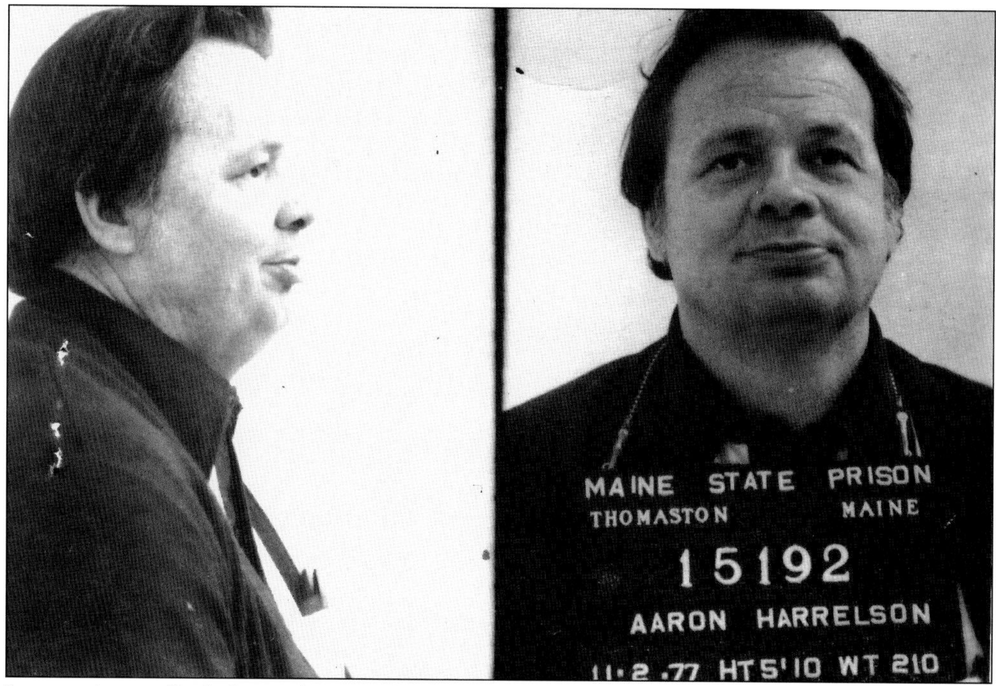

Inmate Aaron "Jack-the-Tack" Harrelson gained notoriety during the 1980 prison lockdown. He was referred to as the "novelty king" because he employed several inmates to work for him producing novelties and rented television sets to other inmates. He became a powerful figure within the prison, and when the lockdown occurred, he was transferred to the U.S. penitentiary at Terre Haute, Indiana. The novelty program was brought back under prison control.

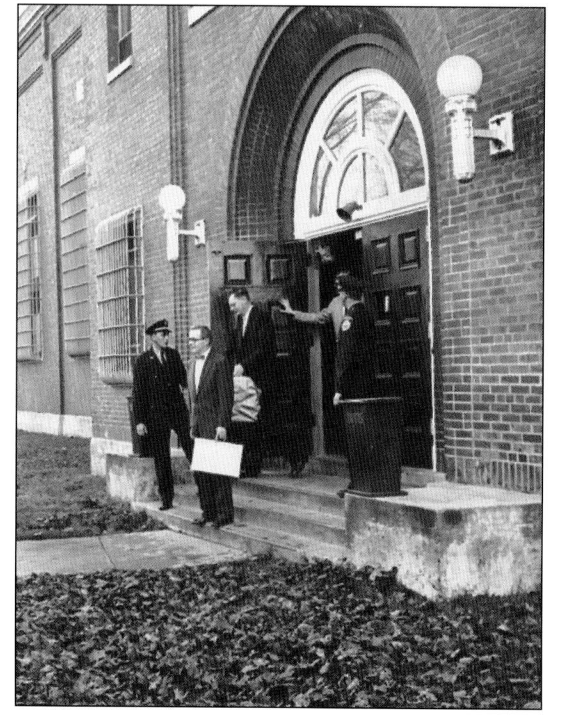

In 1937, Paul Dwyer was convicted of murder and sentenced to life in prison for the slayings of Dr. James Littlefield and his wife. Dwyer later confessed that they were killed by his girlfriend's father, Deputy Sheriff Francis Carroll, after the doctor confronted Carroll alleging that he had taken sexual liberties with his own daughter. Carroll was sentenced to life, and Dwyer was released in 1959. (Courtesy of the Robbins family.)

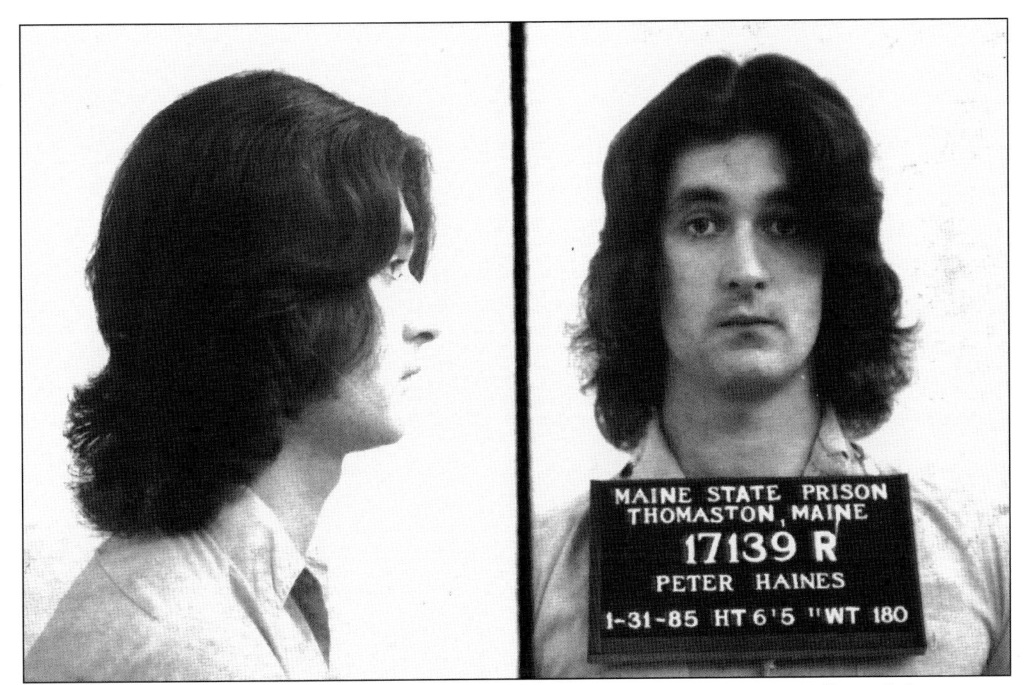

Inmate Peter Haines was stabbed to death at the prison by inmate William Johnson on September 22, 1985. It was later determined that inmate Haines had initiated the attack by trying to stab Johnson with a screwdriver. Inmate Johnson disarmed Haines and stabbed him in the neck, killing him.

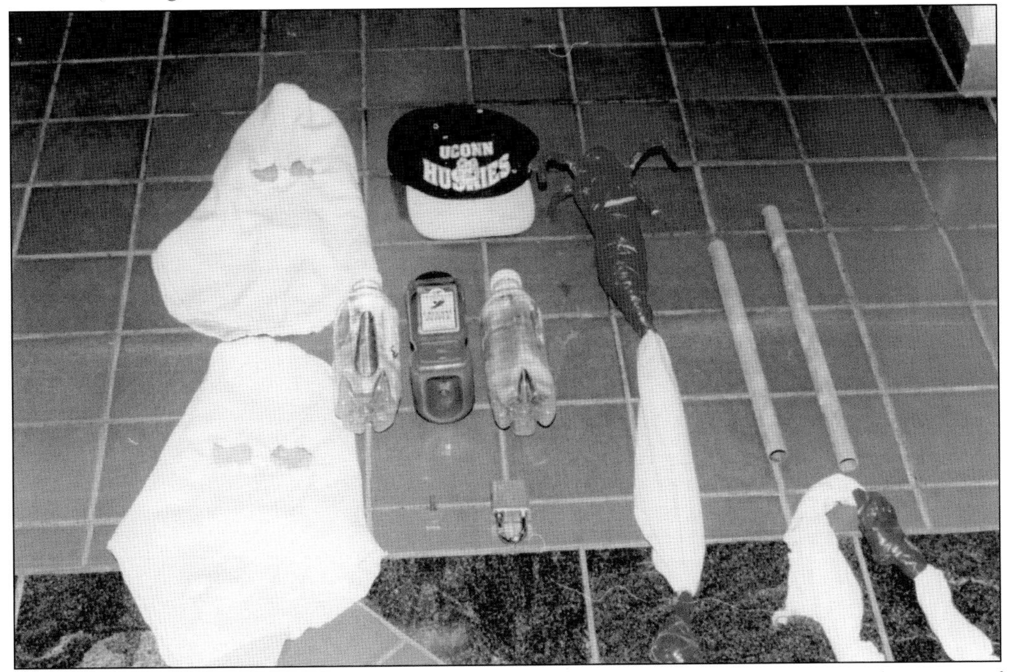

The last escape attempt took place in 1996. Two inmates made a grappling hook and rope out of bed sheets, which they tied together using tape. They were waiting for a foggy night to throw the "hook" over the wall. The white hoods made from pillowcases would camouflage their heads.

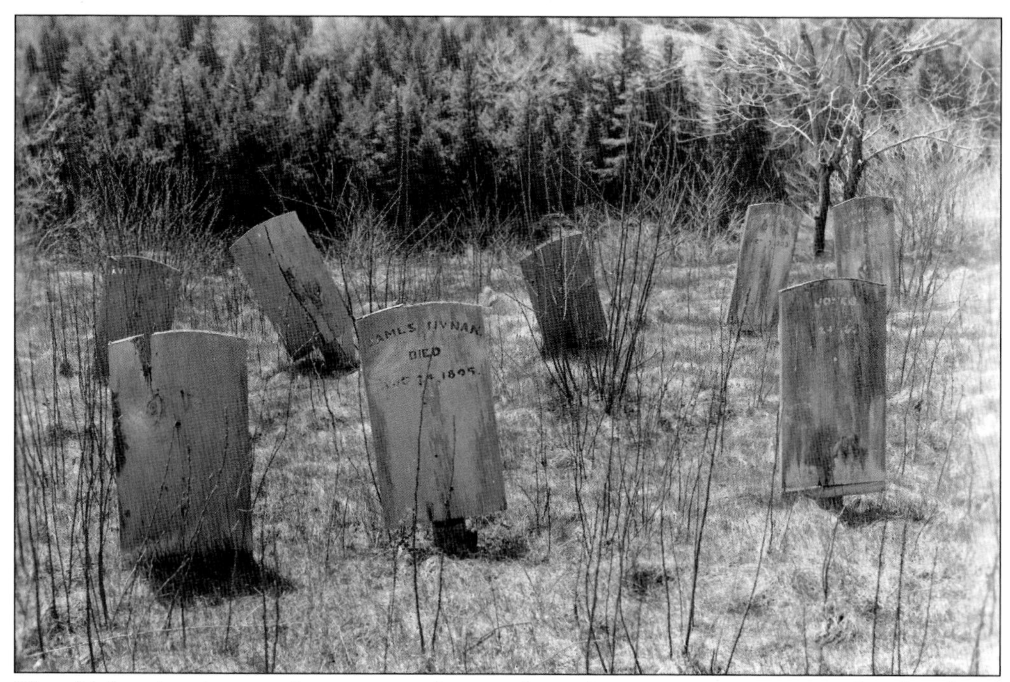

The old deteriorating wooden grave markers in the early cemetery were removed and replaced with granite gravestones. A black wrought iron fence surrounds them today. Ongoing research revealed the identities of many of the inmates buried, but the mystery of their death and felony convictions remain.

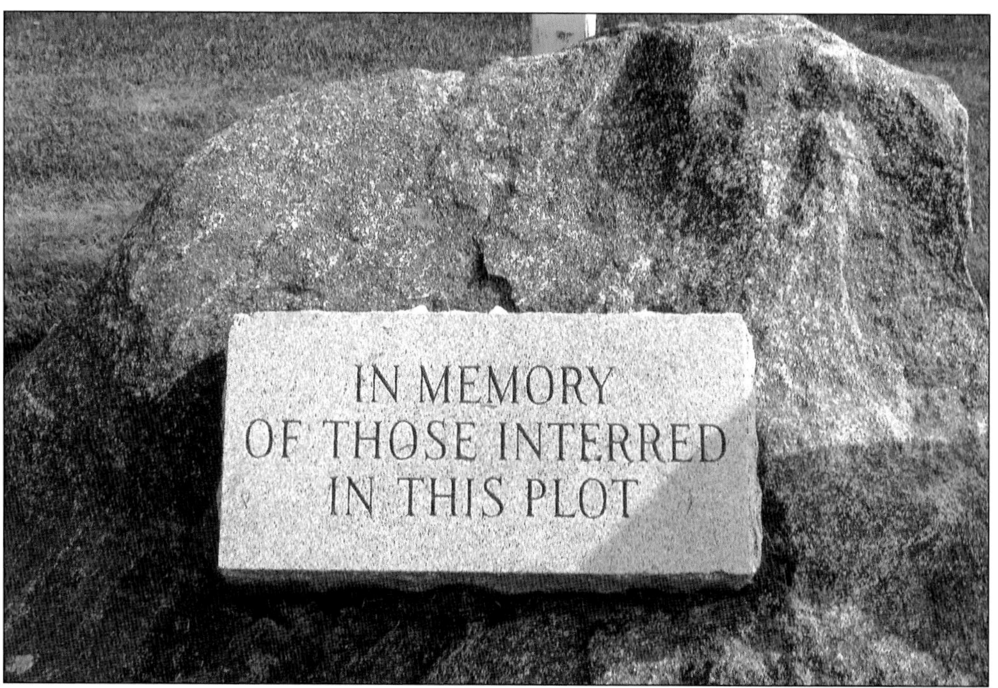

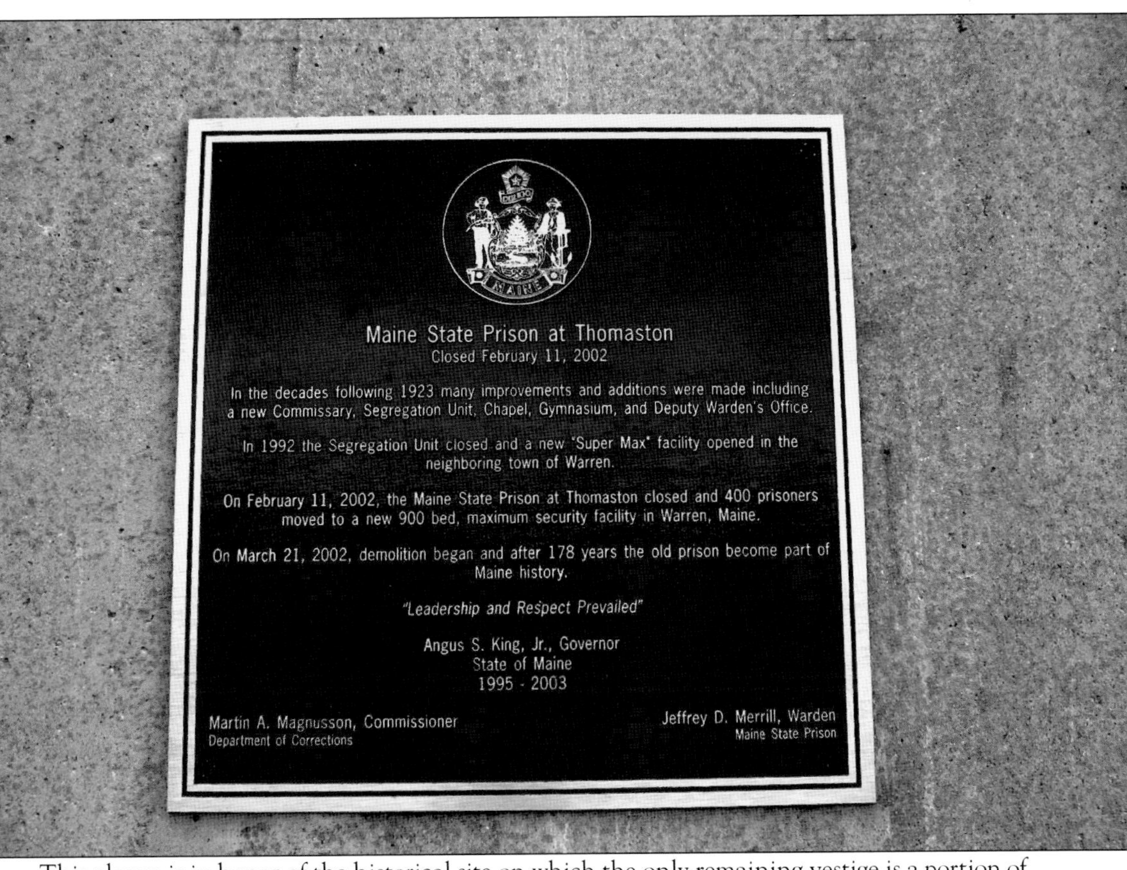

This plaque is in honor of the historical site on which the only remaining vestige is a portion of the wall where the plaque is now embedded.